ISOCRATES II

THE ORATORY OF CLASSICAL GREECE

Translated with Notes • *Michael Gagarin, Series Editor*

VOLUME 7

ISOCRATES II

Translated by Terry L. Papillon

 UNIVERSITY OF TEXAS PRESS, AUSTIN

First edition, 2004

Requests for permission to reproduce material from
this work should be sent to Permissions, University
of Texas Press, Box 7819, Austin, TX 78713-7819.

⊗ The paper used in this book meets the minimum
requirements of ANSI/NISO z39.48-1992 (R1997)
(Permanence of Paper).

Library of Congress Cataloging-in-Publication Data

Isocrates.
   [Selections. English. 2004]
   Isocrates II / translated by Terry L. Papillon.
      p.   cm. — (The oratory of Classical
Greece ; v. 7)
Includes bibliographical references and index.

   ISBN 978-0-292-70246-2 (pbk. : alk. paper)

   1. Isocrates—Translations into English.
2. Speeches, addresses, etc., Greek—Translations
into English.   3. Athens (Greece)—Politics and
government—Sources.   I. Title: Isocrates 2.
II. Title: Isocrates two.   III. Papillon, Terry L.,
1958–   IV. Title.   V. Series.
PA4217.E5P37   2004
885'.01—dc22

                              2003019068

CONTENTS

THE WORKS OF ISOCRATES

ACKNOWLEDGMENTS

This is the seventh volume in The Oratory of Classical Greece. The aim of the series is to make available primarily for those who do not read Greek up-to-date, accurate, and readable translations with introductions and explanatory notes of all the surviving works and major fragments of the Attic orators of the classical period (ca. 420–320 BC): Aeschines, Andocides, Antiphon, Demosthenes, Dinarchus, Hyperides, Isaeus, Isocrates, Lycurgus, and Lysias.

This volume completes the works of Isocrates (*Isocrates I,* translated by David Mirhady and Yun Lee Too, was published in 2000). The "Introduction to Isocrates" represents the combined effort of three translators of Isocrates and the Series Editor.

I would like to thank Ed Schiappa, who read the volume for the University of Texas Press, and the entire staff at the Press, including Director Joanna Hitchcock, Humanities Editor Jim Burr, Managing Editor Carolyn Wylie, and Copyeditor Nancy Moore.

— M.G.

Translating Isocrates is not an easy or quick task, but it is a noble one. I hope that what I offer here will be of use to readers in a variety of intellectual fields, and I am grateful to Michael Gagarin for asking me to contribute to this series. The translation has been helped enormously by his careful and supportive direction; I have learned much from him in the process.

I am, as always, grateful to my wife Carol and my two boys, Greg and Ben, for their support and also for giving up the dining room table to piles of books and my computer during the fall semester of

2000. My life and work are always dedicated to them. Thanks are due to many others as well. Ann-Marie Knoblauch, Katie Rask, and Emily Winslow read portions of the manuscript and offered advice and assistance. Edward Schiappa read the manuscript for the University of Texas Press and provided helpful comments; Nancy Moore worked as copyeditor and saved me from many embarrassments. Virginia Tech granted me a research leave for fall 2000, during which substantial work was completed. Finally, I am grateful to Trudy Harrington Becker and Andrew Becker, who have provided incalculable support for this project, reading much of the manuscript with great care and offering continuous support during an at times difficult process.

This volume is dedicated to the memory of Virginia Holden Hummel (1912–1998), who passed away during the work on this project. She was a resident of Blacksburg from her birth (on campus) in 1912 until her death in 1998; she was a staunch supporter of Classics at Virginia Tech; and most importantly, she was an effective model of lifelong learning for our Classics community as she learned Greek and Latin in her retirement and took every course the Virginia Tech Classical Studies Program had to offer. She is fondly remembered by all and greatly missed.

— T.L.P.

SERIES INTRODUCTION
Greek Oratory

✿✿

By Michael Gagarin

ORATORY IN CLASSICAL ATHENS

From as early as Homer (and undoubtedly much earlier) the Greeks placed a high value on effective speaking. Even Achilles, whose greatness was primarily established on the battlefield, was brought up to be "a speaker of words and a doer of deeds" (*Iliad* 9.443); and Athenian leaders of the sixth and fifth centuries,[1] such as Solon, Themistocles, and Pericles, were all accomplished orators. Most Greek literary genres —notably epic, tragedy, and history—underscore the importance of oratory by their inclusion of set speeches. The formal pleadings of the envoys to Achilles in the *Iliad*, the messenger speeches in tragedy reporting events like the battle of Salamis in Aeschylus' *Persians* or the gruesome death of Pentheus in Euripides' *Bacchae,* and the powerful political oratory of Pericles' funeral oration in Thucydides are but a few of the most notable examples of the Greeks' never-ending fascination with formal public speaking, which was to reach its height in the public oratory of the fourth century.

In early times, oratory was not a specialized subject of study but was learned by practice and example. The formal study of rhetoric as an "art" (*technē*) began, we are told, in the middle of the fifth century in Sicily with the work of Corax and his pupil Tisias.[2] These two are

---

[1] All dates in this volume are BC unless the contrary is either indicated or obvious.

[2] See Kennedy 1963: 26–51. Cole 1991 has challenged this traditional picture, arguing that the term "rhetoric" was coined by Plato to designate and denigrate an activity he strongly opposed. Cole's own reconstruction is not without problems,

scarcely more than names to us, but another famous Sicilian, Gorgias of Leontini (ca. 490–390), developed a new style of argument and is reported to have dazzled the Athenians with a speech delivered when he visited Athens in 427. Gorgias initiated the practice, which continued into the early fourth century, of composing speeches for mythical or imaginary occasions. The surviving examples reveal a lively intellectual climate in the late fifth and early fourth centuries, in which oratory served to display new ideas, new forms of expression, and new methods of argument.[3] This tradition of "intellectual" oratory was continued by the fourth-century educator Isocrates and played a large role in later Greek and Roman education.

In addition to this intellectual oratory, at about the same time the practice also began of writing speeches for real occasions in public life, which we may designate "practical" oratory. For centuries Athenians had been delivering speeches in public settings (primarily the courts and the Assembly), but these had always been composed and delivered impromptu, without being written down and thus without being preserved. The practice of writing speeches began in the courts and then expanded to include the Assembly and other settings. Athens was one of the leading cities of Greece in the fifth and fourth centuries, and its political and legal systems depended on direct participation by a large number of citizens; all important decisions were made by these large bodies, and the primary means of influencing these decisions was oratory.[4] Thus, it is not surprising that oratory flourished in Athens,[5] but it may not be immediately obvious why it should be written down.

The pivotal figure in this development was Antiphon, one of the fifth-century intellectuals who are often grouped together under the

---

but he does well to remind us how thoroughly the traditional view of rhetoric depends on one of its most ardent opponents.

[3] Of these only Antiphon's Tetralogies are included in this series. Gorgias' *Helen* and *Palamedes,* Alcidamas' *Odysseus,* and Antisthenes' *Ajax* and *Odysseus* are translated in Gagarin and Woodruff 1995.

[4] Yunis 1996 has a good treatment of political oratory from Pericles to Demosthenes.

[5] All our evidence for practical oratory comes from Athens, with the exception of Isocrates 19, written for a trial in Aegina. Many speeches were undoubtedly delivered in courts and political forums in other Greek cities, but it may be that such speeches were written down only in Athens.

name "Sophists."[6] Like some of the other sophists he contributed to the intellectual oratory of the period, but he also had a strong practical interest in law. At the same time, Antiphon had an aversion to public speaking and did not directly involve himself in legal or political affairs (Thucydides 8.68). However, he began giving general advice to other citizens who were engaged in litigation and were thus expected to address the court themselves. As this practice grew, Antiphon went further, and around 430 he began writing out whole speeches for others to memorize and deliver. Thus began the practice of "logography," which continued through the next century and beyond.[7] Logography particularly appealed to men like Lysias, who were metics, or noncitizen residents of Athens. Since they were not Athenian citizens, they were barred from direct participation in public life, but they could contribute by writing speeches for others.

Antiphon was also the first (to our knowledge) to write down a speech he would himself deliver, writing the speech for his own defense at his trial for treason in 411. His motive was probably to publicize and preserve his views, and others continued this practice of writing down speeches they would themselves deliver in the courts and (more rarely) the Assembly.[8] Finally, one other type of practical oratory was the special tribute delivered on certain important public occasions, the best known of which is the funeral oration. It is convenient to designate these three types of oratory by the terms Aristotle later uses: forensic (for the courts), deliberative (for the Assembly), and epideictic (for display).[9]

---

[6] The term "sophist" was loosely used through the fifth and fourth centuries to designate various intellectuals and orators, but under the influence of Plato, who attacked certain figures under this name, the term is now used of a specific group of thinkers; see Kerferd 1981.

[7] For Antiphon as the first to write speeches, see Photius, *Bibliotheca* 486a7–11 and [Plut.], *Moralia* 832c–d. The latest extant speech can be dated to 320, but we know that at least one orator, Dinarchus, continued the practice after that date.

[8] Unlike forensic speeches, speeches for delivery in the Assembly were usually not composed beforehand in writing, since the speaker could not know exactly when or in what context he would be speaking; see further Trevett 1996.

[9] *Rhetoric* 1.3. Intellectual orations, like Gorgias' *Helen,* do not easily fit into Aristotle's classification. For a fuller (but still brief) introduction to Attic oratory and the orators, see Edwards 1994.

THE ORATORS

In the century from about 420 to 320, dozens—perhaps even hundreds—of now unknown orators and logographers must have composed speeches that are now lost, but only ten of these men were selected for preservation and study by ancient scholars, and only works collected under the names of these ten have been preserved. Some of these works are undoubtedly spurious, though in most cases they are fourth-century works by a different author rather than later "forgeries." Indeed, modern scholars suspect that as many as seven of the speeches attributed to Demosthenes may have been written by Apollodorus, son of Pasion, who is sometimes called "the eleventh orator." [10] Including these speeches among the works of Demosthenes may have been an honest mistake, or perhaps a bookseller felt he could sell more copies of these speeches if they were attributed to a more famous orator.

In alphabetical order the Ten Orators are as follows: [11]

- AESCHINES (ca. 395–ca. 322) rose from obscure origins to become an important Athenian political figure, first an ally, then a bitter enemy of Demosthenes. His three speeches all concern major public issues. The best known of these (Aes. 3) was delivered at the trial in 330, when Demosthenes responded with *On the Crown* (Dem. 18). Aeschines lost the case and was forced to leave Athens and live the rest of his life in exile.

- ANDOCIDES (ca. 440–ca. 390) is best known for his role in the scandal of 415, when just before the departure of the fateful Athenian expedition to Sicily during the Peloponnesian War (431–404), a band of young men mutilated statues of Hermes, and at the same time information was revealed about the secret rites of Demeter. Andocides was exiled but later returned. Two of the four speeches

---

[10] See Trevett 1992.

[11] The Loeb volumes of *Minor Attic Orators* also include the prominent Athenian political figure Demades (ca. 385–319), who was not one of the Ten; but the only speech that has come down to us under his name is a later forgery. It is possible that Demades and other fourth-century politicians who had a high reputation for public speaking did not put any speeches in writing, especially if they rarely spoke in the courts (see above n. 8).

in his name give us a contemporary view of the scandal: one pleads for his return, the other argues against a second period of exile.

• ANTIPHON (ca. 480–411), as already noted, wrote forensic speeches for others and only once spoke himself. In 411 he participated in an oligarchic coup by a group of 400, and when the democrats regained power he was tried for treason and executed. His six surviving speeches include three for delivery in court and the three Tetralogies—imaginary intellectual exercises for display or teaching that consist of four speeches each, two on each side. All six of Antiphon's speeches concern homicide, probably because these stood at the beginning of the collection of his works. Fragments of some thirty other speeches cover many different topics.

• DEMOSTHENES (384–322) is generally considered the best of the Attic orators. Although his nationalistic message is less highly regarded today, his powerful mastery of and ability to combine many different rhetorical styles continues to impress readers. Demosthenes was still a child when his wealthy father died. The trustees of the estate apparently misappropriated much of it, and when he came of age, he sued them in a series of cases (27–31), regaining some of his fortune and making a name as a powerful speaker. He then wrote speeches for others in a variety of cases, public and private, and for his own use in court (where many cases involved major public issues), and in the Assembly, where he opposed the growing power of Philip of Macedon. The triumph of Philip and his son Alexander the Great eventually put an end to Demosthenes' career. Some sixty speeches have come down under his name, about a third of them of questionable authenticity.

• DINARCHUS (ca. 360–ca. 290) was born in Corinth but spent much of his life in Athens as a metic (a noncitizen resident). His public fame came primarily from writing speeches for the prosecutions surrounding the Harpalus affair in 324, when several prominent figures (including Demosthenes) were accused of bribery. After 322 he had a profitable career as a logographer.

• HYPERIDES (390–322) was a political leader and logographer of so many different talents that he was called the pentathlete of orators. He was a leader of the Athenian resistance to Philip and Alexander and (like Demosthenes) was condemned to death after Athens' final surrender. One speech and substantial fragments of five others have been recovered from papyrus remains; otherwise, only fragments survive.

* ISAEUS (ca. 415–ca. 340) wrote speeches on a wide range of topics, but the eleven complete speeches that survive, dating from ca. 390 to ca. 344, all concern inheritance. As with Antiphon, the survival of these particular speeches may have been the result of the later ordering of his speeches by subject; we have part of a twelfth speech and fragments and titles of some forty other works. Isaeus is said to have been a pupil of Isocrates and the teacher of Demosthenes.

* ISOCRATES (436–338) considered himself a philosopher and educator, not an orator or rhetorician. He came from a wealthy Athenian family but lost most of his property in the Peloponnesian War, and in 403 he took up logography. About 390 he abandoned this practice and turned to writing and teaching, setting forth his educational, philosophical, and political views in essays that took the form of speeches but were not meant for oral delivery. He favored accommodation with the growing power of Philip of Macedon and panhellenic unity. His school was based on a broad concept of rhetoric and applied philosophy; it attracted pupils from the entire Greek world (including Isaeus, Lycurgus, and Hyperides) and became the main rival of Plato's Academy. Isocrates greatly influenced education and rhetoric in the Hellenistic, Roman, and modern periods until the eighteenth century.

* LYCURGUS (ca. 390–ca. 324) was a leading public official who restored the financial condition of Athens after 338 and played a large role in the city for the next dozen years. He brought charges of corruption or treason against many other officials, usually with success. Only one speech survives.

* LYSIAS (ca. 445–ca. 380) was a metic—an official resident of Athens but not a citizen. Much of his property was seized by the Thirty during their short-lived oligarchic coup in 404–403. Perhaps as a result he turned to logography. More than thirty speeches survive in whole or in part, though the authenticity of some is doubted. We also have fragments or know the titles of more than a hundred oth-

ers. The speeches cover a wide range of cases, and he may have delivered one himself (Lys. 12), on the death of his brother at the hands of the Thirty. Lysias is particularly known for his vivid narratives, his *ēthopoiïa*, or "creation of character," and his prose style, which became a model of clarity and vividness.

THE WORKS OF THE ORATORS

As soon as speeches began to be written down, they could be preserved. We know little about the conditions of book "publication" (i.e., making copies for distribution) in the fourth century, but there was an active market for books in Athens, and some of the speeches may have achieved wide circulation.[12] An orator (or his family) may have preserved his own speeches, perhaps to advertise his ability or demonstrate his success, or booksellers may have collected and copied them in order to make money.

We do not know how closely the preserved text of these speeches corresponded to the version actually delivered in court or in the Assembly. Speakers undoubtedly extemporized or varied from their text on occasion, but there is no good evidence that deliberative speeches were substantially revised for publication.[13] In forensic oratory a logographer's reputation would derive first and foremost from his success with jurors. If a forensic speech was victorious, there would be no reason to alter it for publication, and if it lost, alteration would probably not deceive potential clients. Thus, the published texts of forensic speeches were probably quite faithful to the texts that were provided to clients, and we have little reason to suspect substantial alteration in the century or so before they were collected by scholars in Alexandria (see below).

In addition to the speaker's text, most forensic speeches have breaks for the inclusion of documents. The logographer inserted a notation in his text—such as *nomos* ("law") or *martyria* ("testimony")—and the

---

[12] Dover's discussion (1968) of the preservation and transmission of the works of Lysias (and perhaps others under his name) is useful not just for Lysias but for the other orators too. His theory of shared authorship between logographer and litigant, however, is unconvincing (see Usher 1976).

[13] See further Trevett 1996: 437–439.

speaker would pause while the clerk read out the text of a law or the testimony of witnesses. Many speeches survive with only a notation that a *nomos* or *martyria* was read at that point, but in some cases the text of the document is included. It used to be thought that these documents were all creations of later scholars, but many (though not all) are now accepted as genuine.[14]

With the foundation of the famous library in Alexandria early in the third century, scholars began to collect and catalogue texts of the orators, along with many other classical authors. Only the best orators were preserved in the library, many of them represented by over 100 speeches each (some undoubtedly spurious). Only some of these works survived in manuscript form to the modern era; more recently a few others have been discovered on ancient sheets of papyrus, so that today the corpus of Attic Oratory consists of about 150 speeches, together with a few letters and other works. The subject matter ranges from important public issues and serious crimes to business affairs, lovers' quarrels, inheritance disputes, and other personal or family matters.

In the centuries after these works were collected, ancient scholars gathered biographical facts about their authors, produced grammatical and lexicographic notes, and used some of the speeches as evidence for Athenian political history. But the ancient scholars who were most interested in the orators were those who studied prose style, the most notable of these being Dionysius of Halicarnassus (first century BC), who wrote treatises on several of the orators,[15] and Hermogenes of Tarsus (second century AD), who wrote several literary studies, including *On Types of Style*.[16] But relative to epic or tragedy, oratory was little studied; and even scholars of rhetoric whose interests were broader than style, like Cicero and Quintilian, paid little attention to the orators, except for the acknowledged master, Demosthenes.

Most modern scholars until the second half of the twentieth century continued to treat the orators primarily as prose stylists.[17] The re-

---

[14] See MacDowell 1990: 43–47; Todd 1993: 44–45.

[15] Dionysius' literary studies are collected and translated in Usher 1974–1985.

[16] Wooten 1987. Stylistic considerations probably also influenced the selection of the "canon" of ten orators; see Worthington 1994.

[17] For example, the most popular and influential book ever written on the orators, Jebb's *The Attic Orators* (1875) was presented as an "attempt to aid in giving Attic Oratory its due place in the history of Attic Prose" (I.xiii). This modern focus

evaluation of Athenian democracy by George Grote and others in the nineteenth century stimulated renewed interest in Greek oratory among historians; and increasing interest in Athenian law during that century led a few legal scholars to read the orators. But in comparison with the interest shown in the other literary genres—epic, lyric, tragedy, comedy, and even history—Attic oratory has been relatively neglected until the last third of the twentieth century. More recently, however, scholars have discovered the value of the orators for the broader study of Athenian culture and society. Since Dover's groundbreaking works on popular morality and homosexuality,[18] interest in the orators has been increasing rapidly, and they are now seen as primary representatives of Athenian moral and social values, and as evidence for social and economic conditions, political and social ideology, and in general those aspects of Athenian culture that in the past were commonly ignored by historians of ancient Greece but are of increasing interest and importance today, including women and the family, slavery, and the economy.

GOVERNMENT AND LAW IN CLASSICAL ATHENS

The hallmark of the Athenian political and legal systems was its amateurism. Most public officials, including those who supervised the courts, were selected by lot and held office for a limited period, typically a year. Thus a great many citizens held public office at some point in their lives, but almost none served for an extended period of time or developed the experience or expertise that would make them professionals. All significant policy decisions were debated and voted on in the Assembly, where the quorum was 6,000 citizens, and all significant legal cases were judged by bodies of 200 to 500 jurors or more. Public prominence was not achieved by election (or selection) to public office but depended rather on a man's ability to sway the majority of citizens in the Assembly or jurors in court to vote in favor of a pro-

---

on prose style can plausibly be connected to the large role played by prose composition (the translation of English prose into Greek, usually in imitation of specific authors or styles) in the Classics curriculum, especially in Britain.

[18] Dover (1974, 1978). Dover later commented (1994: 157), "When I began to mine the riches of Attic forensic oratory I was astonished to discover that the mine had never been exploited."

posed course of action or for one of the litigants in a trial. Success was never permanent, and a victory on one policy issue or a verdict in one case could be quickly reversed in another.[19] In such a system the value of public oratory is obvious, and in the fourth century, oratory became the most important cultural institution in Athens, replacing drama as the forum where major ideological concerns were displayed and debated.

Several recent books give good detailed accounts of Athenian government and law,[20] and so a brief sketch can suffice here. The main policy-making body was the Assembly, open to all adult male citizens; a small payment for attendance enabled at least some of the poor to attend along with the leisured rich. In addition, a Council of 500 citizens, selected each year by lot with no one allowed to serve more than two years, prepared material for and made recommendations to the Assembly; a rotating subgroup of this Council served as an executive committee, the Prytaneis. Finally, numerous officials, most of them selected by lot for one-year terms, supervised different areas of administration and finance. The most important of these were the nine Archons (lit. "rulers"): the eponymous Archon after whom the year was named, the Basileus ("king"),[21] the Polemarch, and the six Thesmothetae. Councilors and almost all these officials underwent a preliminary examination (*dokimasia*) before taking office, and officials submitted to a final accounting (*euthynai*) upon leaving; at these times any citizen who wished could challenge a person's fitness for his new position or his performance in his recent position.

---

[19] In the Assembly this could be accomplished by a reconsideration of the question, as in the famous Mytilenean debate (Thuc. 3.36–50); in court a verdict was final, but its practical effects could be thwarted or reversed by later litigation on a related issue.

[20] For government, see Sinclair 1988, Hansen 1991; for law, MacDowell 1978, Todd 1993, and Boegehold 1995 (Bonner 1927 is still helpful). Much of our information about the legal and political systems comes from a work attributed to Aristotle but perhaps written by a pupil of his, *The Athenian Constitution* (*Ath. Pol.*—conveniently translated with notes by Rhodes 1984). The discovery of this work on a papyrus in Egypt in 1890 caused a major resurgence of interest in Athenian government.

[21] Modern scholars often use the term *archōn basileus* or "king archon," but Athenian sources (e.g., *Ath. Pol.* 57) simply call him the *basileus*.

SERIES INTRODUCTION   xxi

There was no general taxation of Athenian citizens. Sources of public funding included the annual tax levied on metics, various fees and import duties, and (in the fifth century) tribute from allied cities; but the source that figures most prominently in the orators is the Athenian system of liturgies (*leitourgiai*), by which in a regular rotation the rich provided funding for certain special public needs. The main liturgies were the *chorēgia,* in which a sponsor (*chorēgos*) supervised and paid for the training and performance of a chorus which sang and danced at a public festival,[22] and the trierarchy, in which a sponsor (trierarch) paid to equip and usually commanded a trireme, or warship, for a year. Some of these liturgies required substantial expenditures, but even so, some men spent far more than required in order to promote themselves and their public careers, and litigants often tried to impress the jurors by referring to liturgies they had undertaken (see, e.g., Lys. 21.1–n5). A further twist on this system was that if a man thought he had been assigned a liturgy that should have gone to someone else who was richer than he, he could propose an exchange of property (*antidosis*), giving the other man a choice of either taking over the liturgy or exchanging property with him. Finally, the rich were also subject to special taxes (*eisphorai*) levied as a percentage of their property in times of need.

The Athenian legal system remained similarly resistant to professionalization. Trials and the procedures leading up to them were supervised by officials, primarily the nine Archons, but their role was purely administrative, and they were in no way equivalent to modern judges. All significant questions about what we would call points of law were presented to the jurors, who considered them together with all other issues when they delivered their verdict at the end of the trial.[23] Trials were "contests" (*agōnes*) between two litigants, each of whom presented his own case to the jurors in a speech, plaintiff first, then de-

---

[22] These included the productions of tragedy and comedy, for which the main expense was for the chorus.

[23] Certain religious "interpreters" (*exēgētai*) were occasionally asked to give their opinion on a legal matter that had a religious dimension (such as the prosecution of a homicide), but although these opinions could be reported in court (e.g., Dem. 47.68–73), they had no official legal standing. The most significant administrative decision we hear of is the refusal of the Basileus to accept the case in Antiphon 6 (see 6.37–46).

fendant; in some cases each party then spoke again, probably in rebuttal. Since a litigant had only one or two speeches in which to present his entire case, and no issue was decided separately by a judge, all the necessary factual information and every important argument on substance or procedure, fact or law, had to be presented together. A single speech might thus combine narrative, argument, emotional appeal, and various digressions, all with the goal of obtaining a favorable verdict. Even more than today, a litigant's primary task was to control the issue—to determine which issues the jurors would consider most important and which questions they would have in their minds as they cast their votes. We only rarely have both speeches from a trial,[24] and we usually have little or no external evidence for the facts of a case or the verdict. We must thus infer both the facts and the opponent's strategy from the speech we have, and any assessment of the overall effectiveness of a speech and of the logographer's strategy is to some extent speculative.

Before a trial there were usually several preliminary hearings for presenting evidence; arbitration, public and private, was available and sometimes required. These hearings and arbitration sessions allowed each side to become familiar with the other side's case, so that discussions of "what my opponent will say" could be included in one's speech. Normally a litigant presented his own case, but he was often assisted by family or friends. If he wished (and could afford it), he could enlist the services of a logographer, who presumably gave strategic advice in addition to writing a speech. The speeches were timed to ensure an equal hearing for both sides,[25] and all trials were completed within a day. Two hundred or more jurors decided each case in the popular courts, which met in the Agora.[26] Homicide cases and certain other religious trials (e.g., Lys. 7) were heard by the Council of the Areopagus or an associated group of fifty-one Ephetae. The Areopagus was composed of all former Archons—perhaps 150–200 members at most

---

[24]The exceptions are Demosthenes 19 and Aeschines 2, Aeschines 3 and Demosthenes 18, and Lysias 6 (one of several prosecution speeches) and Andocides 1; all were written for major public cases.

[25]Timing was done by means of a water-clock, which in most cases was stopped during the reading of documents.

[26]See Boegehold 1995.

times. It met on a hill called the Areopagus ("rock of Ares") near the Acropolis.

Jurors for the regular courts were selected by lot from those citizens who registered each year and who appeared for duty that day; as with the Assembly, a small payment allowed the poor to serve. After the speakers had finished, the jurors voted immediately without any formal discussion. The side with the majority won; a tie vote decided the case for the defendant. In some cases where the penalty was not fixed, after a conviction the jurors voted again on the penalty, choosing between penalties proposed by each side. Even when we know the verdict, we cannot know which of the speaker's arguments contributed most to his success or failure. However, a logographer could probably learn from jurors which points had or had not been successful, so that arguments that are found repeatedly in speeches probably were known to be effective in most cases.

The first written laws in Athens were enacted by Draco (ca. 620) and Solon (ca. 590), and new laws were regularly added. At the end of the fifth century the existing laws were reorganized, and a new procedure for enacting laws was instituted; thereafter a group of Law-Givers (*nomothetai*) had to certify that a proposed law did not conflict with any existing laws. There was no attempt, however, to organize legislation systematically, and although Plato, Aristotle, and other philosophers wrote various works on law and law-giving, these were either theoretical or descriptive and had no apparent influence on legislation. Written statutes generally used ordinary language rather than precise legal definitions in designating offenses, and questions concerning precisely what constituted a specific offense or what was the correct interpretation of a written statute were decided (together with other issues) by the jurors in each case. A litigant might, of course, assert a certain definition or interpretation as "something you all know" or "what the lawgiver intended," but such remarks are evidently tendentious and cannot be taken as authoritative.

The result of these procedural and substantive features was that the verdict depended largely on each litigant's speech (or speeches). As one speaker puts it (Ant. 6.18), "When there are no witnesses, you (jurors) are forced to reach a verdict about the case on the basis of the prosecutor's and defendant's words alone; you must be suspicious and examine their accounts in detail, and your vote will necessarily be cast on the basis of likelihood rather than clear knowledge." Even the testimony of witnesses (usually on both sides) is rarely decisive. On the other hand, most speakers make a considerable effort to establish facts and provide legitimate arguments in conformity with established law. Plato's view of rhetoric as a clever technique for persuading an ignorant crowd that the false is true is not borne out by the speeches, and the legal system does not appear to have produced many arbitrary or clearly unjust results.

The main form of legal procedure was a *dikē* ("suit") in which the injured party (or his relatives in a case of homicide) brought suit against the offender. Suits for injuries to slaves would be brought by the slave's master, and injuries to women would be prosecuted by a male relative. Strictly speaking, a *dikē* was a private matter between individuals, though like all cases, *dikai* often had public dimensions. The other major form of procedure was a *graphē* ("writing" or "indictment") in which "anyone who wished" (i.e., any citizen) could bring a prosecution for wrongdoing. *Graphai* were instituted by Solon, probably in order to allow prosecution of offenses where the victim was unable or unlikely to bring suit himself, such as selling a dependent into slavery; but the number of areas covered by *graphai* increased to cover many types of public offenses as well as some apparently private crimes, such as *hybris*.

The system of prosecution by "anyone who wished" also extended to several other more specialized forms of prosecution, like *eisangelia* ("impeachment"), used in cases of treason. Another specialized prosecution was *apagōgē* ("summary arrest"), in which someone could arrest a common criminal (*kakourgos,* lit. "evil-doer"), or have him arrested, on the spot. The reliance on private initiative meant that Athenians never developed a system of public prosecution; rather, they presumed that everyone would keep an eye on the behavior of his political enemies and bring suit as soon as he suspected a crime, both to harm his opponents and to advance his own career. In this way all public officials would be watched by someone. There was no disgrace in admitting that a prosecution was motivated by private enmity.

By the end of the fifth century the system of prosecution by "anyone who wished" was apparently being abused by so-called sykophants (*sykophantai*), who allegedly brought or threatened to bring false suits against rich men, either to gain part of the fine that would be levied or to induce an out-of-court settlement in which the accused would pay to have the matter dropped. We cannot gauge the true extent of this problem, since speakers usually provide little evidence to support their claims that their opponents are sykophants, but the Athenians did make sykophancy a crime. They also specified that in many public procedures a plaintiff who either dropped the case or failed to obtain one-fifth of the votes would have to pay a heavy fine of 1,000 drachmas. Despite this, it appears that litigation was common in Athens and was seen by some as excessive.

Over the course of time, the Athenian legal and political systems have more often been judged negatively than positively. Philosophers and political theorists have generally followed the lead of Plato (427–347), who lived and worked in Athens his entire life while severely criticizing its system of government as well as many other aspects of its culture. For Plato, democracy amounted to the tyranny of the masses over the educated elite and was destined to collapse from its own instability. The legal system was capricious and depended entirely on the rhetorical ability of litigants with no regard for truth or justice. These criticisms have often been echoed by modern scholars, who particularly complain that law was much too closely interwoven with politics and did not have the autonomous status it achieved in Roman law and continues to have, at least in theory, in modern legal systems.

Plato's judgments are valid if one accepts the underlying presuppositions, that the aim of law is absolute truth and abstract justice and that achieving the highest good of the state requires thorough and systematic organization. Most Athenians do not seem to have subscribed to either the criticisms or the presuppositions, and most scholars now accept the long-ignored fact that despite major external disruptions in the form of wars and two short-lived coups brought about by one of these wars, the Athenian legal and political systems remained remarkably stable for almost two hundred years (508–320). Moreover, like all other Greek cities at the time, whatever their form of government, Athenian democracy was brought to an end not by internal forces but by the external power of Philip of Macedon and his son Alexander. The legal system never became autonomous, and the rich sometimes complained that they were victims of unscrupulous litigants, but there is no indication that the people wanted to yield control of the legal process to a professional class, as Plato recommended. For most Athe-

nians—Plato being an exception in this and many other matters—
one purpose of the legal system was to give everyone the opportunity
to have his case heard by other citizens and have it heard quickly and
cheaply; and in this it clearly succeeded.

Indeed, the Athenian legal system also served the interests of the
rich, even the very rich, as well as the common people, in that it provided a forum for the competition that since Homer had been an important part of aristocratic life. In this competition, the rich used the
courts as battlegrounds, though their main weapon was the rhetoric of
popular ideology, which hailed the rule of law and promoted the ideal
of moderation and restraint.[27] But those who aspired to political leadership and the honor and status that accompanied it repeatedly entered
the legal arena, bringing suit against their political enemies whenever
possible and defending themselves against suits brought by others
whenever necessary. The ultimate judges of these public competitions
were the common people, who seem to have relished the dramatic
clash of individuals and ideologies. In this respect fourth-century oratory was the cultural heir of fifth-century drama and was similarly ap-
preciated by the citizens. Despite the disapproval of intellectuals like
Plato, most Athenians legitimately considered their legal system a hallmark of their democracy and a vital presence in their culture.

THE TRANSLATION OF GREEK ORATORY

The purpose of this series is to provide students and scholars in all
fields with accurate, readable translations of all surviving classical Attic oratory, including speeches whose authenticity is disputed, as well
as the substantial surviving fragments. In keeping with the originals,
the language is for the most part nontechnical. Names of persons and
places are given in the (generally more familiar) Latinized forms, and
names of officials or legal procedures have been translated into English
equivalents, where possible. Notes are intended to provide the necessary historical and cultural background; scholarly controversies are
generally not discussed. The notes and introductions refer to scholarly
treatments in addition to those listed below, which the reader may
consult for further information.

---

[27] Ober 1989 is fundamental; see also Cohen 1995.

Cross-references to other speeches follow the standard numbering system, which is now well established except in the case of Hyperides (for whom the numbering of the Oxford Classical Text is used).[28] References are by work and section (e.g., Dem. 24.73); spurious works are not specially marked; when no author is named (e.g., 24.73), the reference is to the same author as the annotated passage.

ABBREVIATIONS:

Aes.   = Aeschines
And.   = Andocides
Ant.   = Antiphon
Arist.   = Aristotle
Aristoph. = Aristophanes
Ath. Pol. = *The Athenian Constitution*
Dem.   = Demosthenes
Din.   = Dinarchus
Herod.   = Herodotus
Hyp.   = Hyperides
Is.   = Isaeus
Isoc.   = Isocrates
Lyc.   = Lycurgus
Lys.   = Lysias
Plut.   = Plutarch
Thuc.   = Thucydides
Xen.   = Xenophon

NOTE: The main unit of Athenian currency was the drachma; this was divided into obols and larger amounts were designated minas and talents.

1 drachma = 6 obols
1 mina   = 100 drachmas
1 talent = 60 minas (6,000 drachmas)

It is impossible to give an accurate equivalence in terms of modern currency, but it may be helpful to remember that the daily wage of

---

[28] For a listing of all the orators and their works, with classifications (forensic, deliberative, epideictic) and rough dates, see Edwards 1994: 74–79.

some skilled workers was a drachma in the mid-fifth century and 2–2½ drachmas in the later fourth century. Thus it may not be too misleading to think of a drachma as worth about $50 or £33 and a talent as about $300,000 or £200,000 in 1997 currency.

BIBLIOGRAPHY OF WORKS CITED

Boegehold, Alan L., 1995: *The Lawcourts at Athens: Sites, Buildings, Equipment, Procedure, and Testimonia.* Princeton.

Bonner, Robert J., 1927: *Lawyers and Litigants in Ancient Athens.* Chicago.

Carey, Christopher, 1997: *Trials from Classical Athens.* London.

Cohen, David, 1995: *Law, Violence and Community in Classical Athens.* Cambridge.

Cole, Thomas, 1991: *The Origins of Rhetoric in Ancient Greece.* Baltimore.

Dover, Kenneth J., 1968: *Lysias and the Corpus Lysiacum.* Berkeley.

———, 1974: *Greek Popular Morality in the Time of Plato and Aristotle.* Oxford.

———, 1978: *Greek Homosexuality.* London.

———, 1994: *Marginal Comment.* London.

Edwards, Michael, 1994: *The Attic Orators.* London.

Gagarin, Michael, and Paul Woodruff, 1995: *Early Greek Political Thought from Homer to the Sophists.* Cambridge.

Hansen, Mogens Herman, 1991: *The Athenian Democracy in the Age of Demosthenes.* Oxford.

Jebb, Richard, 1875: *The Attic Orators,* 2 vols. London.

Kennedy, George A., 1963: *The Art of Persuasion in Greece.* Princeton.

Kerferd, G. B., 1981: *The Sophistic Movement.* Cambridge.

MacDowell, Douglas M., 1978: *The Law in Classical Athens.* London.

———, ed. 1990: *Demosthenes, Against Meidias.* Oxford.

Ober, Josiah, 1989: *Mass and Elite in Democratic Athens.* Princeton.

Rhodes, P. J., trans., 1984: *Aristotle, The Athenian Constitution.* Penguin Books.

Sinclair, R. K., 1988: *Democracy and Participation in Athens.* Cambridge.

Todd, Stephen, 1993: *The Shape of Athenian Law.* Oxford.

Trevett, Jeremy, 1992: *Apollodoros the Son of Pasion*. Oxford.

————, 1996: "Did Demosthenes Publish His Deliberative Speeches?" *Hermes* 124: 425–441.

Usher, Stephen, 1976: "Lysias and His Clients," *Greek, Roman and Byzantine Studies* 17: 31–40.

————, trans., 1974–1985: *Dionysius of Halicarnassus, Critical Essays*. 2 vols. Loeb Classical Library. Cambridge, MA.

————, 1999: *Greek Oratory: Tradition and Originality*. Oxford.

Wooten, Cecil W., trans., 1987: *Hermogenes' On Types of Style*. Chapel Hill, NC.

Worthington, Ian, 1994: "The Canon of the Ten Attic Orators," in *Persuasion: Greek Rhetoric in Action*, ed. Ian Worthington. London: 244–263.

Yunis, Harvey, 1996: *Taming Democracy: Models of Political Rhetoric in Classical Athens*. Ithaca, NY.

ISOCRATES II

Translated by Terry L. Papillon

INTRODUCTION TO ISOCRATES [1]

LIFE AND CAREER

Isocrates (436–338) differs from the other Attic Orators in that his reputation was not based on speeches that he delivered in the courts or the Assembly, or wrote for others to deliver, but rather on "speeches" (*logoi*) that were intended to be circulated in writing and read by others. This is important for his representation of himself and his career (and his dissociation of himself from those he called "sophists") and for understanding the important role he played in the intellectual life of fourth-century Athens.

Early in his career Isocrates did write speeches for others to deliver in the lawcourts, but he soon gave up this practice and opened a school where he taught about education and rhetoric, that is, politics. His views on these subjects put him at odds with Plato (and later Aristotle), who had a rival school, and his generally aristocratic political views brought him into conflict with politicians like Demosthenes. But among his pupils were many prominent Greeks of the time, and in antiquity and the Renaissance he enjoyed a reputation as a political writer, a stylist, and the foremost teacher of rhetoric in his day (e.g., Cicero, *De Oratore* 2.94–95).

Details of Isocrates' life are provided by his own works and by several later biographies, notably those of Dionysius of Halicarnassus and Pseudo-Plutarch (*Moralia* 836–839). But Isocrates was a controversial figure, and so all our sources may be influenced by political agendas,

---

[1] This Introduction to Isocrates is a joint effort of the three translators of Isocrates (David Mirhady, Terry Papillon, and Yun Lee Too) and the Series Editor.

by literary and biographical conventions, and sometimes by misun-
derstanding. He was born into a wealthy Athenian family during the
height of Athens' power before the Peloponnesian War. According
to tradition, his father Theodorus owned a workshop that manufac-
tured flutes; his mother's name was Heduto, and he had three brothers and a sister. He is reported to have studied with several prominent
teachers, including Tisias (one of the traditional founders of rhetoric), the sophists Prodicus and Gorgias, and the moderate oligarch
Theramenes, and to have associated with Socrates, but such reports
may reflect later views of his intellectual roots more than historical
fact.[2] Late in his life he married a woman named Plathane, daughter
of the sophist Hippias, and adopted Aphareus, one of her sons by a
previous marriage.

Isocrates apparently avoided public life during the turbulent years of
the Peloponnesian War (431–404). After the war he had a brief career
as a logographer, writing forensic speeches for others (speeches 16–
21), but he apparently gave this up around 390 and turned to teaching,
in part to recover his fortunes after suffering financial losses in the
Peloponnesian War (15.161). He was so successful at this that he was
later enrolled among the wealthiest 1,200 Athenian citizens, who were
responsible for public liturgies, such as the financing of warships (trierarchies) and choruses (see Series Introduction: xxi). He says that he
and his son voluntarily undertook three trierarchies during his lifetime (15.145).

Isocrates distinguishes himself from those who treat public speaking largely as a means of amassing personal fortunes and instead represents himself as a principled and responsible teacher of what he calls
"philosophy," but later ages down to the present have more often in-
terpreted as "rhetoric." Tradition has it that he taught as many as a
hundred students, including many who became prominent orators
(Isaeus, Hyperides), writers (Theopompus, Ephorus, Androtion), and
military and political leaders (Timotheus, Nicocles). Many of his letters dramatize the teacher offering political instruction and advice to
various potentates of the Greek-speaking world, including the tyrant
Dionysius of Syracuse (*Epistle* 1), Philip of Macedon (*Epistles* 2 and 3),

[2] See Too 1995: 235–239.

Timotheus, ruler of Heracleia (*Epistle* 7), and Archidamus III, king of Sparta (*Epistle* 9).

In 378 Athens established a new naval confederation, the so-called Second Athenian League, and regained much of its former prominence. During the next two decades Isocrates enjoyed the friendship of the leading Athenian general Timotheus, and it was probably during this period that he developed his relationship with Evagoras, king of Cyprus, and his son Nicocles (see speeches 2, 3, 9). The power of Athens and Timotheus' standing in the city both diminished sharply in the 350s, and Isocrates retired from teaching in 351 at the age of 85. He continued to write, however, and became increasingly interested in engaging the leadership of Philip in the cause of panhellenism—the ideal of a unified Greek political and cultural world that the individual Greek cities had thus far been unable or unwilling to achieve. He is reported to have died at the age of 98 by starving himself after hearing the news of Athens' defeat by Philip in the battle of Chaeronea in 338. In any case he did not live to see the actual unification of the Greek world that was achieved rather differently from what he had imagined by Philip's son Alexander the Great (reigned 336–323).

PHILOSOPHIA, EDUCATION, AND POLITICS

Isocrates devoted many of his writings to proclaiming his views (and criticizing those of his opponents) on a broad range of educational and political issues. At the core of his teaching was an aristocratic notion of *aretē* ("virtue, excellence"), which could be attained by pursuing *philosophia*—not so much the dialectical study of abstract subjects like epistemology and metaphysics that Plato marked as "philosophy" as the study and practical application of ethics, politics, and public speaking. His views are most fully expounded in two works, one early in his career, the other near the end of it.

Against the Sophists (13) is a polemic against his rival professional teachers. As he characterizes them, these sophists are primarily interested in disputation ("eristic") as a tool for victory in debates, particularly debates between litigants in court. Although the text breaks off just as Isocrates announces that he will give a more comprehensive account of his teaching, this work can be read as a partial account of his pedagogical methods: his essential point is that in order to become a skilled practitioner of public speech, a student requires both the appropriate natural ability, including a capacity for hard work and a good memory, and also the guidance of a good teacher.

Antidosis (15), in which Isocrates seeks to justify his life as a professional teacher in Athens, offers a fuller account of his own pedagogical views.[3] He stresses that his teaching (*paideia*) is practical and is aimed at preparing young men broadly as gentlemen. It includes more than what later ages called rhetoric—instruction in the art of public speech and persuasion—and is essentially an education in political leadership, a mechanism for the construction of authority among the traditional elite groups that comprise Isocrates' ideal pupils (15.304). He demonstrates that Athens was founded and made great through the oratorical skills of men like Solon, Themistocles, and Pericles, and he argues that because public speaking is the basis of the ideal democratic community, it should continue to be a structuring principle of Athens. Despite the six forensic speeches that are preserved in his name, Isocrates denies having had anything to do with the lawcourts, and he repudiates any possible identification with the culture of forensic oratory (15.36). Only the sophists concern themselves with private lawsuits (15.45–46); by contrast, Isocrates asserts that he has devoted himself only to the interests of the Greek people.

Isocrates' political agenda is thus conservative, verging on oligarchy, though he is always careful to designate it democracy. As an advocate of public speaking, he promotes an earlier culture of public discourse, reminding his audience that although the contemporary culture of oratory has caused wealthy, respectable citizens like himself to be involved in trials motivated by personal grudges and jealousy, public discourse originally and ideally constitutes the basis of the community. He returns frequently to the historical role of discourse (as he sees it) in the establishment of Athenian military and cultural supremacy, which has allowed the people (the *dēmos*) to wield the

---

[3] In *Antidosis* Isocrates devises the elaborate scenario of a trial in which he was accused of being an unscrupulous teacher who corrupted his pupils and failed to disclose his true earnings. This trial is the pretext for writing the *Antidosis*, in which Isocrates assumes the role of the philosopher wrongly attacked by his community, explicitly modeling himself after the Socrates of Plato's *Apology* (see Papillon 1997).

power it does. Through speech (*logos*) men persuaded one another, associated with one another, created cities, established customs and laws (*nomoi*), educated others, disputed with one another, and invented the arts (3.5–9, 15.253–257). For Isocrates *logos* (discourse) and *philosophia* (the study of and training in discourse) are at the core of any orderly, civilized community and have been essential to the success of Athens, the classical democratic city *par excellence.* Discourse institutionalizes morality and makes possible debate, persuasion, and the instruction of others; and an individual who provides a true education in this subject demonstrates his own civic virtue (*aretē*) and deserves the gratitude of the city for helping to maintain its ideals and power.

Isocrates' political views also found expression on contemporary issues, primarily in his advocacy of panhellenism—the promotion of a united Greek opposition to Persia. He sees Athens as the natural leader of Greece and urges cooperation among the leading cities in the fourth century, Athens, Sparta, and Thebes, with Athens assuming a leading role. These views are first set forth in *Panegyricus* (4), composed for the panhellenic Olympic festival in 380. In this work he argues that freedom and other common values divide Greeks from non-Greeks, so that Greek cities should put aside their differences and unite against the common enemy. Isocrates returns to these themes often, but as time revealed the inability of Athens and the other Greek cities to give up their long-standing independence from and distrust of one another, he increasingly saw Macedonia—on the fringe of the Greek world and ambiguously straddling Greek and "barbarian" elements—as the best hope for unifying the Greek states in common cause against Persia. To this end, in speeches such as *To Philip* (5) and *Panathenaicus* (12), in particular, he lobbied for a panhellenic military expedition against Persia led by Philip. He still hoped for a leading role for Athens, a hope that was dashed at Chaeronea, just before his death.

Another feature of Isocrates' rhetorical teaching, which may be partly responsible for both ancient and modern devaluing of him,[4] is

---

[4] Marrou (1956: 131), for instance, judges that despite his preeminent position as a teacher of rhetoric in antiquity, Isocrates is to be regarded as standing in second place to his contemporary Plato where personality, temperament, depth of intellect, and art are concerned.

that he challenges the common perception of discourse as predominantly oral. Indeed, he explicitly rejects the spoken word as a political medium, claiming that a "small voice" and lack of courage prevent him from speaking in public (cf. 5.81, 15.190–191, *Epistle* 8.7). This account may best be understood as the product of a paradoxical self-fashioning, since in claiming to be unable to speak in public, Isocrates conveniently excuses himself from his contemporary culture of public oratory, which he characterizes as petty, litigious, and promoted by self-interested and unscrupulous sophists.[5] By preserving his distance from contemporary oratory and its limited concerns, Isocrates could explore larger political issues, in particular those concerning Athens' leadership of the Greek states. For him, the written word was the basis of interactions with the larger Hellenic community. His works were thus a testimony to his political interactions with individuals and states outside Athens.

STYLE

Like several other Athenian orators, Isocrates was and continues to be known for his distinctive literary style. Although he was influenced by the stylistic innovations of Gorgias, verbal assonance is not nearly as prominent in his work as in Gorgias' writings, and he generally employs parallelism and antithesis at the level of whole clauses and sentences rather than individual words and short phrases. The result may not rival the forcefulness of Demosthenes, but Isocrates' prose has generally been admired for its smoothness and charm.

Isocrates seems to offer an account of his literary method in *Against the Sophists* (13.16–17), where he speaks of the hard work and superior natural ability required in order to choose from the various forms of discourse

> the necessary forms for each subject, to mix them with each other and arrange them suitably, and then, not to mistake the circumstances (*kairoi*) but to embellish the entire speech properly with considerations (*enthymēmata*) and to speak the words rhythmically and musically.

---

[5] For discussion of this aspect of the rhetorician's self-representation, see Too 1995: 74–112.

In following this method Isocrates developed a style characterized by long, artfully constructed, "periodic" sentences, which by their architectural structure of balanced clauses convey a strong sense of order and reason. For example, in a translation that tries to follow as closely as possible the Greek word order, a single sentence from *Antidosis* (15.48 – 49)[6] might read as follows (Isocrates is distinguishing between those who write for the courts and those like himself who do not):

> [48] [Many men] recognize that the one group (*tous men*)[7] through political meddling have become experienced in legal contests, but the others (*tous de*) through philosophy have developed their skill in the speeches I have just described, and that those (*tous men*) who appear to be skilled in forensic speeches, on that day only are tolerated on which they happen to be pleading, whereas the others (*tous de*) are honored in all gatherings all the time and have acquired a high reputation; [49] and furthermore, that the former (*tous men*), if they are seen two or three times in the courts, are hated and derided but the latter (*tous de*), the more people they associate with and the more often, the more they are admired; and in addition to this, those (*tous men*) who are skilled in legal pleadings are far from the eloquence of the others, but the others (*tous de*), if they wished, could quickly master that kind of speaking.

The structure of this sentence (which needless to say is impossible to reproduce consistently in a readable English translation) reinforces the polarization Isocrates seeks to convey and supports his assertion of the superiority of his own endeavor, while at the same time giving the reader no specific information about the exact nature of that endeavor.[8]

----

[6] It should be noted that in Isocrates' day punctuation marks such as the period did not exist, so that the determination of sentence end is the work of modern editors. In places a period could arguably be substituted for a semicolon or comma and vice versa.

[7] The particles *men* and *de* are used in Greek as early as Homer to designate antithetical words and clauses.

[8] Isocrates' style is also characterized in Greek by the avoidance of hiatus—the collision of vowels between two successive words. In English hiatus is avoided by, e.g., inserting an "n" between the vowels ("an apple" instead of "a apple"). Greek avoids hiatus primarily by the careful placement of words. Our translations do not attempt to reproduce this effect.

A NOTE ON TERMINOLOGY

As noted above, Isocrates never uses the term "rhetoric," (*rhētorikē,* i.e., *rhētorikē technē,* "the rhetorical art") to refer to public speaking or instruction in the art of discourse, though he does occasionally use the adjective "rhetorical" (*rhētorikos*).[9] Instead, to designate his own work he uses *philosophia* and various expressions involving *logos* ("word, speech, argument, discourse," etc.) in both singular and plural (*logoi*). The use of these terms and the avoidance of *rhētorikē* must be intentional on Isocrates' part and may be linked to his rivalry with Plato, who uses *rhētorikē,* most notably in the *Gorgias,* to condemn the teaching of public speaking.[10] Isocrates instead seeks to appropriate the term *philosophia* to describe his intellectual activity and teaching, thereby implicitly challenging Plato, who was seeking to appropriate the term for his own work.[11]

In view of this, although *philosophia* and other expressions may overlap with various meanings of the English term "rhetoric," we do not use "rhetoric" in our translations (though we do use "rhetorical" for *rhētorikos*). We generally translate *philosophia* as "philosophy" (with an occasional reminder that this means something close to our "rhetoric"), and use such terms as "speaking," "speech," "discourse," "oratory," and "eloquence" as the occasion requires for various expressions with *logos.*

Finally, a note of caution to the reader. Interest in Isocrates has been growing rapidly in recent years, and scholars in different fields have been exploring new ways of reading him. As a result, a diversity of views is reflected in the three translators, and although we have co-ordinated our translations and discussed our differences among ourselves with a view to achieving consensus wherever possible, this diversity is still evident, both among the three translators and perhaps even within the translators themselves. Thus the reader should not al-

---

[9] He also uses *rhētoreia* ("[artful] speaking") in 5.26, 12.2, and 13.21, and *rhētoreuō* ("to speak publicly") in 5.25 and *Epistle* 8.7. *Rhētores* ("public speakers," always in the plural) is fairly common (21 instances).

[10] *Gorgias* 448–466 *passim.* As Schiappa 1990 and Cole 1991 argue, Plato may have created the term *rhētorikē* as part of his attack on this competing cultural force.

[11] See Too 1995: 180, 193; Papillon 1995; Timmerman 1998.

ways expect to find a single voice in these two volumes but will, we hope, enter into our discourse and create his or her own voice for Isocrates.

TEXT

A number of medieval manuscripts of Isocrates' works have survived, one dating back to the late ninth or early tenth century, and a very recent papyrus find in Egypt has given us the earliest texts of speeches 1–3 (fourth century AD). The most notable modern editions of Isocrates are the Budé edition in four volumes by Georges Mathieu and Emile Brémond, *Isocrate: Discours* (Paris, 1929–1966), and the Loeb text in three volumes by George Norlin and LaRue Van Hook, *Isocrates* (Cambridge, MA and London, 1928–1945).

The translations in this volume are based on the Budé text, except where noted.

THE WORKS OF ISOCRATES

According to Pseudo-Plutarch as many as sixty works were associated with Isocrates' name, but not all these are authentic. Today thirty works are generally ascribed to him. They are traditionally numbered as in Table 1 (the Roman numerals indicate the volume of Isocrates in this series that contains the work; most dates are approximate guesses).

There is no obvious or generally accepted arrangement of the speeches of Isocrates. In this translation we use the traditional numbering of the manuscripts but do not follow this order in our translations. Instead, Mirhady translates the earlier speeches; Too, the speeches that concern education in its various manifestations; and Papillon, the remainder.

Scholars have offered various generic descriptions and classifications of these works. To cite just one example, Richard Jebb proposed a generic scheme that divided them into the following four categories: *A.* Scholastic, which included hortatory, display, and educational works (1, 2, 3, 9, 10, 11, 12, 13, 15). *B.* Political works (4, 5, 6, 7, 8, 14). *C.* Forensic speeches (16–21). *D.* Letters and fragments.[12] Such broad

---

[12] See Jebb 1876: 2.82–84.

TABLE I

The Works of Isocrates

Oration	Date	Volume
1. *To Demonicus*	(374–370)	I
2. *To Nicocles*	(374)	I
3. *Nicocles*	(372–365)	I
4. *Panegyricus*	(380)	II
5. *To Philip*	(346)	II
6. *Archidamus*	(366)	II
7. *Areopagiticus*	(ca. 357)	I
8. *On the Peace*	(355)	II
9. *Evagoras*	(370–365)	I
10. *Encomium of Helen*	(370)	I
11. *Busiris*	(391–385)	I
12. *Panathenaicus*	(342–339)	II
13. *Against the Sophists*	(390)	I
14. *Plataicus*	(373–371)	II
15. *Antidosis*	(354–353)	I
16. *On the Team of Horses*	(397–396)	I
17. *Trapeziticus*	(393)	I
18. *Special Plea against Callimachus*	(402)	I
19. *Aegineticus*	(391–390)	I
20. *Against Lochites*	(394)	I
21. *Against Euthynus, without Witnesses*	(403)	I
Epistle 1. To Dionysius	(368)	II
Epistle 2. To Philip 1	(342)	II
Epistle 3. To Philip 2	(338)	II
Epistle 4. To Antipater	(340)	II
Epistle 5. To Alexander	(342)	II
Epistle 6. To the Children of Jason	(359)	II
Epistle 7. To Timotheus	(345)	II
Epistle 8. To the Rulers of the Mytileneans	(350)	II
Epistle 9. To Archidamus	(356)	II

generic descriptions may help a modern reader understand the conventions governing the writing of a particular work, but they may also conceal the extent to which works in all categories form part of a larger whole, which Isocrates identifies as *logos politikos*.[13] Thus although Isocrates at times seems to insist on generic differentiation (e.g., 1.5), at other times he resists such classifications, and a generic taxonomy may sometimes conceal the complexity of his literary self-representation.

---

[13] See Poulakos 1997.

INTRODUCTION TO
ISOCRATES, VOLUME II

This volume contains the six discourses of Isocrates not treated in *Isocrates I* of this series, and all the letters. If the second section of *Isocrates I* shows Isocrates as a teacher,[1] then we could say that the discourses in this volume demonstrate how Isocrates uses his ideas on education and public discourse to address situations affecting the city or *polis.* Thus, they might be called Isocrates' political works. All of them—and we can include the letters in this—demonstrate his ability to present ideas called forth by a given political and rhetorical situation.[2] Three discourses, *Panathenaicus, On the Peace,* and the most famous, *Panegyricus,* focus on Isocrates' home city of Athens; other discourses focus on other cities: *Archidamus* is in the voice of the Spartan prince to his assembly; *Plataicus* is in the voice of a citizen of Plataea asking Athens for aid; the discourse *To Philip* is Isocrates, *in propria persona,* calling on Philip of Macedon to lead a unified Greece against Persia.

Two speeches, *Panathenaicus* and *Panegyricus,* represent what Greek rhetorical theory called epideictic or display oratory, where the speaker addresses a public gathering to offer praise, in these instances praise of the city. The other four, *To Philip, Archidamus, On the Peace,* and *Plataicus,* represent deliberative rhetoric, the rhetoric of the Assembly considering issues of interest to the city and its future. In fact, how-

---

[1] See Too in Mirhady and Too 2000: 137.

[2] For the seminal statement of the concept of the "rhetorical situation," see Bitzer 1968; cf. Papillon 1998b: 2–3, 113–116.

ever, Isocrates did not deliver any of these in public; all were pamphlets written and circulated to interested parties.

We do not even know if they actually addressed the specific situation. To take one example, we do not know if the discourse *To Philip* was ever actually sent to Philip. It may have been sent to him at the dramatic date of the discourse, 346, or it may have been written at that time or later as a sample speech for Isocrates' students. This is generally true of all the discourses included in this volume: we do not know if they were written at the time claimed and if they were sent to the party interested (or written for the person speaking, as in the case of *Archidamus* or *Plataicus*). But even if they are fictionalized presentations, Isocrates carefully set these discourses into the appropriate time to address the given situation, and thus they can tell us much about the political realities of the periods represented as well as Isocrates' notion of what it means to be an active citizen.

The dramatic date of each discourse is thus quite important because each speech reacts to a specific situation. *Panegyricus* represents Isocrates' celebration of the greatness of Athens at a time, 380, when Greek politics was complicated by competition between cities and the intervention of the Great King of Persia. Isocrates presents one of his main ideas in this speech, and one of the central ideas of his career: the need for Greece to unite in a panhellenic campaign against Persia. The speech celebrates Athens at a public gathering, but it must also recognize that Sparta led Greece at the time. Isocrates thus celebrates the past of Athens and argues for a joint leadership for Greece between Athens and Sparta. This is perhaps Isocrates' most famous and most carefully constructed speech, dealing effectively with the political and rhetorical realities of the period while lifting up the greatness of Athens and its culture. *Panathenaicus* is similar—it too celebrates the greatness of Athens in a public assembly—but it is among the last of Isocrates' works, completed when he was 98, and shows signs of lack of care and weakness even while it presents the glory of Athens at the very end of Greek freedom in 338. Yet it has its own points of interest, such as the discussion he reports with a former pupil about compositional technique.

In both *Plataicus* and *Archidamus,* Isocrates writes in the voice of another. It is common enough in Greek oratory for a speechwriter, called a logographer, to compose a speech for another person to present in a lawcourt, but it is unusual for a logographer to compose a deliberative speech, as Isocrates does in these two speeches. In *Plataicus,* a citizen of Plataea asks Athens for aid after Plataea had been destroyed by Thebes in 373. It represents a vivid picture of the troubles of a smaller Greek city in the very chaotic times of the late 370s. *Archidamus* presents the Spartan prince addressing the Assembly on how to deal with the difficult times after Sparta lost power in the battle of Leuctra in 371. It is a rare view of Spartan affairs from the Spartan point of view, or at least Isocrates' attempt to present what he thought a Spartan point of view would be.

The two speeches *On the Peace* and *To Philip* address Greek politics in Isocrates' own voice. In *On the Peace,* Isocrates addresses the newly signed peace treaty in 355 that settled the Social War between Athens and its allies. It was a difficult time in Athens' history because the allies had revolted from Athens' control, and Isocrates takes advantage of the occasion to broaden the issue from peace with the allies to peace with all Greek cities, again representing the notion of Greek unity that Isocrates continually advocates. The speech *To Philip* also addresses this theme of unity, summoning Philip II of Macedon in 346 to lead a unified Greece against Persia. When Philip actually did take control of Greek affairs after the battle of Chaeronea in 338, Isocrates is said to have committed suicide by starvation because he was disillusioned about Philip's military solution.[3] Philip did not lead the Greeks the way Isocrates had envisioned him doing it.

The letters are smaller images of the affairs of the day and offer similar kinds of information about Greece and Isocrates. The fifth letter, to Alexander the Great, is particularly interesting because it represents Isocrates' advice to the future ruler and Isocrates' views of Alexander's training under Aristotle, Isocrates' contemporary and rival. The last piece of writing we have from Isocrates also comes from the letters, the second letter to Philip (*Ep.* 3), which was written just after Philip's victory at Chaeronea, when Isocrates was 98 years old. This letter is more

---

[3] So Pseudo-Plutarch in *Lives of the Ten Orators* (837E–F) and picked up later in Milton (*Sonnet* 10).

hopeful about Philip's intentions and plans than the tradition of his disillusionment implies. Perhaps, as Michael Edwards has suggested,[4] it was his frustration at the continued opposition on the part of Athens rather than Philip's actions that led to his choice to die.

THE TRANSLATION

Translating Isocrates is often difficult. So, too, is reading Isocrates. The style Isocrates employs in all the speeches collected in this volume shows an elaborate periodicity that can be difficult to represent in English and difficult to grasp, in English or Greek. This is particularly true of his greatest speech, *Panegyricus*. In most cases I have broken up longer periods to make them more readable in English. I have also changed many Greek participial phrases, the heart of Greek periodic prose, into subordinate clauses in English because English more comfortably uses subordinate clauses than it does participial phrases. The elaborate nature of Isocratean prose has limited appeal in the early twenty-first century, when discourse tends to be much more direct, and his prose can seem foreign at times. To the extent that this translation helps its readers understand, appreciate, and enjoy Isocrates, his periodic style, and his thought, it will have succeeded.

A second facet of Isocrates' discourse that may seem foreign to modern readers is his self-conscious speech. Isocrates talks of himself often, and often in very glowing terms. This may seem arrogant to modern readers, but a person's claim to superiority was a natural part of discourse in ancient times. Homeric characters, Pericles (as Thucydides presents him), and Cicero do not shy away from stating their own greatness. Isocrates himself faults his confidence in his *Panathenaicus* (12.230–232). This is the exception that proves the rule, however, in that he mentions it here, where he does not fault himself on the many other occasions when he speaks so highly of himself. This presentation of self-confidence can be different from modern notions, but we must remember that we are entering a different world with different assumptions; one thing this translation tries to do is to take

---

[4] On the end of Isocrates' life, see Edwards 1994: 27.

readers to another world, and it asks them to be open to the culture that the other world offers, even if it may seem odd at first.

I rarely translate the Greek word *logos* as "speech." Instead, I often use the word "discourse." This is partially a function of the complicated question of how Isocrates presented his works; he probably did not present them orally himself (see the introductory essays in this volume) but circulated written versions. I have also hesitated to translate *logos* as "speech" because of modern notions of speech and discourse. Just as the Speech Communication Association recognized that the word "speech" is too limiting in the study of persuasion and communication when it changed its name to the National Communication Association, so too I want to stress that what Isocrates does and what he argues for is not limited to oral contexts but can be applied to many different areas. When Isocrates presents rhetorical theory, it need not be restricted to oral presentation but can be considered in all areas of persuasive discourse and communication. This awareness of the ubiquity of persuasion and communication is one of the advances that modern rhetorical theory has emphasized in the history of rhetoric, and it is one of the truly modern aspects of Isocrates.

For the translation I have relied on both the Budé edition of Mathieu and Brémond and the Loeb Classical Library edition of van Hook and Norlin. I have also consulted the Teubner edition of Benseler-Blass and the Italian edition of Ghirga and Romussi.

SPEECHES

4. PANEGYRICUS

❧❧

INTRODUCTION

The Greeks often gathered for public celebration in their own cities, but they also celebrated (though less often) at panhellenic gatherings, which were called *pan-egyreis* or panegyric festivals because *all* Greeks *gather together* to celebrate. Isocrates praises panegyric festivals in sections 43–44 of this speech:

> Those who established panegyric festivals are justly praised for handing down such a fine custom to us where we make a peace treaty, break off any existing hostilities, and come together in the same place; after this, as we make prayers and sacrifices, we recall the common heritage we have with each other, establish our goodwill toward each other for the future, and renew ancient ties of guest friendship and make new ones. The time spent here is not wasted, for either the private observer or the superior athlete, but in this gathering of the Greeks, the athletes come to display their good fortune and the observers to see the athletes competing against each other; neither group is unmoved but each takes pride: the observers in seeing the athletes competing on their behalf and the athletes in knowing that all are there to see them compete.

Examples of such festivals include the four panhellenic athletic festivals at Olympia, Delphi (Pythian games), Nemea, and Corinth (Isthmian games), as well as two notable gatherings in Athens: the Panathenaic festival and the Greater Dionysia.[1] As occasions for all of Greece

---

[1] Lysias' panegyric speech, the *Olympiacus* (33.1–2), credits Heracles with founding the Olympic festival, the earliest of the panhellenic festivals.

to gather together, these festivals were natural opportunities for oratory, and addresses to the crowds seem to have stressed Greek unity.[2] An officially recognized oration to celebrate the festival came to be called a panegyric (*panegyrikos logos*), and Isocrates himself calls the present speech by that name.[3] He follows in an oratorical tradition, including the Olympic orations of Gorgias in 392 and Lysias in 388, that celebrates the glory of Greek history and culture. Parallel to such panegyrics and showing similar themes is the tradition of the funeral oration (*epitaphios logos*), which celebrates both those who died in war and the city for which they died. Nicole Loraux (1986) has shown the importance of such discourse for creating and sustaining cultural values in the community.[4]

Isocrates' *Panegyricus* was published in 380 after ten years of composition.[5] This was a time of discord in Greece, with city-states competing against each other for political supremacy. Sparta had led the Greek states since 404, when it defeated Athens at the end of the Peloponnesian War, but it had suffered setbacks in the late 390s and was trying to consolidate its power in the face of the reemergence of Athens and opposition from Corinth and Thebes. Persia also played a major part in Greek politics in this period, notably with the King's Peace of 387—also called the Peace of Antalcidas—when it negotiated a treaty with Sparta identifying which cities would be independent and which would be under Spartan, Athenian, or Persian control. Isocrates seizes the opportunity presented by the confusion in these years to propose a solution: the way to relieve the stresses on the Greek city-

---

[2] Cf. Kennedy 1963: 166–167 and Loraux 1986.

[3] There are references to Isocrates' speech by this name in the works of Aristotle and later authors, but I know of no prior reference to *panēgyrikos logos* as a technical term (cf. Schiappa 1999: 190–192). Isocrates called another speech *Panathenaicus* (12) in the tradition of speeches to be delivered at the Panathenaea in Athens.

[4] Cf. below, 74n.

[5] The exact number of years Isocrates worked on the speech varies with the sources. One sign of the long period of composition is the appearance of references to the Peace of Antalcidas (387/6) in the second half of the speech but none in the first (Sandys 1872: xlii–xliii).

states is to induce them to give up their animosity toward each other and join in a unified campaign against Persia.

Oratory in the classical world became thoroughly systematized, and speeches took on prescribed structures. Speeches in the lawcourts, for example, have a fairly strict structure.[6] The proem (introduction) introduces the topic, seeks the goodwill of the audience, and gets their attention. It is followed by a narration of the events relevant to the issue. After this comes the proof, with arguments for the speaker's case and refutation of his opponent's points. The peroration or conclusion follows, summing up the points and rousing the audience to the speaker's side. There are additional options: after the narration, the orator may offer a partition, a statement of the significant issues to be treated. This reasserts the important points after the narrative and clarifies them for the jury, serving as a sort of second proem. Between proof and peroration the orator may add what has been called an "ethical digression" to serve as a transition from the rigorous logical work of the proof to what is often an emotional appeal in the peroration.[7] Such a structure, often discussed by ancient and modern theorists, appears with varied strictness in lawcourt speeches, and deliberative and epideictic oratory are even less rigorously structured. These usually have an introduction and conclusion and may have a narrative, but the argumentation often occurs through topics rather than logical progression.[8] Such is the case in *Panegyricus*.

This speech combines the epideictic function of praise with the deliberative function of advice, which Isocrates presents in two major subsections.[9] After an introduction that is quite combative and programmatic (1–14) and a partition (15–20), Isocrates treats the epideictic theme of Athens' greatness (21–128). Traditional aspects of such praise include the city's gifts to the world (22–50), its actions in war

[6] For a brief, clear, and persuasive summary of classical rhetorical theory, see Kennedy 1984: 3–38.

[7] On ethical digression, see May 1988.

[8] On epideictic patterns of composition, see the fine edition of Menander Rhetor by Russell and Wilson (1981) and the treatise on epideictic rhetoric by Burgess (1902).

[9] On the mixture of rhetorical species, see Papillon 1998b: 14–18.

(51–99), and its stature in comparison with its rival, Sparta (100–128). This borrows much from the epideictic tradition of funeral orations that praise virtues.[10] A brief transition (129–132) leads to the treatment of the deliberative section (133–169), which stresses the need for a campaign against Persia and uses the topics of the Greeks' inaction (133–137), the specific weakness of the Persian King himself (138–149), the general weakness of the Persians as a people (150–159), and the present problems facing Persia that give Greece an advantage (160–169). The peroration (170–189) reasserts the notions of advantage, justice, possibility, and the Greeks' ability to carry out what Isocrates suggests.

Both major sections of the discourse focus on the main theme of this work, which is also a main theme of Isocrates' life work as a whole: panhellenic unity. He announces this early in *Panegyricus* (3) and then states it again clearly in the peroration (173):

> The plan for this is simple and easy; it is impossible to have a secure peace unless we join together to make war against the barbarians, and it is impossible for us to be unified until we gain our advantages from the same sources and run our risks against the same enemies.

The theme is stated baldly in this section of the conclusion to make sure that the reader has a clear sense of where the epideictic and deliberative portions of the discourse have been aiming.[11]

Because of the historical context mentioned above, the speech shows an awkward tension in the question of leadership of the unified Greeks. As a devoted Athenian, Isocrates wants to assert Athens' historical claim to superiority, but he must recognize the reality of Spartan supremacy in the present. There are times when Isocrates seems to call for Athens' leadership and other times when he seems to call for joint leadership of Athens and Sparta. The extensive period of composition could account for this tension (cf. Usher 1990: 19–21): Isoc-

---

[10] Loraux (1986: 89) makes much of the political importance of the funeral oration and comments specifically on the influence of the funeral oration on Isocrates' *Panegyricus*. See also Hudson-Williams 1948.

[11] This two-sided proposal, taken from the praise tradition of funeral and panegyric oratory before him, can be seen in *To Philip* in 346 and again in *Panathenaicus* in 339 (both translated in this volume).

rates began with the idea of joint hegemony and, as the political situation changed, ended by proposing the sole leadership of Athens. Such a hypothesis would make Isocrates a bad editor, however, who could not clean up the discrepancies through the body of the text. It is perhaps more likely that Isocrates wanted to suggest multiple options for the reader, and he thus created a fiction of a long process of composition to allow for the variation. If this is the case, it would be another instance of biographical manipulation on the part of Isocrates, such as has been argued about his claims to have a weak voice and nervous disposition (Too 1995: 75–81). Finally, it is also possible that Isocrates struggled to reconcile the political reality of Spartan prominence with his own desire for Athenian supremacy. It would be difficult for an Athenian to accept the leadership of Sparta, and at a time of political instability such as the late 380s, even a joint leadership might strike Isocrates as unfair, albeit politically necessary. Isocrates thus proposes joint leadership, but he makes it clear in the argumentation that all should recognize Athens' moral claim to sole leadership.

Isocrates tells us that he published this speech when he was 56 years old, about 380, after working for ten years. We are to imagine that Isocrates began work at about the time he opened his own school in 390 or slightly earlier, and he would have planned for it to serve as an advertisement of both his abilities and his ideas. He meant to set his abilities against other popular teachers, orators, and speechwriters of the day such as Gorgias and Lysias, both of whom presented Olympic orations. He also meant to set his own ideas, especially the ubiquitous idea of the unity of the Greeks in a common expedition against Persia, against other politicians of the day. Tradition says that Isocrates did not present the speech himself. As with most of his discourses, *Panegyricus* was probably written and circulated for a wider reading audience. We do not know for sure whether it was actually read at one of the festivals.

The speech is often considered the finest of the Isocratean corpus. It treats topics found in other discourses of his but does so with a unity of composition and polish of style that makes it superior to the others. It had a long and influential literary reputation from the classical world into the modern period as an example of high prose style. The artistic use of extremely elaborate sentences marks his style, highlighted by periodic sentences that have great length but are carefully organized through the development of subordinate clauses and phrases that give context to the point presented in the main clause. It is not unusual for an Isocratean period to comprise two sections in the Greek text. Sections 47–50 offer a particularly elaborate example, one sentence extending over four sections of original Greek. In addition, Isocrates was famous for his attention to word order and particularly to the avoidance of hiatus, that is, the clashing of vowel sounds in the Greek.

The influence of *Panegyricus* on political history is less clear. Scholars disagree on whether Isocrates was able to influence the thinking of the day. The Second Athenian League promoted ideas akin to those seen in the speech, and its leaders, Timotheus and Callistratus, were directly or indirectly connected to Isocrates' school.[12] Others argue that Isocrates' notions of unity and a return to an almost Homeric opposition to the east may have been too idealistic for most Athenians (Usher 1990: 21; Jebb 1962: 2.20–21); this dream was eventually rendered moot by the intervention of Philip in 338 at the battle of Chaeronea. But whether or not Isocrates influenced contemporary politics, by championing the greatness of Athens, he certainly presented an influential form of cultural pride that would continue into the modern age (Jebb 1962: 2.166).

There are commentaries by Sandys (1872), Mesk (1903), and Buchner (1958). I have found the more recent translation with commentary by Usher (1990) especially helpful.

4. PANEGYRICUS

[1] I have often marveled that those who established panegyric festivals and set up athletic contests considered athletic success worthy of

---

[12] For a survey of views, see Adams 1912; Laistner 1930: Bringmann 1965: 28 (cf. Usher 1990: 21). For positive views of his influence, see Mathieu 1925; de Romilly 1992; Too in Mirhady and Too 2000: 137–138; and the Introduction to Isocrates above (pp. 4–5). Some have argued that the digression on Agamemnon in *Panathenaicus* of 339 (12: 74–89) is a veiled picture of Philip of Macedon and a call for him to assert his power (Blass 1892: 2.321). Isocrates made requests to Philip more openly with his discourses *To Philip* (5) in 346 and the first *Epistle to Philip* (*Ep.* 2) in 342.

such great prizes but established no such prize for those who work hard as private citizens for the public good and prepare their own lives so that they can benefit others.[13] [2] They should have given more thought to the latter, for even if the athletes acquired twice their current strength, there would be no greater benefit for the people, while if one person has good ideas, all who wish to share in those ideas would benefit. [3] Nonetheless, I have not lost heart about these things or chosen to give up. Rather, I think that there is sufficient reward for me in the glory this discourse will bring, and so I have come to advise you about the war against the barbarians[14] and the need for unity among ourselves. I know that many who claim to be sophists[15] have attempted this task, [4] but I expect to speak so much better that people will think nothing has ever even been spoken on these matters before, and I consider those discourses most beautiful that treat the greatest subjects, best demonstrate the speaker's talent, and most help those who hear them.[16] This is just such a discourse. [5] Moreover, the moment has not yet passed that would have made it vain to recall these matters, for we should only stop speaking either when the situation comes to a close and we no longer need to consider it or when someone sees that a discourse has reached its goal and no possibility for improvement is left for any other speaker. [6] But as long as things remain as before and other speeches are ineffective, how can we not devote our attention and study to the argument that will, should it

---

[13] Isocrates immediately introduces the theme of competition that will run through the discourse. Cf. 23, 44, 85. He makes a similar argument at *Epistle* 8.5. The complaint that athletes are more highly honored than intellectuals goes back at least to the sixth century and Xenophanes 2 (Campbell 1967).

[14] The word *barbaros* in Greek usually refers to any people who do not speak Greek, but it has greater specificity for Isocrates on most occasions, when he usually means the Persians. The proper name Persians appears only 12 times in the whole corpus, 7 times in this speech (though he uses the adjective Persian about the same number of times to refer to the Persian Wars specifically). He uses the word *barbaros* 145 times in the corpus, 45 in this speech.

[15] On the sophists, see below, 8n.

[16] The tripartite analysis of discourse in terms of the topic, the speaker, and the audience that Isocrates uses here will form an important part of Aristotle's organization in the *Rhetoric* (1.3).

come off successfully, free us from war against each other, from the current confusion, and from the direst troubles?

[7] In addition, if it were possible to explain the same issues in only one way, someone could consider it unnecessary to trouble the audience by saying the same things as others. [8] But since discourses can naturally be set out in many ways about the same matters, and one can make great things small and give greatness to small things,[17] or set out old issues in a new way and speak in a traditional way about things that have happened recently, we must not avoid issues about which others have spoken before, but rather, we must try to speak better than they have. [9] What happened in the past is available to all of us, but it is the mark of a wise person to use these events at an appropriate time, conceive fitting arguments about each of them, and set them out in good style. [10] I think that other arts, and especially the study of discourse (*tēn peri tous logous philosophian*), would be best improved if we would admire and honor not those who first undertook these tasks but those who brought each of them to their highest level of accomplishment, and not those who are eager to speak about things no one else has addressed before but those who speak so wisely that no one else would be able to speak afterwards.

[11] Nonetheless, some criticize speeches that are beyond ordinary citizens and are too carefully composed. They have so misjudged things that they analyze elaborate speeches by comparing them to those written for trials about private contracts, as if the two types must be similar, when in fact one is plain (*aphelōs*),[18] and the other is demonstrative (*epideiktikōs*), or as if they themselves observe the middle course while those who know how to speak precisely (*akribōs*) cannot speak

---

[17] Aristophanes makes such a complaint against Socrates in *Clouds*. His parody of sophistic education probably represents a criticism of the alleged deceit of the sophists of the day by "making the lesser the greater cause." On this phrase, see Schiappa 1999: chap. 6, and Gagarin 2002: 24–26; cf. 12.239. Socrates defends himself against this charge in Plato's *Apology*.

[18] I prefer the emended reading *aphelōs* (plain) to the manuscript reading *asphalōs* (safe, certain). O'Sullivan (1992: 42, 56–58) points out that Isocrates uses *aphelōs* as a negative term in comparison to his own style, which he often calls demonstrative (*epideiktikōs*) or precise or elegant (*akribēs*). See also Sandys 1872: *ad loc.*

simply (*haplōs*).¹⁹ [**12**] It is obvious that the men who make such criticisms are praising those who work like they do themselves. I am not
concerned with such men but rather interested in those who have no
patience for randomly composed speech, who are annoyed by such
discourse, and who seek to find something in my discourse that they
will not find in others. To these people I shall speak on the issue at
hand, after first boasting about myself a bit more. [**13**] I see that others in their introductions soften up their listeners and make excuses
about the speech to come, some saying that their speech was prepared
at short notice, others that it is difficult to find words equal to the
magnitude of the subject.²⁰ [**14**] But in my case, if I do not speak in a
way worthy of the topic, of my reputation, and of the time allotted to
me—not only the time spent on this speech but also my whole life—
I encourage you to have no mercy but to mock and scorn me. For
there is nothing I do not deserve to suffer if I make such great promises when I am no different from the rest.²¹

Let that suffice for an introduction about me personally. [**15**] As for
the public issue, they speak the truth who, as soon as they come forward to speak, show us that we must resolve our hostilities against
each other and turn them against the barbarians and who catalogue
the calamities we have suffered from war against each other and the
benefits we will reap from a campaign against the King,²² but they do
not begin their speeches at the point where they could compose the

---

¹⁹ On the precision of *akribeia* in Isocrates, see Usher 1990: *ad loc.*, where he
points out that this word represents the kind of sophisticated precision that gives
Isocrates' work the sense of polish and elegance for which it is famous.

²⁰ Cf. section 82 for an example of how he does this with the Athenians. It
is a commonplace of epideictic oratory, especially funeral orations, to point out
that words cannot match deeds. Cf. 4.74, 6.100; Thuc. 2.35; Lys. 2.1; and, later,
Hyp. 6.2 and Dem. 60.1. On funeral orations, see below, 74n.

²¹ Isocrates will change his approach at the end of the speech (187) and confess
his own inability, just what he criticizes in section 13.

²² This is a very clear partition. Isocrates wants this occasion to be deliberative,
dealing with the future. Lysias' Olympic speech (33.3–6) also shows this interest
in the future, as perhaps did Gorgias' (cf. Kennedy 1963: 166). Isocrates recalls this
deliberative theme and its presentation here when he addresses Philip of Macedon
(see 5.9, 16).

best arguments.[23] [16] Now, some of the Greeks follow us, others follow the Spartans, and the governments by which they manage their cities have divided most of them along these lines. Thus, whoever thinks that the others will accomplish anything good before the two leading cities are reconciled is quite naive and out of touch with the situation. [17] But someone who is not only seeking to make a display (*epideixis*), but also wishes to accomplish something,[24] must look for the kind of arguments that will persuade these two cities to share equally with each other, to take up joint leadership, and to gain advantages from the Persian King that they currently want to get from the other Greeks. [18] It would be easy to get our city to take this approach, but the Spartans are still hard to persuade, since they have accepted the false argument that it is their ancestral right to lead. Nevertheless, if someone should point out[25] to them that this right is ours rather than theirs, they might perhaps give up arguing and consider their own advantage. [19] Others should have started with this topic and should not have given recommendations about matters already agreed upon before they taught us about controversial ones.[26] It is fitting for me, then, to spend most of my time on these matters for two reasons: first and foremost, so that something useful might happen, and we might end our rivalry against each other so that we can make a joint campaign against the barbarians, [20] but if this is not possible,

---

[23] This is a more general example of Isocrates' tendency to introduce his discourse as a corrective example for a weaker attempt by some other orator. The Introductions to *Busiris* (11.4–9) and *Helen* (10.14–15) are more explicit in their criticism of another orator's attempt, in those cases, Polycrates and perhaps Gorgias (cf. Papillon 1997a).

[24] Isocrates makes a traditional comment here on the distinction between epideictic and deliberative discourse. Epideictic is criticized as being only for display, only to show off the prowess of the speaker; deliberative seeks to recommend useful actions for future benefit (Arist., *Rhetoric* 1.3).

[25] Isocrates uses the verb *epideiknumi* here and recalls his use of the noun *epideixis* in section 17. In 17 he seems to criticize *epideixis* as mere show, while here he uses the verb in one of its usual senses, to point out and prove. This is a situation that calls for traditional display oratory, a panegyric, but also must address the needs of the Greeks in the future, a deliberative topic.

[26] As he said in section 15.

then so that I might show who stands in the way of prosperity for the Greeks and make it clear to all that in the past, our city ruled the sea with justice and now with just cause stakes a claim to hegemony.[27]

[21] [28] If in any given situation honor should be given to those who are the most experienced and have the greatest power, then it is indisputably right that we should again take up the hegemony that we had before. For no one could show (*epideixeien*) another city as preeminent in land war as ours is in war at sea. [22] If some people do not consider this a fair assessment of the situation, since changes often occur and power never stays in the same hands, but think that hegemony, like any other prize, should go either to those who first had it[29] or to those who have brought the most benefit to the Greeks, I believe that such people are on our side, [23] for the further back one investigates these two, the further behind we will leave those who dispute our claim.[30] Indeed, everyone agrees that our city is the oldest, the greatest, and the most renowned among all people. And though this claim is a fine one, we deserve even more honor for what follows from this: [24] we inhabit this city not because we expelled others from it or found it abandoned or gathered a group together here from many peoples but rather because we were born so nobly and purely that we continue to hold the land where we were born, for we are autochthonous[31]

---

[27] Isocrates presents his two main points in the *partitio* (15–20), which he will treat in reverse order in the discourse (see the Introduction to the speech): the need for a campaign against Persia and Athens' claim to leadership. For Isocrates' ambivalence on the matter of leadership, that is, whether Athens should hold it alone or jointly with Sparta, see the Introduction to this speech. There are references to Athens alone (18, 20, 21), but the historical situation of 390–380 constrains Isocrates to recognize Sparta's leadership at the time (16, 17, 19; cf. 185, 188).

[28] Sections 21–128 make the claim that Athens is superior and therefore justly deserves the leadership role. On its themes, see the Introduction to the speech.

[29] He opposed this idea in 10.

[30] A good example of the motif of the athletic context that Isocrates began in section 1.

[31] The notion of autochthony (lit. "born from the earth," i.e., indigenous) is common in praise of Athens (cf. Lys. 2.17; Hyp. 6.7; Dem. 60.4; Plato, *Menexenus* 237b; and Herod. 7.161. It is hinted at in Thuc. 2.36; cf. Loraux 1986: 148–150). Athenian autochthony contrasts sharply in Athenian minds with Sparta's

and can address our city with the same names as we address our kin, [25] for we alone can rightly call it our nurse, our fatherland, or our mother.[32] And those who have reasonable grounds for their ambition, who wish to make a just claim for hegemony, and who often recall their ancestral history must clearly have this sort of origin to their race.

[26] Thus, the magnitude of our initial resources and the gifts of fortune are very great. Now, we might best examine the extent to which we have been a source of benefits for others as well if we should recount the history and accomplishments of our city in order from the beginning, for we will find that the city has been in charge not only of the dangers of war [27] but of other preparations too—how we run our government, how we act as citizens, in general how we are able to live. In choosing examples of good deeds, we must not pick out those that are forgotten in silence because of their insignificance but rather those that, because of their greatness, are recounted and recalled by all people, both now and in the past.

[28] First of all then, that which our nature first needed was provided by our city. For even if the account has become mythical, nevertheless it should be told even now.[33] Demeter once came to our land, wandering about after her daughter Kore was kidnapped, and since she looked favorably on our ancestors because of their kindness— which no one other than the initiates is allowed to hear[34]—she gave

---

origins from migration and conquest. Isocrates presents an account of Spartan origins in the mouth of the Spartan Archidamus in 6.16–21, 24.

[32] Though Isocrates employs a fairly romantic notion here with the virtual personification of the land because of the Athenians' autochthonous nature, it is also the case that Athenian tradition named some of the demes, or local neighborhoods, after local heroes or founders (cf. Whitehead 1986: 208–211).

[33] On Isocrates' notion of myth and the mythic, see Papillon 1996b. Thucydides (1.22.4) questions the value of stories that are "mythical" (*to mythōdes*), criticizing such stories as providing "sentimental and chauvinistic accounts" with a view only to pleasure in contrast with more useful accounts (cf. Flory 1990).

[34] The Eleusinian Mysteries were instituted by Demeter as a gift to humans. The initiate into this religious group (*mystēs*) must keep silent (*muō*) about its activities. The myth of Demeter and Kore/Persephone, with the gift of grain and the institution of the Eleusinian Mysteries, is told more fully in the *Homeric Hymn to Demeter* (cf. Foley 1994).

two gifts to Athens that are, in fact, our two most important possessions: the fruits of the earth that have allowed us to live civilized
lives and the celebration of the mystery rites that grant to those who
share in them glad hopes about the end of their life and about eternity.
[29] As a result, our city was not only loved by the gods but also was
considerate of other people so much that when it gained such great
goods, it did not begrudge these gifts to others but shared what it had
with everyone else. Even now, we still share the mystery rites every
year, and we have taught others about the use, the care, and the
benefits coming from the fruits of the earth. And if I add a bit more
detail, no one would disbelieve this. [30] First, the reason one might
scorn this story—because it is ancient—might also make someone
accept that the events probably happened. Since many have told the
story, and everyone has heard it, it is right to consider the story not
something new but rather trustworthy.[35] Second, we not only have re-
course to the argument that we received the fabled story a long time
ago, we can use even greater proofs than this. [31] To commemorate
our ancient gift, most cities send the first part of their offerings to us
each year; and those who do not are often ordered by the Pythia[36] to
bring a portion of their crop and perform the ancestral duties toward
our city. Furthermore, what should we trust more than something
ordered by the god and approved by most Greeks, where the ancient
reports agree with current practice, and current practice agrees with
what was spoken by the ancients? [32] Apart from this, if we set this
all aside and examine the matter from the beginning, we will find that
when the first people appeared on earth, they did not immediately
find life as it now is, but they progressed little by little.[37] Who then

---

[35] This section seems to reveal an increased skepticism in the fourth century
about the old stories and a tendency to see new information as dependable.

[36] The Pythia was the priestess of the oracle of Apollo at Delphi who spoke the
pronouncements of the god.

[37] There were at least two different views of human development among the
ancient Greeks. One view, seen in Hesiod's *Theogony* and *Works and Days,* argued
that human existence devolved from a golden age to a current difficult bronze age.
The other view, seen in Aeschylus' *Prometheus Bound* and the philosophic thought
of Xenophanes and other Presocratic philosophers and sophists, argues that humans began in a state close to animals and gradually advanced to the civilization

should we think received this gift from the gods or found it themselves by searching? [33] Is it not those whom all agree came into existence first, have natures best suited to the arts (*technai*), and are the most pious towards the gods? There is no need to show how much honor those responsible for such great goods should have, for no one could find a gift so great as to equal what they did.

[34] So much then for the greatest and first and most famous of the benefits we brought. About the same time, though, seeing that the barbarians had most of the land, that the Greeks were closed up in a small space and, because of the scarcity of land, were plotting and sending forces against one another, and some were dying through want of daily necessities and others through war, [35] Athens did not allow this situation to continue but sent leaders to the other cities who, assembling those in the greatest need, assumed the role of generals for them and, defeating the barbarians in battle, founded many cities on both sides of the Aegean, established colonies in all the islands, and ensured the safety of both those who came with them and those who remained behind.[38] [36] To those who stayed back they left sufficient land at home, while to the ones who came along they provided more land than they had before, for they gained possession of all the land we now have. Thus, they made it very easy for those who later wished to establish colonies in imitation of our city, for they did not need to endure the dangers of obtaining land but could go and settle in land we had already appropriated. [37] So who could demonstrate a hegemony either more ancestral than this, which came into existence before most Greek cities were founded, or more advantageous, since it got rid of the barbarians and brought the Greeks to such prosperity?

[38] Furthermore, after this major accomplishment, Athens did not ignore other things but began its assistance to others by finding daily sustenance for those in need, which is necessary if they are to manage their own affairs well. The city thought that a life based on these ne-

---

they knew in the classical period. Isocrates follows the latter view and later in the discourse (47–50) gives credit for this advance to *logos*.

[38] Isocrates refers to the Ionian Migration, led by Attica, which took the Greeks to the islands and to Asia Minor during the eleventh and tenth centuries BC. He refers to it more specifically in *Panathenaicus* (12.42–44). Thucydides describes this briefly (1.2, 12). Cf. Hammond 1986: 72–91.

cessities alone was not good enough to make people want to live, and so the city devoted so much care to their remaining needs that none of the goods that humans have—those that do not come from the gods, that is, but from our own mutual efforts—none of these exist apart from our city, and most of them have come because of our city. [39]³⁹ It found the Greeks living scattered about, without law, some of them abused by tyrannies, others perishing through lack of government (*anarchia*). It freed them from these troubles by assuming power over some and offering itself as a model for others, for it was the first to set up laws and establish a government (*politeia*).⁴⁰ [40] This priority is clear because those who in the beginning brought homicide charges and wanted to settle their differences with reason, not violence, established trials for these cases according to our laws.⁴¹ Indeed, of the arts (*technai*) that are useful for the necessities of life as well as those that have been devised for pleasure, the city discovered some, determined the value of others, and then handed them on for the rest to enjoy.⁴² [41] Furthermore, Athens has arranged the rest of its affairs in

---

³⁹ Usher (1990: 157) points out the characteristic method of Isocratean composition in 39. Wanting to praise Athenian government, he begins with the opposite condition in others, then presents the contrary side to these to end up at his theme of the greatness of Athenian government.

⁴⁰ Perhaps a reference to the unification (synoecism) attributed to Theseus. Athens prided itself on its civic organization, traditionally attributed to Theseus, and to the origins of democratic rule, attributed to Draco (ca. 620) and Solon (ca. 590). According to tradition, it is likely that other cities established law codes before Athens, particularly in Italy and Sicily, but Athens' priority on the Greek mainland is possible (cf. Usher 1990: 157).

⁴¹ This may refer to the trial of Orestes at Athens, where a jury of Athenian citizens acquitted him of homicide. This was said to be the first homicide case settled in a court with a jury, and it is described in Aeschylus' *Eumenides*. Isocrates may also be referring to Draco, the first Athenian lawgiver, who was famous for his homicide laws, which were still in effect in his time (more than two centuries later). From Draco's beginnings, the Athenians created an elaborate system of homicide courts and procedures, described by Demosthenes in his speech *Against Aristocrates* (23.65–79). Cf. MacDowell 1963: 39–84.

⁴² Athens' great talents are mentioned and listed in various ways throughout history. Pliny the Elder talks of brick kilns, silver, pottery, carpentry, and the olive and its products (*Natural History* 7.194–200). Aelian (*Variae Historiae* 3.38) adds

such a hospitable and convenient way for all people that it serves well both those who are in need and those who want to profit from what they already have. It meets the needs of those who are fortunate and those who are unfortunate in their own cities; each has something from us: the fortunate have pleasant opportunities; the unfortunate have a secure sanctuary. [42] Further, since each city had land that was not self-sufficient, but lacked some things while producing more than it needed of others, and since they did not know where they should send the surplus and where they should obtain what they lacked, our city helped them overcome these troubles too. It established Piraeus as a trade center in the midst of Greece.[43] This port had such an inventory that what was difficult to get from other cities individually could easily be gotten from Athens.

[43] Next, those who established panegyric festivals[44] are justly praised for handing down such a fine custom to us where we make a peace treaty, break off any existing hostilities, and come together in the same place; after this, as we make prayers and sacrifices, we recall the common heritage we have with each other, establish our goodwill toward each other for the future, and renew ancient ties of guest friendship and make new ones. [44] The time spent here is not wasted, for either the private observer or the superior athlete, but in this gathering of the Greeks, the athletes come to display their good fortune and the observers to see the athletes competing against each other; neither group is unmoved but each takes pride: the observers in seeing the athletes competing on their behalf[45] and the athletes in knowing that all are there to see them compete. Such are the benefits we derive from these gatherings, and here too our city is not inferior. [45] For it has many very fine displays, some outstanding for their

---

justice, athletics, and chariot racing. Milton calls Athens the "mother of arts and eloquence" (*Paradise Regained* 4.120).

[43] Themistocles first began to build walls around Piraeus as Athens' port (instead of the smaller harbor at Phalerum) in 493/2 because it was more easily defended (cf. Thuc. 1.93). Cf. Garland 2001.

[44] On panhellenic festivals, see the Introduction.

[45] That is, the observers see the athletes competing on behalf of the cities of the observers, much as modern Olympic athletes represent countries. Pindar's victory odes demonstrate that praise goes not only to the athlete but also to the athlete's family and city. Cf. Nisetich 1980 and Race 1997.

expense, others notable for their artistry, still others superior in both these regards.[46] The number of people who visit our city is so great that if there is any benefit in simply gathering together, our city has gained this too. In addition, here especially one can find the most dependable bonds of friendship and join groups of all sorts; one can also see contests not only of speed and strength but also of speech and thought and all other activities, not to mention the greatest prizes for all these. [46] In addition to the prizes our city offers, it persuades others to give similar ones,[47] for what is judged best by us has such weight that it is approved by all people. Apart from this, other panegyric festivals are held only at long intervals and end quickly, whereas our city is a festival (*panēgyris*) for all time for those who come.[48]

[47][49] Moreover, our city revealed philosophy (*philosophia*),[50]

---

[46] From sections 43 to 45, Isocrates has moved from festivals in general, perhaps with Olympia in mind, to Athens specifically. He probably refers here both to the building programs of Peisistratus and Pericles, which made the city more impressive for visitors, and to the festivals themselves that attracted many visitors to the city.

[47] This probably means that the greatness of their prizes compels other cities to give better prizes at their own games (Norlin 1928: *ad loc.*) but may also, though less likely, mean that the city leads others to give additional gifts to victors at Athens (Usher 1990: *ad loc.*).

[48] Isocrates means this both literally and figuratively. The two major Athenian festivals, the Panathenaea and the Dionysia, were held every year, while the other four famous festivals were held either every four years (Olympian, Pythian) or every two years (Nemean, Isthmian). But more figuratively, Isocrates probably wants to equate the good qualities of a panegyric festival he has been describing with the normal life of Athens as the gathering place (*panēgyris*) for all Greece, much as Thucydides (2.41.1) made Pericles say that Athens was the education (*paideia*) of Greece.

[49] Sections 47–49 are one long period in Isocrates' Greek. A period is a long and complex sentence. Usher (1990: 10–12) nicely points out that Isocrates concentrates his greatest compositional periods for important topics, as he does here. It is difficult to carry such a long period in one English sentence, so I have broken up the sections. For this complete period in one English sentence, see Kennedy 1999: 43–45. For an example in this translation of a long period in one English sentence, see below, sections 93–95.

[50] *Philosophia* comprises something like all intellectual activity for Isocrates, and this can only be actualized through discourse (*logos*), and so the transition in

which has discovered and provided us with everything. It has taught us about public affairs, made us gentle towards one another, showed us which misfortunes come through ignorance and which through necessity, and taught us to guard against the former and to endure the latter nobly. The city has also honored the power of discourse (*logos*); everyone desires it and is envious of others who have it. [48] The city knew that we alone of all animals possessed *logos* as part of our nature and therefore used this advantage to become superior in all other ways. The city also saw that in other matters, fortune is so confused that often the wise have troubles and the foolish prosper. But common people have no share in discourse that is fine and artistic, since this is the task of an intelligent mind, [49] and those who appear wise or foolish differ most in this way. Further, those who are raised from the very beginning like free men are not known so much for their courage or wealth or other such good qualities, as they become particularly distinguished for what they say, and this has become the surest sign of each person's education. Those who use discourse well not only have authority in their own cities but are also honored among other cities. [50] Our city has so far surpassed other men in thought and speech that students of Athens have become the teachers of others,[51] and the city has made the name "Greek" seem to be not that of a people but of a way of thinking; and people are called Greeks because they share in our education (*paideusis*) rather than in our birth.[52]

[51] So that I do not seem to waste time on details when I should be addressing the whole situation, or to eulogize the city on these topics because I am at a loss to praise her regarding her conduct in war, let this suffice for those who pride themselves in such things.[53] I think

---

the middle of this period is an easy one for him. He talks of *logos* also in his discourse *Nicocles* (3.5–10) and in *Antidosis* (15.253–260). His ideas on *philosophia* are developed in *Antidosis* (15.261–285); for discussions of how Aristotle "disciplined" genres, see Timmerman 1998 and Schiappa 1999: chaps. 10 and 11.

[51] Cf. *Antidosis* 15.295 and Thuc. 2.41.1.

[52] The Gennadion Library in Athens displays an inscription taken from Isocrates' words: "People are called Greeks because they share in our education."

[53] Isocrates clearly marks the transition from one major section (the gifts of Athens to Greece, 22–50) to the next major section (Athens' leadership in wars, 51–99). In ancient rhetorical theory of the ideas of style promulgated by Hermogenes of Tarsus (cf. Wooten 1987), this is called Distinctness (*eukrineia*).

our ancestors should gain honor no less from their risks in war than from other good deeds. [52] For they endured wars that were not small or few or insignificant but many and fearsome and great; some fought for their own territory, some for the freedom of others. For all this time they always made their city the common defender of Greeks who were wronged. [53] Because of this, in fact, some have even accused us of bad policies since we usually help the weak, as if such arguments were not consistent with those who wish to praise us. We did not develop this policy because we were ignorant of how stronger allies are more advantageous to our own security. Although we knew much more clearly than others the results of such actions, we still chose to give aid to the weak—even though it was against our own interests—rather than to join in injustice with the stronger for the sake of profit.

[54] One could also recognize the character and strength of the city from the supplications that people have made to us. I will pass over those that happened recently or concerned minor matters; however, long before the Trojan War—for those who argue about ancestral traditions rightly find evidence in this period—the children of Heracles came as suppliants and, a little before them, Adrastus, the son of Talaus, king of Argos.[54] [55] Adrastus had suffered defeat in a campaign against Thebes and could not recover the dead from beneath the Cadmea[55] by himself so asked our city to assist him in this misfortune that concerned all men and not let those who died in war go unburied or let the ancient practice and ancestral custom be violated. [56] Again, when the children of Heracles were fleeing the hostility of Eurystheus, they passed over the other cities, realizing that they could not help them in their troubles, and decided that our city was the only one able to repay the kindness their father had provided to all people.

[57] From this it is easy to see that even at that time our city was a leader, for who would dare seek help from weaker cities or from those under the control of others and pass over those with greater power, especially when it concerned not private matters but public issues, about which no one would likely be interested except those who thought they

----

[54] After Heracles died, Eurystheus exiled his children. When they came to Athens for help, Eurystheus invaded and was killed by Hyllus, one of the sons of Heracles. See section 58. Isocrates also talks of Adrastus at 14.53–54 and 12.168–171 (cf. 12.168n and 172n) and the children of Heracles in 6.17–24.

[55] The Cadmea was the citadel of Thebes.

were foremost among the Greeks? [58] Moreover, they were clearly not disappointed in their hopes when they fled to our ancestors. The Athenians took up the war on behalf of those who died at Thebes and also on behalf of the children of Heracles against the power of Eurystheus. They attacked and forced the Thebans to give back the bodies to their families for burial, and when the Peloponnesians invaded our land under Eurystheus, our ancestors met and defeated them in battle and put an end to that man's arrogance. [59] Already admired for other acts, they became even more famous for these accomplishments, for they had no small effect but completely reversed the situation in both cases: by seeking our help, Adrastus succeeded in gaining everything he needed in spite of his enemies, and Eurystheus expected to overwhelm us but was himself made prisoner and forced to become a suppliant. [60] He had passed his whole life ordering and mistreating Heracles, a man who surpassed human nature by being born from Zeus and having divine strength, though he was still a human. Yet when Eurystheus wronged us, his situation changed so completely that he fell under the power of Heracles' children and died in shame.[56]

[61] There are many benefits we have rendered to Sparta, but I need only mention this one. Taking the security they got from us as a starting point, the offspring of Heracles, the ancestors of those who now rule in Sparta, came back into the Peloponnese; took control of Argos, Lacedaimon, and Messene; founded the city of Sparta; and became the authors of all their present blessings. [62] They should have remembered our help and never attacked our land, from which they first set out and gained such great prosperity, and they should never have put this city into danger when it had risked so much on behalf of the children of Heracles. They also should not have handed over the kingship to Heracles' descendants and then decided that the city responsible for the safety of his family should serve them as slaves. [63] Now, if we may return to the main point, leaving aside issues of gratitude or fairness, and make the most precise argument, then surely it is not tradition that newcomers should be leaders of the original

---

[56] A slight against the Spartans, who looked to Heracles as their patron and founding hero. Heracles could not resist Eurystheus, but the Athenians could.

inhabitants of a land (*autochthones*),[57] or that those who benefited should be leaders of those who conferred the benefits, or that those who were suppliants should be leaders of those who took them in. [64] I can make this point even more briefly. Besides our city, Argos, Thebes, and Sparta were and continue to be the greatest Greek cities, but our ancestors were clearly so superior to all of them that on behalf of the Argives, they gave orders to the Thebans even though the Thebans considered themselves the greatest, [65] they defeated the Argives and the rest of the Peloponnesians in battle on behalf of the children of Heracles, and they kept the founders and leaders of Sparta safe from the dangers posed by Eurystheus. Thus, I do not know how anyone could demonstrate (*epideixei*) domination over the Greeks more clearly.[58]

[66] It seems appropriate to me to take up the city's accomplishments against the barbarians, especially when I have made the question of leadership against them the subject of this discourse. Since I would go on too long if I were to mention every danger we encountered, I will try to use the same approach I did before and treat only the greatest examples. [67] The races that are the most powerful and had the greatest empires are the Scythians, the Thracians, and the Persians. It happens that all these people plotted against us, and our city faced great danger against all of them. And indeed, what will be left for our opponents to argue if it is shown that the Greek cities that could not find justice themselves decided to come to us as suppliants and if the barbarians who wanted to enslave the Greeks attacked us first?[59]

[68] The most famous of our wars were those against Persia, but for those who argue about our ancestral claim, the older wars are no less

---

[57] On Athenians as autochthonous, see sections 23–27. On the Spartans as settlers, see *Archidamus* (6.16–21, 24).

[58] Isocrates continues to use the verbal stem *epideix-* in his discussion of this section. It is acceptable to take it to mean "show" or "demonstrate" or "argue," but its connection with epideictic (praise) discourse keeps the goal of this first half of the speech in mind, that Athens is superior and has a rightful claim to hegemony.

[59] This is an effective transitional sentence from the topic of the prior sections (51–65) to the new subject of wars against the barbarians (66–99).

significant. For example, while Greece was still small in power, our land was attacked by the Thracians under Eumolpus, son of Poseidon, and by the Scythians together with the Amazons, daughters of Ares; they did not attack at the same time but when each of these two groups were trying to annex Europe. They hated the whole race of Greeks, but they made their complaints against us specifically, thinking that by taking their risk this way against just one city, they would conquer all of them at once. [69] They were not successful, however. Even though they attacked our ancestors alone, they were destroyed as if they had warred against all the Greeks together. The magnitude of the troubles they encountered is clear, for the reports about them would not have lasted so long if these events were not far more important than others. [70] It is said that none of the Amazons who came against us escaped and that those who stayed home were thrown from power because of the disaster here. As for the Thracians, they say that before then, they lived as our neighbors, but after that campaign, they withdrew so far from us that many races and nations of all kinds and great cities were established in the area between us.[60]

[71] These are noble examples and appropriate ones for those who want to contend for leadership, but those who fought against Darius and Xerxes accomplished deeds akin to those described and appropriate for those born from such ancestors. When that most important war occurred and the greatest dangers fell upon us all at the same time, when our enemies thought they were unstoppable because of their numbers and our allies thought they themselves had unsurpassable courage (*aretē*),[61] [72] we bested both the Persians and our allies with respect to each claim.[62] We succeeded against all the dangers, were immediately awarded the prize for valor, and soon took command of the

---

[60] Scione, Potideia, and Amphipolis are the most prominent examples.

[61] The Greek word *aretē* can have a variety of meanings. In general, it refers to the excellence of something; thus the *aretē* of a knife would be sharpness, of a runner, speed. In some contexts I will translate it "courage," as here, while elsewhere I will use the word "excellence." At times I will also use the common translation "virtue," which is not always the best choice because of the moral weight of the English word, but it works at other times.

[62] One might expect an explanation that the Athenians defeated the Persians physically in battle and the allies morally by displaying their superior *aretē*.

naval empire; the other Greeks gave us this with no opposition from those who now are eager to strip us of it.

[73] Let no one think me unaware that the Spartans also were responsible for many benefits for the Greeks during those crucial times. Yet even this allows me to praise my city even more, because even with such rivals, it still rose so far above them. Now, I want to speak a bit longer about these two cities and not run by them too quickly, so that we might have reminders both of the excellence of our ancestors and of their hatred toward the barbarians. [74] It has not escaped me, however, that it is hard to come forward so late and speak about deeds that were treated long ago and about which those citizens who are the best speakers have already spoken many times at public funerals.[63] By necessity, all the most important topics have already been used up, and only minor topics are left. Nevertheless, since it is relevant to my theme, I must not shrink from recalling some of those that remain.

[75] I think that those responsible for the most benefits and worthy of the greatest praise are those who risked their lives for Greece. But we should also not forget those who lived before the Persian Wars[64] or who held power in each of these cities, for they prepared those who followed and turned the people to virtue (*aretē*) and made them fierce opponents of the barbarians.[65] [76] They did not scorn the common good, either by profiting from it like it was their own property or by neglecting it like it was someone else's concern; rather, they cared for it like it was their own, although they kept an appropriate distance, as is fitting for something that does not belong to them. They did not

---

[63] Ceremonial funeral orations (*epitaphioi*) were common in Athens from the fifth century on. There are six extant examples: the funeral oration of Pericles reported in Thucydides' *History* (2.34–46), those of Gorgias, Lysias, Demosthenes, Hyperides, and the one preserved in a discussion of funeral orations in the Platonic dialogue *Menexenus*. For a useful summary discussion, see Kennedy 1963: 154–166. For their importance as a cultural and social constructive force, see Loraux 1986. The most famous of the six examples is Pericles' funeral oration in Thucydides (2.34–46), to which much of this section of *Panegyricus* is indebted (cf. Hudson-Williams 1948).

[64] 490–479.

[65] Usher (1990: *ad loc.*) points out that Isocrates offers an educational system in his school that fulfills the goals described here.

judge their happiness in terms of money but thought that a person obtained the surest and most noble wealth if he did the sorts of things that would bring him a particularly good reputation and produce the greatest glory for his children. [77] They did not emulate the rashness of others or practice their own daring but thought that it was more terrible to have a bad reputation among the citizens than to die nobly for the city; they were more ashamed at the city's errors than we are now at our own mistakes. [78] The reason for this is that they took care that laws would be precise and fair, not so much those about private contracts as those concerning daily activities, for they knew that good men do not need many written rules, but that from a few accepted principles they could easily come to agreement on both private and public matters. [79] Their public spirit was such that when they divided into factions against each other, they did so not in order that whichever group destroyed the other would rule over the remainder but in order to see which group would be the first to treat the city well. They formed associations not for their own private advantage but for the benefit of the whole people. [80] In the same spirit they managed the affairs of others, tending to their interests but not treating them arrogantly; they thought that they should lead them as generals but not rule them as tyrants, and they wanted to be addressed as leaders more than as despots, to be called saviors rather than destroyers, and to lead the other cities through their good deeds rather than subduing them by force. [81] They kept their word more faithfully than we keep our oaths, and they honored treaties as if it were the natural thing to do. They did not so much exult in their political power as they sought honor by living prudently, and they thought they should have the same attitude toward the weak as they expected the strong to have toward them, supposing that their own cities were their private communities and that Greece was their common homeland.[66]

[82][67] Using such ideas and teaching the young such habits, they produced men to fight against those from Asia who were so brave that

---

[66] Though Isocrates begins this portion of the speech (75) on the assumption that he is praising those before the Persian Wars, the description sounds much like an idealized picture of the Delian League when it was formed in 477 just after the Persian Wars. Section 83 returns to things before the Persian Wars.

[67] Sections 82–84 present many themes that are common in funeral orations and should be compared with those mentioned in 74n.

no one, neither poet nor sophist, was ever able to speak about them in words worthy of their deeds. I have great sympathy for them, for it is just as difficult to praise those who surpass the virtues of others as it is to praise those who have done nothing good. For the latter, there are no deeds to speak of, and for the former, there are no words that match their deeds. [83] For how might words match men who were so superior to those who fought at Troy that whereas these spent ten years fighting for one city, they overcame the power of all Asia in just a short time and not only preserved their own country but also won the freedom of all Greece? Would they have shunned any deed or labor or danger so that they might live with a good reputation, when they were ready to die for the glory that they would have in death? [84] I think that one of the gods brought about this war out of admiration for their courage (*aretē*) so that men who were by nature born to be great would not die in obscurity but would be worthy of the same honors as those born from the gods, who are called demigods; the gods gave even the bodies of those men over to the necessities of nature, but they made the memory of their courage immortal.

[85] To be sure, our ancestors and the Spartans have always been rivals, but during that time, they competed for the noblest goals, considering themselves not enemies but competitors;[68] they did not curry the favor of the barbarians in hope of enslaving the Greeks, but joining together for their common security, they conducted their rivalry about who would achieve that security. They first demonstrated their courage against the men sent by Darius,[69] [86] for when they landed in Attica, the Athenians did not wait for their allies but made this common war their own private struggle,[70] and with just their own force, only a few against tens of thousands,[71] they met those who scorned all

[68] Much like the factions he described in section 79. Here is another instance of the contest motif begun in section 1. The image of the Spartans in these sections is quite positive; it will become more negative in sections 120–128.

[69] Isocrates now moves to the Persian Wars specifically, beginning with the battle of Marathon in 490.

[70] Certainly the Persians were a threat to Greece as a whole, but they were particularly focused on revenge against Athens and Eretria for the aid those two gave to cities on the coast of Asia Minor during the Ionian Revolt a few years earlier.

[71] Herodotus does not give the number of soldiers involved, only those slain. Estimates for the Persians in ancient sources, which are exaggerated, run from a low

Greece as if they were about to risk the lives of others rather than their own. The Spartans, on the other hand, did not hesitate once they heard about the war in Attica; ignoring everything else, they came to help us as quickly as though their own land were being sacked.[72] Here is a sign both of their speed and of their rivalry: [87] they say that on the same day that our ancestors learned of the invasion of the barbarians, they rushed to defend the borders of their land, defeated them in battle, and set up a victory trophy over the enemy. The Spartans, meanwhile, in three days and nights came 1,200 stades marching in formation.[73] Such was their haste, the Spartans to share in the dangers and the Athenians to join battle before the Spartans could get there.

[88] After this came the second campaign, which Xerxes himself led, leaving his palace and daring to become the leader of the force after he gathered together everyone from Asia.[74] What speaker is there whose words have not fallen short of these events even when he tried to exaggerate? [89] Xerxes became so arrogant that he thought subduing Greece was just a small task; even so, he still wished to leave behind a memorial of something beyond ordinary human ability, so he did not stop before he devised and accomplished a feat that everyone keeps talking about, namely, that he made his army sail through the land and march across the sea, yoking the Hellespont and digging a canal through Mount Athos.[75] [90] Against a man who was so arro-

---

of 210,000 (Nepos) to as high as 600,000 (Justin). How and Wells (1928: 2.114) argue that there were 10,000 Athenians and 1,000 Plataeans against 40,000 Persians.

[72] This account is very positive toward the Spartans, even more than historical evidence would indicate, for the Spartans, in fact, delayed their arrival for religious reasons, and the Athenians waited for them as long as possible before engaging the Persians on their own.

[73] A stade was 600 feet. The Attic foot was just less than 12 inches, the Olympic foot just larger. This distance, if measured in Attic feet, was about 132 miles.

[74] Xerxes, the Persian king after his father Darius, invaded Greece in 480. Darius did not come to Greece himself in 490 but sent Datis and Artaphernes to lead the Persian forces.

[75] Mt. Athos, to the west of the Hellespont on the northern coast of Greece, was a peninsula that jutted out into the northern Aegean. Herodotus (7.22–24) tells the story of Xerxes cutting a canal through it and comments on his arrogance, since he could have simply dragged the ships across the isthmus. Herodotus also (7.33–36) tells the story of Xerxes building a bridge across the Hellespont. Once

gant, did such amazing things, and was the leader of such impressive forces, the Athenians and Spartans made their defense, splitting the danger between them. Against the Persian land force at Thermopylae the Spartans selected a thousand of their men and took a few of the allies as well, intending to use the narrow pass there to keep the Persians from getting further.[76] Meanwhile, our ancestors at Artemisium manned sixty triremes against the whole naval force of the enemy.[77]

[91] The two cities had the courage to do these things not so much because they thought little of the enemy but out of rivalry with each other: the Spartans, envious of the battle at Marathon, wanted to make themselves equal to the Athenians and feared that twice in succession our city would be the cause of Greek salvation; and our city wished especially to protect its existing reputation and to make it clear to all that they won before because of their courage (*aretē*), not because of chance. They also wanted to lead the Greeks into a naval battle to show them that at sea just as on land, Greek courage could overcome Persian numbers.

[92] Although they showed equal courage, they did not meet with equal fortune, since the Spartans perished; though victorious in spirit, they were worn down in body, though surely it would be impious to say that they were defeated, for not a one of them dared to abandon his post. Our ships, on the other hand, conquered the advanced fleet, but when they heard that the enemy had taken control of the pass at Thermopylae, they sailed home to make plans for dealing with the engagements still to come. As a result, although they had already ac-

---

completed, a storm destroyed it, and in anger, Xerxes ordered the waves whipped, verbally abused, and chains dropped in for symbolic subjugation; he then rebuilt the bridge.

[76] The battle of Thermopylae (Herod. 7.196–233) became legendary among the Greeks as a sign of the dedication and valor of the Spartans, even though it ended in defeat. The Spartans were able to hold the Persians off at the pass because it was narrow, and they could cut down the few Persians at a time that could come through. They were eventually betrayed when a Greek showed the Persians a route around the pass, and the Persians then ambushed the Spartans from behind. Even in defeat, however, the Spartans were able to delay the Persians enough to allow the Greeks to regroup in Attica.

[77] At the naval battle of Artemisium in 480, the Greeks defeated the larger Persian force when a sudden storm drove the Persian fleet into confusion.

complished many noble things, they distinguished themselves even more in the final stages of the danger. [93]⁷⁸ For even when all the allies were down-hearted, and the Peloponnesian states were building defensive walls at the isthmus, trying to find security just for themselves, while the other cities—save those that were ignored because they were too small—were now controlled by the barbarians and had joined them in their campaign, when twelve hundred triremes were approaching and countless foot soldiers were about to attack Attica and there was no salvation in sight for our ancestors because they were bereft of allies and losing all hope, [94] although they could have not only escaped the dangers they faced but also gained special privileges that the King was offering them because he thought that if he could add our city's fleet to his own, he would immediately take control of the Peloponnese too, our ancestors refused to accept the King's bribes, nor did they clamor for a treaty with the barbarians out of anger at other Greeks for betraying the cause, [95] but our city prepared to fight on their own for freedom and excused those who had chosen slavery. Our ancestors considered it appropriate for weak cities to seek safety in any way they could but thought that those who claimed to be leaders of Greece should not be able to avoid danger; as men of good character prefer to choose a noble death over a shameful life, so they thought it better for the leading cities to be obliterated rather than be seen living as slaves.

[96] It is clear that the Athenians thought this way, for when they were not able to arrange their forces against the Persians on both land and sea at the same time, they took their whole population from the city and sailed to the neighboring island⁷⁹ so they might risk battle

---

⁷⁸ I have tried to render the period of sections 93–95 in one sentence, but it is labored in English more than in Greek. See Usher (1990: 11–12) for a good analysis of the period and a brief discussion of how style is not just ornamental but serves to highlight and demonstrate the importance of the topic being treated. This period begins with multiple subordinate phrases and the main thought does not appear until late in section 94 ("our ancestors refused to accept the King's bribes . . ."). The main thought is expanded by using the parallelism of "not A and not B, but C and D," a favorite way to develop and demonstrate the complexity of a thought in Isocrates.

⁷⁹ The island of Salamis in the Saronic Gulf.

against each force separately. And yet how could men show themselves
to be better or more devoted to the Greek cause than those men, who,
to avoid causing the rest to be enslaved, had the courage to see their
city abandoned, their land laid waste, their holy places plundered,
their temples burned, and the whole war focusing on their own homeland?[80] [97] And as if this were not enough, they were about to enter
a naval battle all alone against twelve hundred triremes. In the end,
they were not allowed to do this, for the Peloponnesians were compelled to share in the danger, shamed by the Athenians' courage and
realizing that if our forces were destroyed, they themselves would not
be safe and that if the Athenians succeeded without them, they would
bring their own cities into dishonor. I do not think I need to spend
time describing the uproar rising from that battle and the shouts and
the encouragements that are common to all naval battles. [98] My task
is to tell the special features that fit with a claim of leadership and are
consistent with what I have already said. For our city was so superior
when it was unharmed, that even when destroyed, it provided more
triremes for the battle for control of Greece than all the other naval
forces. No one is so hostile toward us that he would not agree we won
the war because of this sea battle and that our city was responsible for
this victory.

[99] Who then should have the leadership role if there is going to
be a campaign against the barbarians? Is it not those who gained the
greatest reputation in the former war and who often endured dangers
by themselves and in the joint campaigns were judged worthy of the
greatest battle prizes? Is it not those who abandoned their own city for
the security of the rest and who in ancient times were the founders of
very many cities and then later rescued those cities from their greatest
troubles? How would we not be gravely mistreated if, having taken on
the greatest share of evils in that war, we were then thought to deserve
a lesser share of honors, drawn up in the front ranks at that time on
behalf of all Greeks but now forced to follow others?

[100] Up to this point, then, I know all would agree that our city

---

[80] The Athenian general Themistocles convinced the Athenians to abandon
the city to the attack of the oncoming Persians. The Persians burned Attica and the
Athenian Acropolis as they moved south. The Greeks then met and defeated the
Persian navy at Salamis as Xerxes looked on from shore.

was responsible for the most benefits and that the hegemony of Greece was justly ours. But after the Persian Wars, some accuse us of being responsible for many troubles for the Greeks after we took our naval empire. They bring up the enslavement of the Melians and the destruction of the Scionians in these charges.[81] [101] But in my opinion, first, it is no sign that we rule badly if some of those who fought against us clearly were severely punished; this is much more a sign that we manage the affairs of our allies well because none of the cities under our control ever fell into these sorts of troubles. [102] Next, anyone else who managed the same situations more leniently could reasonably be able to fault us. As it is, however, this has never happened, and it is impossible to have power over so many cities if one does not punish those who commit crimes. How then is it not right to praise us, since we were harsh least often and were able to maintain our empire for the longest time? [103] I think all agree that the strongest leaders of the Greeks will be those under whom obedient subjects happen to fare best. In that case, we will find that under our leadership, private households achieved the greatest prosperity and cities grew largest.[82] [104] [83] We

---

[81] Scione was besieged in 423 (Thuc. 4.120–123, 129–133) and destroyed in 421 (5.32). The Plataeans colonized the area until they were thrown out again at the end of the Peloponnesian War. In 416 the people of Melos wanted to assert their independence, while Athens wanted them to join their side in the war. Thucydides describes this situation in an unusual and famous passage called the Melian Dialogue (5.84–116). The two cities talk as if characters in a play, the Melians asserting their rights based on justice, the Athenians asserting their plans based on the interest of the stronger. The Athenians eventually took the island, killed all the men, and enslaved the women and children. Thucydides makes the act look tyrannical on the part of Athens, bullying a small independent island. Inscriptional evidence, however, may show that Melos was contributing to the Spartan cause; if this is true, the action of the Athenians might seem slightly more understandable from a military point of view (cf. Meiggs and Lewis 1969: 181–184). Cf. 12.63.

[82] Isocrates treats the time between the Persian Wars and the outbreak of the Peloponnesian War, called the Pentecontaetea by Thucydides, roughly, 479–431.

[83] Sections 104–105 represent another large period presenting an elevated and unified view of the blessings of Athenian leadership. Isocrates presents an ideal image of democratic Athens leading the other Greeks, rebuking those interested in oligarchy—as he makes explicit in 105—with many critical phrases meant to signify oligarchic government ("the many ruled by the few," "giving help to the

did not envy our allied cities when they grew, and we did not cause instability by promoting opposing forms of government so they might fight against one another and each try to curry our favor. On the contrary, we thought that the unity of the allies was for the common good, and so we managed all the cities with the same laws, making policy for them as an ally and not as a despot, overseeing affairs as a whole, but allowing each city its own individual freedom, [105] giving help to the people and opposing autocratic governments, thinking it terrible that the many be ruled by the few, that those who are poorer but in no other respect inferior should be excluded from leadership positions, that even when we share a common homeland, some rule like tyrants while others live as if they were aliens, not citizens, and finally, that the people who are citizens by nature, by convention are deprived of a voice in government.[84]

[106] Because we had these complaints against oligarchies, and in fact even more than these, we established the same government in other cities that we had ourselves, a government that certainly needs no lengthy praise, especially since the subject can be treated briefly. The Athenians lived for seventy years under this government without tyranny, free of threat from the barbarians or from internal factionalism, at peace with all people.[85] [107] For this, anyone with good

---

people and opposing autocratic governments," the notion that under oligarchy those who are poor, but equal in other respects, are denied leadership positions, among others).

[84] Isocrates alludes to the philosophic and political controversy of "nature or nurture." In Greece there was intense discussion about the difference between *physis* and *nomos,* nature and convention (cf. Heinimann 1945). Are we who we are naturally or because of social construction? As Isocrates sets up the distinction, he uses words that mark the contrast, citizens by nature (*physis*) but by convention (*nomos*) deprived of rights. Isocrates also plays on a pun here, for the word for convention (i.e., *nomos*), what is agreed upon by the community rather than recognized as externally true, is the word for law. Thus Isocrates sets up the dichotomy where "all men are created equal" but where the laws of the land (or an oligarchic government in this scenario) deprive people of that natural position.

[85] Isocrates approximates the length of time, as do all funeral orators; he is referring to the period 479–404 when Athens had a free democracy. The idealized description here characterizes epideictic oratory. It could even be argued to be true in some sense (cf. Usher 1990: 176), but the description is much too simple, as Usher 1990: 175–177 and Cloché 1963: 63 show.

sense should be very grateful to us much more than fault us for our cleruchies,[86] which we sent into states that were depopulated to guard the land, not out of greed. The evidence for this is that we had a land that was very small in relation to the population, but an empire that was very great, and we had twice as many triremes as all the other allies together [108] and also ships that could face twice their own number. Euboea, lying within reach of Attica,[87] was naturally suited to a naval empire and surpassed all the other islands in other assets as well. Still, we had control over it almost more than our own land. In addition, although we knew that the Greeks and barbarians who have an especially good reputation are the ones who uprooted their neighbors and thus made their own lives plentiful and easy, none of this moved us to harm those on the island, [109] but we alone among great powers accepted a life more frugal for ourselves than for those who are accused of being our slaves. Furthermore, if we had wanted simply to profit, we surely would not have set our sights on the land of the Scionians—which everyone knows we then gave to those who fled to us from Plataea—and passed over this land of Euboea, which would have made us all richer.[88]

[110] Although this is the kind of people we are, and there is strong evidence that we did not covet the land of others, some still dare to ac-

---

[86] A cleruchy is a system of control in which Athenian colonists were given a portion of land in an allied city but retained their Athenian citizenship. Athens often did this to cities it had overthrown or where they had put down revolt. While protecting Athenian interests, the colonists would also serve as a reserve force for defense purposes, thus Isocrates' reference to guarding the land.

[87] Sandys (1872: *ad loc.*) points out that the verb shows not just geographical proximity but also political dependence.

[88] That is, Euboea was a strong island, but it was still easily under Athens' control. Also, Euboea was an important strategic island for Athens because it was an important food source as well as being located along a large part of the shipping routes to the north, where Athens got much of its resources. Isocrates argues that the Athenians spent time on places like Scione and Plataea, which were not nearly so useful to them, when it would have helped them more to take complete control of Euboea. They did not do this, so this is proof that they were not motivated solely by self-interested notions of expansion. On Scione and Plataea, see 100n.

cuse us, namely, those who were part of the decarchies,[89] thereby hurting their own homeland and making the crimes of those before seem small by comparison while leaving no possibility that those who might want to be evil afterwards could ever surpass them. They claim to follow Spartan customs but in fact do the opposite. They lament the sufferings of the Melians but dare to commit incurable crimes against their own people.[90] [111] What sort of crime escaped them? What sort of shameful or shocking behavior did they not engage in? They thought that the most lawless people were the most trustworthy; they flattered traitors as if they were benefactors.[91] They chose to be slaves to one of the helots[92] so that they could act violently toward their own cities; more than they honored their own parents, they honored killers and murderers among their citizens. [112] They drove us all to such savagery that even though each of us found many who, before this time because of our general prosperity, would sympathize with us even in our slight misfortunes, once these men came to power, because of the multitude of our own troubles, we stopped taking pity on each other. They left no one any time to feel someone else's pain. [113] Whom did they not affect? Who was so far removed from the affairs of the city that they were not compelled to experience the troubles that such beasts sent to us? And then they are not ashamed, though they treated their own cities so lawlessly, to attack our city so unjustly; in addition

---

[89] At the conclusion of the Peloponnesian War, the Spartans set up oligarchic panels of ten men from each city (decarchies) to oversee their government. These were supported by a Spartan garrison and commander and were often perceived as tyrannical by the cities they occupied.

[90] It is important to remember here that Isocrates is not criticizing Spartans as a whole but those who sided with the decarchs, the most reactionary oligarchic members of the political spectrum. Isocrates elsewhere praises Spartan actions (85–89) but here points out the insincerity of the minority. In fact, the subject of these few sentences is unclear, but Isocrates is probably aiming his criticism at the Thirty (Usher 1990: 178).

[91] Usher (1990: *ad loc.*) points out the similarities to Thucydides' analysis of the change in meanings of words (3.80–82).

[92] Lysander was said by some to be the child of a helot (a kind of "serf"; cf. 5.49n) and not from one of the two ruling houses of Sparta. There is a similar anti-Spartan remark about helots in authority in Xenophon's *Hellenica* (3.5.12).

to all the rest, they dared to speak about private and public trials that took place in our city, when they themselves killed more people in three months without trials than our city put on trial since the beginning of our empire. [114] Exiles and factionalism and violations of laws and overthrow of governments; violence against children, rape of the women, seizure of property; who could list everything? I can say only this much about all this: with one vote one could easily put an end to such atrocities under our regime, but no one could cure the slaughter and lawlessness that took place under them.

[115] Now, neither the present peace nor the autonomy that is inscribed in the treaty,[93] even if it is not in our constitutions, deserves to be preferred to our rule; for who would want a situation where pirates control the seas and second-rank mercenaries[94] take control of the cities? [116] Instead of making wars against other people to defend their territory, the citizens fight against each other within their own walls, and more cities have been taken captive than before we made the peace; because of the frequency of revolutions, those living in the cities are more disheartened than those who were punished with exile. The former fear the future, while the latter always hope to return. [117] They are so far from freedom and autonomy that some are ruled by tyrannies, others by harmosts;[95] a few have been destroyed, and in others, barbarian rulers hold sway. These same barbarians, who dared to cross into Europe and thought more highly of themselves than they ought, [118] we dispatched in such a way that they not only stopped making campaigns against us but also endured the destruction of their own land. We also humbled them so much that they

---

[93] The treaty of the Peace of Antalcidas of 387/6, in which cities were said to belong to the Persian King (the cities of Asia Minor, Clazomene, and Cyprus) or to Athens (Lemnos, Imbros, Scyros) or be autonomous (the rest of Greece). The treaty is quoted in Xenophon's *Hellenica* (5.1.31).

[94] Isocrates uses the word peltasts (*peltastai*) here, which refers to the lightly armed troops rather than the heavily armed hoplites. Mercenaries were more often hoplite warriors than peltasts. Thus Isocrates says that under Sparta the cities could not even oppose second rank mercenaries, a bleak and insulting picture. Cf. Usher 1990: *ad loc.*

[95] A harmost was a Spartan military governor put in charge of an occupied region with the support of a garrison.

brought no war ships to this side of Phaselis[96]—though they had a navy of 1,200 ships—but held their peace and waited for a better time, not trusting the military force that was theirs at the time. [119] That these things happened as a result of the excellence of our ancestors, the subsequent troubles of the city clearly demonstrated. For just when we were stripped of our empire (*archē*), that was the beginning (*archē*) of troubles for the Greeks.[97] After the misfortune at the Hellespont[98] and other leaders took charge, the Persians defeated us in a naval battle,[99] ruled the sea, subdued most of the islands, landed in Spartan territory, took Cythera by force, and sailed all around the Peloponnese, wreaking havoc as they went. [120] One might best see the extent of change if he compared the treaties we made in the past with those written recently. You will see clearly that at that time we divided the King's empire,[100] imposing taxes on some parts and keeping him from using the sea; now, however, he is the one running the affairs of the Greeks, imposing duties on each state, and all but setting up commanders in the cities. [121] Except for this, what else is left for him to do? Is the King not in charge of the war? Does he not manage the peace and put himself in control of present affairs? Do we not travel to his court as if to a despot when we intend to lodge complaints against each other? Do we not address him as "The Great King" as if we were prisoners of war? During wars against each other, do we not put our hopes for security in him, the one who would just as soon destroy us both?

---

[96] A town on the southeast coast of Lycia in Asia Minor that had marked the eastern limits of the Athenian empire. Cf. Talbert 1985: 44.

[97] Isocrates also puns on the Greek word *archē,* meaning both "beginning" and "empire," at 5.61 and 8.101. There is an interesting variation here, since it is the *loss* of empire that is the beginning of troubles. Elsewhere it is the empire *itself* that is the beginning of trouble.

[98] The battle of Aegospotami in 405. Athenian orators commonly used some such euphemism to avoid saying the name of this devastating defeat, which effectively ended the Peloponnesian War.

[99] The battle of Cnidus in 394.

[100] The Greeks regularly referred to the Persian King simply as the King. The earlier treaty was the so-called Peace of Callias, ca. 450 (cf. Demand 1996: 210–211), and the recent one was the Peace of Antalcidas in 387/6.

[122] Keeping these things in mind, we should be angry at the present situation and desire our hegemony back; we should also fault the Spartans because at first they took up war on the pretext of freeing the Greeks but in the end made so many of them slaves; they made the Ionians revolt from our city, from which they originally came and through which they many times found safety, and then they betrayed them to the Persians, against whose will they possess their land and toward whom they never stopped making war. [123] And then the Spartans were upset when we lawfully decided to expand our rule over certain cities. Now, however, they have no concern that those cities are driven into such extremes that it is not enough for them to have to pay taxes and see their citadels controlled by the enemy, but in addition to these common difficulties, they also suffered more terrible physical abuse than our slaves do. For none of us injure our slaves as much as they punish these free men. [124] But the greatest crime is when they are compelled to join the Persians in fighting for the cause of slavery against those who think they should be free, and to endure such dangers that if they lose, they will die immediately, and if they win, they will be further enslaved for the rest of time. [125] Who else should we hold responsible for these troubles other than the Spartans, who, even when they have such great power, allow their former allies to suffer such things and allow the King to set up his own empire using the strength of the Greeks? Formerly, the Spartans used to throw tyrants out and give aid to the people, but now they have changed so completely that they fight against legitimate governments and help set up monarchies. [126] They destroyed the city of Mantinea, for example, although the peace was already in force; they seized the citadel of Thebes, and they now besiege the Olynthians and Phliasians.[101] On the other hand, they work together with Amyntas, king of Macedon, Dionysius, the tyrant in Sicily, and the Persian King, who rules over Asia, so that they will have as big an empire as they can.[102] [127] Is it not absurd that the leading power in Greece should make a single man despot

---

[101] Mantinea: 384; Thebes: taken by the Spartans in 382, who held it until 379; Olynthus: 382; Phlius: 380/79. See Hammond 1986: 466–470 and Xen., *Hellenica* 5.

[102] On Amyntas and Dionysius, see Hammond 1986: 469–482 and Xen., *Hellenica* 5.

over a population so large that you can barely count it, and not allow
the greatest of the cities to govern themselves, but instead forces those
cities to live as slaves and meet with the greatest troubles? [128] And
most terrible of all is when someone sees those who claim to have the
right to lead Greece actually marching against the Greeks every day
and making permanent alliances with the barbarians.

[129] [103] And let no one assume I am embittered just because I have
recalled these things rather harshly, since, as I said before,[104] I make
this argument for the sake of reconciliation; it is not to slander Sparta
in front of others that I said this but so that I might stop them, to the
extent that any argument can, from having this attitude. [130] It is impossible to turn people from their errors or persuade them to desire
other sorts of behavior unless someone strongly rebukes their present
actions. We must call it prosecuting (*katēgorein*) if one criticizes someone in order to hurt him, but advising (*nouthetein*) if one reproaches
him with a view to his benefit. For one must not understand the same
argument in the same way, unless it is spoken with the same intent.
[131] Indeed, we also have these further criticisms to bring against
them, namely, that they compel their neighbors to live like helots for
their own city, but for the common good of the allies they arrange no
such thing, even though they could resolve their disputes with us and
then make all the barbarians subservient neighbors (*perioikoi*)[105] to
the whole of Greece. [132] Those who pride themselves on their natural ability and not just on their luck must attempt such deeds rather
than impose taxes on the islanders; the latter deserve pity, seeing that
they are compelled to till the mountains because of the lack of arable
land, while the mainlanders[106] have abundant land and can leave the
greatest part of it untilled, getting such wealth as they need from the
part that bears fruit.

---

[103] Sections 129–132 are transitional between the epideictic portion of the
speech (21–128) and the deliberative portion (133–169). See Usher's very useful
note on this section: 1990: 184.

[104] 15–20.

[105] Cf. 12.178n. Isocrates uses the term *perioikoi*, which strictly applies only to
a specific group of Sparta's neighbors, as he uses "helots" earlier in this section,
somewhat metaphorically to apply to the situation of Greece as a whole.

[106] The inhabitants of Asia Minor.

[133] [107] Now, I think that if a person came from somewhere else and saw our current situation, he would judge both of our cities mad, since we risk so much on small matters when it is possible to get many things safely, and when we destroy our own land, while we ignore the fertility of Asia. [134] Nothing is more profitable for the King than watching for ways in which we might continually fight among ourselves. But we are so far from harming any of his affairs or making his people revolt that we even try to help end the troubles that happen to him by chance. For example, when there are two armies in Cyprus, we allow him to use one for his attack and allow him to besiege the other, even though both are Greek.[108] [135] But the Cypriots who revolt from Persia are favorable to us and also seek the protection of Sparta; and of those campaigning with Tiribazus against the Cypriot king, the best of the infantry were gathered from these regions, and the best of the naval force came from Ionia.[109] These would be much better off in a common attack on Asia than in warring against each other over trivial matters. [136] We pay no attention to these matters, but we fight over the Cyclades islands[110] when we have so rashly handed over to the King so many cities and such great forces. Thus he holds some of these and will soon hold others; he plots against still

---

[107] Sections 133–169 present the deliberative argument that the Greeks should adjust their efforts and unite against Persia. This includes standard topics: prior inactivity (133–137), the opposition's military weakness (138–149), the opposition's moral weakness (150–159), and finally that the opposition's problems can become an advantage for the Greeks (160–169).

[108] The island of Cyprus was led in a war against Persia by Evagoras that lasted from 391–381, and Greek mercenaries fought on both sides. Isocrates wrote an encomium of Evagoras (9).

[109] The infantry came from the Greek regions of Asia Minor; the naval forces came from Ionia, which is also a part of Asia Minor. Tiribazus was the satrap who led the army against Evagoras. Thus, both Evagoras' opposition force and Tiribazus' attacking force were manned by Greeks.

[110] The islands of the central and southern Aegean Sea, called the Cyclades ("circle") islands because they form a ring around the central holy island of Delos. They represent both problems mentioned in section 133: fighting over trivial matters and not moving hostilities from Greece into Asia Minor against Persia. The islands represent an internal struggle, and of small importance at that.

others and quite rightly he thinks us all fools, [137] for he has accomplished what none of his ancestors ever could. It is agreed by both us and the Spartans that Asia belongs to the King, and he has taken such authoritative control of the Greek cities there that he has destroyed some and has fortified the citadels of others. All these things have come about through our neglect, and not through the power of the King.[111]

[138] And yet there are those who admire the greatness of the King's deeds and say he would be difficult to fight against, recounting the many changes he has brought to the Greeks. But I think that those who say this are not working against a war but promoting it. For if it will be hard to fight against him when we are united while he has troubles, then indeed we should be very afraid of that time when the Persians are settled and unified in purpose, while we are as hostile to each other as we are now. [139] Moreover, even if my opponents agree with what I have said, they do not correctly understand about the King's power. For if they demonstrated that at some time in the past he prevailed against both of us at the same time, then it would be logical for them to try to frighten us now. But if he merely added his forces to one side at a time when we and the Spartans were adversaries, thus making that side's accomplishments greater, this is no sign of his power, for very often in such situations a small force has tipped the balance substantially. We can cite the example of the Chians: whichever side they chose to join was the stronger at sea.[112]

[140] Thus it is not right to judge the King's power from cases where he joined one side or the other but only from cases where he has

---

[111] Sections 136–137 represent negative preparatory arguments (complaints about current behavior) that are characteristic not only of Isocrates, as Usher points out (1990: 187), but of deliberative oratory as a whole. Demosthenes will do similar things in his speeches against Philip. Demosthenes says, for example, that things would be much worse if the Athenians were as bad off as they are while they were trying their hardest, but in fact they have done nothing, so there is room for hope (Dem. 2.22–23, 4.2, 9.11–12, 10.7–8).

[112] Chios sided with Athens in the Peloponnesian War until Athens' loss at Syracuse in 415. They sided with Sparta from this point until Sparta's defeat at Cnidus in 394. Then they returned to Athens' side.

fought on his own. First, when Egypt revolted, what did he do to those who held it?[113] Did he not send the most renowned of the Persians to that war, Abrokomas and Tithraustes and Pharnabazus? These men stayed three months, suffered more harm than they inflicted, and finally escaped so shamefully that the rebels of Egypt are no longer content with freedom but are now seeking to gain control over their neighbors too. [141] After this, he made a campaign against Evagoras, who rules over just one city but was handed over to the King according to the treaty.[114] He inhabits an island, earlier suffered a loss at sea, and on land he has only three thousand peltasts. Nevertheless, even though his power is so slight, the King is not able to prevail in war and has already wasted six years.[115] And if one should predict the future on the basis of past actions, there is much more hope that someone else will revolt before the King takes the city by siege. Such is the sluggish pace of the King's actions. [142] In the Rhodian War,[116] he had allies from the Spartans who were on his side because of the strictness of their government, he had rowers from us, and he had Conon as commander of his forces, who was the most careful of the generals, the most trusted by the Greeks, and the most experienced in the risks of war. Even with such a great general on his side, he allowed his fleet, which had earlier guarded Asia, to be hemmed in by only one hundred triremes, and he deprived the soldiers of their pay for fifteen months. The result was that if the fleet had been under his control, it would have disbanded on many occasions, but because of his commander and the alliance established at Corinth, he achieved a naval victory, but just barely. [143] These are the most regal and awesome of the

---

[113] Perhaps in 383; see Usher 1990: *ad loc.*

[114] That is, the Peace of Antalcidas of 387/6; above, 115n. It is true that Evagoras started with one city, Salamis on Cyprus (9.65; Diodorus Siculus 14.110.5), but he expanded to most of the island before being attacked by Persia. To emphasize one city makes the King's inability all the more pronounced.

[115] Evagoras' war against Persia lasted from 386 to 380, according to Diodorus Siculus (15.2–4).

[116] A struggle between Sparta and Persia that was located near Rhodes, ending with the battle of Cnidus in 394 (Hammond 1986: 449–460). Conon joined the Persians after his disgraceful loss at the end of the Peloponnesian War at Aegospotami.

King's accomplishments, repeatedly mentioned by those who want to amplify his actions. So no one can say that I have used my examples unfairly or that I have dwelt on minor accomplishments and passed over the important ones. [144] Indeed, to avoid such an accusation I have related his most famous actions, not forgetting, however, those of his men: for example, Dercylidas with one thousand hoplites[117] gained control of Aeolis; Draco took Atarneus and with three thousand peltasts, wasted the Mysian Plain; Thibron with only a few more men than these crossed into Lydia and ravaged the whole countryside; and Agesilaus, using Cyrus' army, almost conquered all the area of Asia this side of the Halys river.[118] [145] There is no need to fear the army that follows the King either, or the Persians' courage, for these have been clearly shown by the troops under Cyrus to be no better than the naval forces.[119] I pass over most battles that his forces lost, for I admit that they were factionalized and were not eager to fight against the King's brother. [146] But after Cyrus died and they all united in such favorable circumstances, they fought so shamefully that no argument remains for those who usually praise Persian courage. They faced six thousand Greeks, not chosen for merit but because, through poverty, they could not survive in their own land; these Greeks had no knowledge of the land, they had no allies, they had been deserted by those who came with them, and they had lost the general with whom they had come.[120] [147] Nonetheless, the King's forces were so inferior to these that the King, at a loss what to do and lacking confidence in his own forces, dared to capture the leaders of the mercenaries, even

---

[117] See above, 115n.

[118] Dercylidas was commander of Spartan forces in 399. Draco was harmost at Atarneus after he sacked it in 398, assigned there by Dercylidas. Thibron was commander of the Spartan navy in 400, before Dercylidas took over. Agesilaus took over the Spartan forces in 395. These examples are not put in chronological order but in the order that makes them most effective rhetorically for Isocrates (Usher 1990: 189). Dercylidas, Draco, and Agesilaus were successful against the King; Thibron was not.

[119] The story of this expedition under Cyrus is told in detail by Xenophon in the *Anabasis.* Cyrus' troops were highly successful until Cyrus was killed during his victory at Cunaxa in 401. Cf. *To Philip* 5.90–92.

[120] With the death of Cyrus at Cunaxa in 401.

though they were protected by a truce,[121] in the hope that by committing such a crime, he would unnerve their army. He chose to sin against the gods rather than fight against the troops openly. [148] When this plan failed, since the army remained together and endured their loss nobly, the King sent Tissaphernes and the cavalry with the Greeks as they departed. Although the Greeks were harassed all along the way, they got through just as if they were being escorted in a procession. They especially feared the uninhabited parts of the land and thought that the best thing for them would be if they should meet as many of the enemy as possible. [149] In sum, those men came not to plunder or to capture a town but to march against the King himself, and they went away more safely than ambassadors who visit him seeking friendship. Thus the Persians seem to me to have shown their weakness clearly in all areas: on the coast of Asia they lost many battles; crossing over into Europe they paid the price when some of them were destroyed completely and others escaped in shame; and finally they have become a joke even inside the King's palace.

[150] And none of this happened without reason, but everything turned out just as you would expect, for those raised in the Persian manner and living under their form of government cannot set up victory trophies over their enemies or share in any other virtue. How could there be either a fearsome general or a good soldier who lives like these people? For the most part they are an undisciplined mob, unused to danger, fainthearted in war, and schooled for slavery better than our own slaves. [151] Those with the greatest reputation never lived with a view to equality or the common good or participation in government but spend all their time treating some people arrogantly but acting like slaves toward others, in a way that would most degrade men's natures. Their bodies are soft because of their wealth, and their

---

[121] Isocrates gives more detail about this incident in *To Philip* (5.91): "Still, even though such a disaster struck his enemy, the King thought so little of the force around him that he summoned Clearchus and the other opposition leaders to come into a meeting. He promised to give them great gifts and to give the rest of the troops their full salary and then let them go. But after leading them on with such hopes and offering them pledges that in Asia were considered the most binding, he arrested them all and killed them, preferring to offend the gods rather than enter battle against soldiers who were so isolated without Cyrus."

souls are humble and timid because of their monarchy: they present themselves before the royal palace, falling prostrate before the King, and in every way learn to be meek, honoring a mortal man and addressing him as a divinity and showing less respect for the gods than for men. [152] Moreover, those whom they call satraps[122] and who go down to positions on the sea coast do not discredit this upbringing but keep the same ways, behaving faithlessly toward friends and cowardly toward enemies, alternating between humility and arrogance, scornful of their allies and servile toward their enemies. [153] The satraps supported the army of Agesilaus for eight months at their own expense[123] but did not pay those who fought under them for twice as long. They gave one hundred talents to those who recaptured Cisthene[124] but treated those fighting with them against Cyprus more arrogantly than their prisoners. [154] To speak simply, in general terms without excessive detail, who of those who fought against them did not go away prosperous, and who of those under their command was not mistreated until their death? Certainly not Conon, who campaigned for Asia and thus ruined the power of Sparta. Did they not dare to arrest him and punish him with death? In the case of Themistocles, however, who defeated them in a naval battle to save Greece, did they not bestow the greatest gifts on him? [155] Why should we esteem the friendship of those who punish their benefactors and so openly flatter those who injure them? Against which of us did they not commit crimes? When did they let any time go by without plotting against the Greeks? What is there of ours that is not hateful to these people, who in the prior war dared to plunder and burn the seats of the gods and their temples? [156] We should praise the Ionians because, when their temples were burned, they cursed anyone who would move them or want to restore them to their original conditions, not because they did not know how to rebuild them but so that they might be a memorial for people in years to come of barbarian impiety. They did this so that no one would trust those who dared to commit such crimes against

---

[122] Satraps are governors of provinces under Persian control.

[123] Xenophon describes Tithraustes' payment to Agesilaus in the *Hellenica* (3.4.25–26).

[124] This place has not been positively identified. Cf. Sandys 1872, *ad loc.* Its connection with Agesilaus is also unclear.

the gods and also so that people might be cautious and fearful, seeing that they had fought not only against our bodies but also against our religious offerings.

[157] In contrast, I can say the following about our own citizens: While they forget the hostility they once had as soon as they make peace with a people they have been fighting, so unforgettable is their anger toward the Persians that even when they are well treated by them, they feel no gratitude. Further, our fathers condemned many to death for Medizing,[125] and even now in public meetings, before conducting other business, they put curses on any citizen who makes proposals for a treaty with the Persians. During the rite of the Mysteries, the Eumolpidae and the Ceruces[126] even ban other foreigners from the rites as if they were murderers because of the hatred toward the Persians. [158] We are so naturally hostile toward the Persians that even in our stories (*mythoi*)[127] we devote most time to those about the Trojan Wars and the Persian Wars, which tell about their troubles.[128] One finds that after the war against the barbarians, hymns were composed, but wars against the Greeks have produced laments; the hymns are sung during festivals, but the laments are remembered during times of suffering.[129] [159] I think even the poetry of Homer has a greater reputation because it celebrated those who fought well against the barbarians, and because of this, our ancestors wished to give his art a place of honor in poetic contests and in the education of the young, so that we might hear his words many times and learn the fundamental ha-

---

[125] Medizing is the word to describe a Greek siding with the Medes or Persians. The most famous instance was when the Thebans sided with the Persians during the Persian Wars. Cf. 12.93 and 14.30.

[126] These two families traditionally provided the priests for the Eleusinian Mysteries. On the Mysteries, see above, 28n.

[127] Both the Trojan Wars and the Persian Wars are *mythoi*. On Isocrates' use of myth, see Papillon 1996b.

[128] For Isocrates there is no distinction among easterners; the Trojans and the Persians fall into the same category. Such ethnocentrism is common among the Athenians.

[129] See Usher (1990: 194) on this Isocratean idealization of a motif from the funeral oration of Gorgias. Where Gorgias says that wars against Greeks *ought* to be cause for corporate lament, Isocrates says that they *are* the cause.

tred we have toward them, and in admiration of the courage of those who fought against the barbarians, we might desire to emulate their deeds.

[160] Thus it seems to me that many factors encourage us to make war against the Persians, but especially the present opportunity (*kairos*) that must not be missed. It would be a shame not to seize the present opportunity, only to remember it with regret when it has passed. For what more could we want beyond what we have if we are going to fight the King? [161] Have not Egypt and Cyprus revolted from him?[130] Have not Phoenicia and Syria been ravaged by war? Has not Tyre—of which he thinks highly—been captured by his enemies?[131] Most of the cities in Cilicia are controlled by people on our side, and it would not be difficult to gain the rest. No Persian ever conquered Lycia. [162] Hecatomnus, the governor of Caria, has been in revolt a long time, if truth be told, and will acknowledge this whenever we wish. From Cnidus to Sinope, Greeks inhabit Asia;[132] we do not need to persuade these men to fight but simply not prevent them from doing so. Indeed, with such great incentives and with so much war throughout Asia, why must I set out what will happen in great detail? For when the Persians are defeated by small parts of our force, it is clear how they will fare if forced to fight against all of us. [163] This is how it is. If the King more firmly controls the cities on the coast by establishing more garrisons in them than he now has, the islands near the coast, such as Rhodes and Samos and Chios, would perhaps incline toward his fortunes. But if we take the coastal cities before this happens, it is likely that those who live in Lydia and Phrygia and the rest of the land further inland would come under the control of those who make their base there. [164] Therefore, we must hurry and make no delay so we do not suffer what our ancestors did, for they were slower than the barbarians and thus were compelled to abandon some of the allies and face the danger with only a few troops against the Persians'

---

[130] See sections 140–141 with 140n.

[131] All these cities suffered in the war with Evagoras of Cyprus mentioned in section 141.

[132] The phrase "from Cnidus to Sinope" was a traditional way to identify the whole of Asia Minor.

many, when they could have crossed over to Asia sooner with the whole Greek force and handled each nation in turn. [165] For it has been shown that whenever someone makes war against people gathered from many places, he must not wait until they come against him but must attack them while they are still scattered. Our ancestors made a mistake early, but they corrected the whole affair by undergoing the greatest struggles. So if we are wise, we will take precautions from the beginning and will try to establish a force in Lydia and Ionia first, [166] knowing that the King rules over the mainland peoples not by their consent but by having a greater army there than any one of them individually does. When we transport a force over there greater than his—which we can do easily if we wish—we will safely enjoy the fruits of all of Asia. And it is much better to fight against him for his kingdom than to argue among ourselves about hegemony.

[167] It is right to make this campaign during this generation so that those who shared in our troubles may also enjoy the benefits and not spend their whole lives in misfortune. Has not enough time passed when every terrible thing has happened?[133] Although many evils come naturally to humans, we ourselves have devised more than necessary, [168] bringing wars and factionalism upon ourselves. As a result, some of us die in our own lands contrary to law, others wander in foreign lands with their wives and children, and many through want of daily needs are compelled to hire themselves out and end up dying while fighting against friends on behalf of enemies. No one has ever become angry at these things; they think it right, however, to weep over the sufferings recounted by the poets, overlooking terrible sufferings that happen because of real wars. Far from feeling pity, they actually take more pleasure from the troubles of others than from their own good fortune. [169] Perhaps many would laugh at my naïveté if I should mourn for people's misfortune at a time when Italy has been ravaged and Sicily enslaved, many cities have surrendered to the barbarians, and the remaining parts of Greece are in the gravest danger.[134]

---

[133] Sandys (1872: *ad loc.*) comments on the emphatic nature of this statement.

[134] Dionysius of Syracuse led an attack on Italy in 389 and 387/6. The greater part of Sicily was under his control until he surrendered parts to the Carthaginians. A number of cities were given to Persian control in the Peace of Antalcidas of 387/6 (cf. above, 115n).

[170] [135] I am amazed at those who hold power in our cities, if they believe they should think so highly of themselves even though they can never articulate or form any ideas about such important issues. If they deserved their current reputation, they should have put off everything else to propose ideas and make plans for a war against the barbarians. [171] Perhaps that might have helped accomplish something. But even if they had given up on that before they accomplished something, at least they would have left behind discourses that would be useful for the future. Now, however, those who have the greatest reputation are busy about trivial matters, while it is left to us who are outside the political realm to give advice about such important issues. [172] Not only this, but since our leaders are small-minded, the rest of us must look more vigorously at how we might escape from the current hostility. Now we make peace treaties in vain, for we do not put an end to wars; we merely put them off and wait for a time when we can inflict an incurable injury on each other.

[173] But we must put these intrigues aside and set about making our cities safer for their citizens and establishing more trusting relationships among ourselves. The plan for this is simple and easy; it is impossible to have a secure peace unless we join together to make war against the barbarians, and it is impossible for us to be unified until we gain our advantages from the same sources and run our risks against the same enemies. [174] When this happens and we have removed the confusion in our lives—a confusion that dissolves friendships, causes relatives to hate one another, and drives all people to war and faction-

---

[135] Sections 170–189 comprise the peroration, where Isocrates sums up the arguments he has made. Usher (1990: 197) points out that the conclusion summarizes three important argumentative topics of the speech: advantage, justice, and possibility. The statement of advantage (*sympheron*) begins here in section 173, that of justice (*dikaion*) in 175, and that of possibility (*dynaton*) in 185. Note that the greatest space is given here to the issue of justice; this topic guided the epideictic portion of the speech, which was the longest topic in the speech. But justice appeared much earlier in the oration, so Isocrates needs to remind the audience of it more thoroughly. The idea of advantage is usually attributed to deliberative discourse, and the idea of justice to judicial discourse. Possibility would then be the topic of epideictic. John Poulakos (1995: 53–73) has argued for the importance of the possible for the sophists and epideictic discourse; for a contrary view, see Schiappa 1991: 174–177.

alism—then there is no way that we will not be unified and feel honest goodwill toward one another. For this reason, we must try as hard as we can to move the war here in Greece over to Asia as quickly as possible. The only benefit we might enjoy from our present struggles among ourselves is if we think we can take advantage of the experience gained during these wars in the war against the Persians.

[175] [136] However, perhaps we ought to hold back because of the treaty and not be too quick to press on and begin a campaign. The cities that are free because of the treaty are grateful to the King, for they think that he is responsible for their autonomy; those cities that were surrendered to the King fault the Spartans especially and also the others who shared in the peace, for they think these cities compelled them to be slaves. Yet how can we not dissolve this agreement [137] that has given rise to the view that the King cares about Greece and is the guardian of the peace, while it is some of us who inflict pain and suffering on it? [176] But most ridiculous of all is that we abide by the worst provisions of the agreement. Those provisions that make the islands and the cities in Europe autonomous were long ago violated and are inscribed on the treaty stones without any force. [138] But the sections that bring shame on us and betray many of our allies remain in force throughout the land, and we all treat them as authoritative, when we should have taken them down and not let them remain even one day more, treating them as nothing but an order, not as a treaty. For who does not know that a treaty is something that holds equally for and serves the interests of all parties, whereas orders make one side subordinate in violation of justice? [177] Therefore, it would have been fair to accuse those who negotiated this peace of being sent by the Greeks but making the treaty for the benefit of the barbarians. For

---

[136] Beginning of the summary of arguments based on justice (*dikaion*). He begins it by bringing up an expected objection, the status of the Peace of Antalcidas.

[137] Isocrates changes from the technical term for "treaty" (*synthēkai*) in 175 to a more general and less technical term, "agreement" (*homologiae*), later in 175 and in 176. Rhetorically, it will be less disturbing for the audience to dissolve an agreement than a treaty.

[138] Public documents like a treaty would be inscribed on stone tablets called steles and set up in a public place such as near a temple (for treaties) or in the central marketplace (for laws). See below, 180.

whether they thought it right that each city control its own territory
or that each should also be able to take over those they defeated in war,
or should have power over those they got under the terms of the peace,
they should have selected one of these principles and written this into
the treaty, making it apply justly to everyone alike. [178] But in fact,
they gave no honor to our city or to Sparta but set up the King as despot over all Asia, as if we had waged our war for his benefit or as if the
Persian empire had existed for a long time and we only recently settled
our cities, whereas, in fact, the Persians acquired their position just recently, while we have been powers among the Greeks since the beginning. [179] I think that I will better clarify the dishonor that has be-
fallen us and the greed of the King by putting it in this way: if all the
world under the heavens were cut into two and called Asia and Europe, he gained half through the treaty as if he were dividing up land
with Zeus rather than making a treaty with humans. [180] He forced
us to write it on stone pillars and set them up in the precincts of the
temples, a much finer victory trophy than all those set up after a battle.
For these resulted from minor actions and a stroke of luck, whereas
the treaty was set up to represent the whole war at the expense of all
Greece.

[181] Thus, it is right to be angry about this and consider how we
might get revenge for what happened and correct our course in the future. For it is shameful if privately we approve having barbarians as our
slaves but publicly allow so many of our allies to be enslaved to them,
and equally shameful if our ancestors during the Trojan Wars, when
a single woman was kidnapped, were all so angry on behalf of the
victim that they did not stop fighting until they destroyed the city of
that man who dared such a crime, [182] while we, even though the
whole of Greece is being violated, make no joint attempt to punish the
guilty, although we have the chance to accomplish all we desire. This
war alone is better than a state of peace because it is more like a religious mission than a military campaign.[139] Also it will benefit both

---

[139] One of the characteristics of a peroration in classical theory is the rousing
of emotion. An example here is the increased number and power of religious ideas.
Isocrates presents the religious impiety of the Persian King in section 179 and here
in section 182 presents the Greek campaign against Persia as if it were a religious
duty (*theoria*). A *theoria* can be a delegation sent to religious or athletic festivals

sides, those wanting to keep the peace and those wanting to make war, for it would make it possible for those interested in peace to enjoy their lives without fear and those interested in war to gain great riches from the enemy.

[183] [140] Anyone who thinks about it would find many kinds of important advantages in these actions. Consider this: against whom should people make war when they want no gain but aim only at justice? Is it not against those who abused Greece in the past, are plotting against us in the present, and will feel this way about us for all time? [184] When people are not entirely lacking in courage, but use it in moderation, whom should they likely envy? Should they not envy those who have aimed at greater power than is appropriate for humans but are worth less than the most wretched among us? And when people want to be pious and at the same time think of their own interests, against whom should they campaign? Is it not against those who are by nature hostile and by tradition hateful, who possess the most good things but are least able to defend them? Do not the Persians turn out to meet all these criteria?

[185] [141] And indeed, we will not even bother the cities by levying troops from them, which is the most vexing aspect for them in this current war against each other, for I think that those who want to stay behind will be many fewer than those who are eager to go with us. Who is so lazy, whether young or old, who will not want to share in this expedition that will be led by the Athenians and Spartans, has been assembled for the freedom of our allies, is sent forth by the whole of Greece, and sets out with the aim of punishing the barbarians? [186] Fame, reputation, and glory; how much of these should we imagine those who show themselves the best in this endeavor will have if they come out alive or will leave behind if they die? When those who fought against Alexander and captured just one city were thought

---

(which are themselves religious), and the contrast with a military campaign makes it seem more pious (cf. Jebb 1962: 2.164–165) than relaxing, which is an option Usher chooses in his translation "sightseeing" (1990: 111).

[140] Sections 183–184 present a hybrid argument, bringing advantage together with justice.

[141] Beginning of the summary of arguments based on possibility (*dynaton*).

worthy of such great praise,[142] how much praise must those who conquer the whole of Asia expect to receive? For which of the poets or of those who know about the art of discourse will not work and study, wanting to leave behind for all time a monument of both his own intelligence and their greatness?

[187] [143] Now I do not have the same opinion at present as I had at the beginning of the discourse, for then I thought I would be able to make my speech worthy of the topic, but now I am not reaching the greatness of it. Many of the thoughts I had escape me now. Therefore, you must work with me to consider how much prosperity we will attain if we transfer the war we are currently fighting against each other and make it against those in Asia as well as consider the prosperity we would bring from Asia back to Greece. [188] You must not go away from this Assembly having been only spectators, but as people of action, you must encourage each other to reconcile our city and that of the Spartans.[144] Also, those who contend against each other in public discourses must stop writing about deposits of money and other such trivial things that they prattle on about[145] but must concentrate their rivalry on this topic and see how they can speak about this topic better than I did, [189] taking to heart that those who promise great things should not waste their time on trivial matters, nor say things that will not improve the life of those who are persuaded by them, but they should speak so that when their recommendations are accomplished, they will free themselves from their present difficulties and be thought by others to be responsible for the greatest benefits.

---

[142] The Trojan War, in which the Greeks fought for Helen against Alexander, otherwise known as Paris. Homer's *Iliad* tells us that the Greeks captured other cities along the way as well, but Isocrates is fair in saying that Troy is the sole focus of their expedition.

[143] Isocrates closes with a very personal comment about his abilities and the quality of the discourse, referring to the boasts he made at the beginning in section 14.

[144] In sharp contrast, Aristotle will say later that the audience of an epideictic discourse (such as a panegyric oration) is only a spectator and not a judge (*Rhetoric* 1.3). On the difficulties of epideictic as a category, see Kennedy 1991: 48n77.

[145] Isocrates refers to private lawsuits. Cf. Bonner 1920.

5. TO PHILIP

〰〰〰

INTRODUCTION

This discourse was written in 346 when Isocrates was 90 years old.
Athens and Macedon had been involved in hostilities for some years
prior to this and had just concluded a peace treaty, the so-called Peace
of Philocrates, in which the famous orators Demosthenes and Aeschines were the leading delegates for Athens. Isocrates now writes to
Philip, asking him to help with what has been the main political
agenda of Isocrates' career: unifying the Greek states in a campaign
against Persia. Isocrates had presented this policy earlier in his career
(380) in his *Panegyricus* (4.173). At that time, he talked of Athens and
Sparta sharing leadership (4.16–17), but he also revealed his desire that
Athens alone should lead the unified Greek forces (4.99). By the time
of this discourse to Philip, however, the realities of history and politics compelled Isocrates to admit that Athens' leadership was no longer a feasible idea. He turned now to the most powerful man of the
day in the Greek world, Philip of Macedon.[1] This approach was seen
as treason by some. Demosthenes, for example, vehemently opposed
Philip in many of his speeches. He and others saw Philip as a man who
did not want to lead the Greeks but to conquer them. Isocrates saw
Philip as a way for a Greek to lead the Greeks, but Demosthenes and
others saw him as a barbarian, that is, as a non-Greek or as uncivilized,
or both. The question whether Philip was, in fact, a Greek or a barbarian was much debated.[2]

---

[1] Isocrates says later (*Ep.* 3.3) that he had not yet met Philip when he wrote this
discourse.

[2] Macedon stood geographically on the border of Greek and non-Greek territory. This led to questions about the legitimacy of Macedon as a part of Greece

To Philip is notable in that it begins with the separate but related issue of the city of Amphipolis in northern Greece and the contest for it between Philip and Athens. Aristotle points out that Isocrates often adds a preface unrelated to the rest of the speech (*Rhetoric* 3.14). Calling it unrelated may be too harsh, since Aristotle's own example, *Helen* (10)—as well as *Busiris* (11), *To Philip* (5), and perhaps *Against the Sophists* (13)—shows a prefatory section that is, in fact, connected to the body (see Papillon 1996a).

There is a useful commentary on *To Philip* by Laistner (1927) to which this translation is often indebted. See also Perelman (1957, 1969).

5. TO PHILIP

[1] Do not be amazed, Philip, because I do not begin with the discourse that will be spoken and presented to you shortly, but one written about Amphipolis.[3] I want to make a brief preface (*proeipein*) about this city so that I might show you and others that I did not set out to write this discourse in ignorance or because I was deceived about the weaknesses of my present vexing age, but did it with thought and deliberation.[4]

[2] I saw that the war over Amphipolis that was occupying you and Athens was causing many difficulties, and so I tried not to give the same advice about this city and its territory as either your advisors or the rhetors here, but to differ as much as I could from their point of view. [3] These men have been constantly urging you toward war, saying just what you yourself were feeling. I, on the other hand, did not give any opinion about the controversy over Amphipolis. Rather, I spent my time on an approach that I thought would be the most likely to bring peace. My advice was that both you and we were making a

---

and arguments about whether or not the Macedonians were Greeks (arguments that have continued down to the present). Isocrates argues for their Greek ancestry. See Markle 1976; Borza 1990; and Hall 2001.

[3] Amphipolis was a city in Macedon, captured by the Athenians in the fifth century and taken back by Philip in 358. The latter incident led to hostilities between the two states until the Peace of Philocrates in early 346. It is unclear whether these comments on Amphipolis were ever distributed as a separate discussion.

[4] During these later years of his life, Isocrates often spoke of the difficulties of writing with advancing age.

mistake in this matter: you were fighting for our advantage, and our city was fighting for the benefit of your empire, for I thought that it was more advantageous for you if we have control of this territory, and it was in no way advantageous for Athens to take it. [4] Those who heard me thought so highly of my treatment of the matter that no one praised the arrangement of the speech or the clarity and purity of its style—as people often do—but rather they marveled at the truth of the advice. They thought that the only way we could put an end to our strife was [5] if you should be persuaded that friendship with Athens is more valuable to you than the profits you would receive from Amphipolis and if Athens could understand that one must avoid the kinds of colonies that four or five times over destroy those who settle in them, but should seek instead to colonize places that are far from neighbors who could take control over them, but are near to neighbors who are used to being subservient, as, for example, when the Spartans colonized Cyrene.[5] [6] In addition, you should know that by handing over this territory to us in word, in actuality you will take control of it yourself, and you will also gain the goodwill of our city, for all those we send out as colonists into your sphere of influence you will receive as hostages of our friendship. Further, someone should teach our own people that if we take Amphipolis, we will be compelled to have the same goodwill toward your affairs because of the colonists there as we had done formerly toward Amadocus[6] because of those who set up farms in the Chersonese.

[7] Those who heard me say all these things hoped that when this discourse was published, you and Athens would put an end to the war, change your opinion, and make some common plan for your own good. Now, whether they were foolish or wise in holding this opinion, certainly they alone are responsible. But you two made peace while I was still working on the discourse, and wisely so, for however you did it, peace was better for you than being oppressed by the troubles

---

[5] According to standard accounts (cf. Herod. 4.151–159), Cyrene, in North Africa, was colonized by the island of Thera, which was itself a Spartan colony. Isocrates may be following a Spartan version of the story.

[6] Amadocus was king of Thrace in the early part of the fourth century. Athens made an alliance with him in 390, primarily to protect its settlers in the Chersonese, which is adjacent to Thrace.

brought on by war. [8] Although I agreed with this decision about the peace and thought it would be advantageous not only for us but also for you and all the rest of the Greeks, I could not keep my thoughts from the situation, but I was so agitated that I immediately investigated how this treaty could endure so our city would not quickly begin to desire other wars once more. [9] Going over these matters in my mind, I found that Athens would stay peaceful only if all the greatest cities would decide to put off hostilities among themselves and carry the war into Asia, and if they should plan to gain from the barbarians,[7] the advantages that the barbarians now think they should get from the Greeks. This plan I advocated before in my discourse *Panegyricus*.[8]

[10] Considering all this, I concluded that I would never find a theme nobler than this one, nor of more general interest, nor more advantageous to all of us, and so I was inspired to write about it again. I was not ignorant of my own situation. Rather, I knew that such a discourse demanded someone not my age but a youthful man who is naturally superior to others. [11] I saw also that it is difficult to speak two discourses on the same theme adequately,[9] especially when the first one published was written in such a way that even those who malign me emulate it and wonder at it even more than those who praise it excessively. [12] Nonetheless, overlooking these difficulties, I have become so ambitious in my old age that by speaking to you, I wished at the same time both to make a demonstration by example for my students[10] and to make it clear to them that being an annoyance at panhellenic gatherings and speaking to everyone who gathers together for

---

[7] On Isocrates use of the general term "barbarian," see 4.3n.

[8] Cf. 4.15–17. *Panegyricus*, written some thirty-four years earlier in 380, has very similar phrasing.

[9] The verb in the Greek is *eipein*, usually rendered into English as "speak." Within the discourses, Isocrates often uses the vocabulary of delivery (speaking) rather than the vocabulary of composition (writing) to fit with the conventions of oratory. The opening section of *Antidosis* is a good example: He begins by talking of a discourse (*logos*) to be read out loud (*anagignesthai*), then refers to a prefatory spoken section (*prodialechthēnai, proeipein*), and then back to writing (*graphein*). This is a result of the awkward reality that Isocrates avoided oral performance in a very performance-dependent genre. I will maintain the fiction of a spoken discourse and the tension that it produces in the rest of the speech.

[10] Cf. sections 85 and 155.

them is tantamount to speaking to no one.[11] Such speeches turn out to be just as ineffective as laws and constitutions written by the sophists. [13] Those who wish to avoid trivial speech and do something of value, or who think they have found something of common interest, ought to let others give panhellenic speeches (*panēgyreis*) and should instead find someone to be the spokesman for their cause—someone with a wide reputation and who is able to speak well and do what is needed—if anyone is to take it seriously. [14] With this in mind, I chose to address you. I did not choose to curry favor, and although I would value it if I could speak in a way that pleased you, I did not make my decision with this intent. Rather, I saw all the other men of good reputation living in cities with constitutions and laws such that it was impossible for them to do anything except what those laws and constitutions prescribed.[12] And furthermore, they also were not at all up to the tasks I will mention. [15] To you alone fortune has given the power to send delegates to whomever you wish, to receive delegates from whomever you wish, and to say whatever you think best. In addition, you have obtained wealth and power such as no other Greek has, and these alone are naturally suited both for persuading and for compelling. What I am about to suggest will require, I believe, both of these, [16] for I am about to advise you to stand at the head of a Greek alliance and lead a Greek campaign against the barbarians. Persuasion will be useful with the Greeks; compulsion will be advantageous against the barbarians. This, then, is the goal of the whole discourse.

---

[11] The inconsistency between this statement and Isocrates' own speech *Panegyricus* (published in 380), a speech written for a panhellenic gathering, is only apparent. In fact, that speech was not delivered, since Isocrates communicated only through written discourses that took the form of oral speeches. One aspect of his criticism here may be that those who try to move the crowd with a speech do not give the hearer time for consideration before a vote. As Isocrates does it—through publication—the reader has much more time to consider and reflect before making a decision to act. He also has in mind that trying to get the gathered people of a democracy to act is much more complicated than getting a monarch to act.

[12] Herodotus points out this same problem with democracy in his presentation of the Persian debate over constitutions (3.80–83).

[17] But I will not hesitate to tell you why some of my students criticized me, for I think that it will serve a purpose. When I revealed to them that I was going to send you a discourse that would not make a display of my talent (*epideixis*) and would not praise (*enkōmiazō*) the wars that you have waged—for others will do this—but one that tried to encourage (*protrepein*) you toward deeds that were more fitting, more noble, and more advantageous for you than those you have now chosen, [18] they were so upset, thinking that I might have taken leave of my senses because of my old age, that they dared to reproach me, although they had not been accustomed to doing this before. They said that I was setting upon tasks that were strange and quite odd: "You are on the verge of sending a discourse that will give advice to Philip. Even if in the past he used to think there were others more intelligent than he, now, because of the greatness of his success, there is no chance that he will not consider himself better able to plan than anyone else. [19] Also, he has around him the best advisors in Macedon, who surely, even if they might have little experience in other matters, know better than you what is advantageous for him. Further, you will see that there are many Greeks living there who are not without reputation or wisdom; after consulting with them, he did not make his kingdom smaller but achieved results to match his desire. [20] What is left? Has he not made the Thessalians, who formerly had control over Macedon, so favorably disposed toward him that each of them trusts him more than their own fellow citizens? Of the cities in that area, has he not made some his allies through his benefactions, while others that were too troublesome to him he simply destroyed? [21] Has he not subdued the Magnesians, the Perrhaebians, and the Paeonians and made them all his subjects?[13] Has he not become lord and master of the people of Illyria,[14] except for those who lived along

---

[13] Paeonoia is a region to the north of Macedon; Philip took control of it in 352. Perrhaebia is just to the south of Macedon, on the northern border of Thessaly. Magnesia is just to the southeast of Perrhaebia. These latter two regions were under Thessalian control and served as a buffer between Thessaly and Macedon until Philip took control of them, Perrhaebia in 352 and Paeonia in 356.

[14] Illyria is the region extending north of Epirus, northwest of Macedon, in modern-day Albania. Borza (1990: 180–181) describes it as "not a nation in any strict sense, but rather a collection of tribes." Illyria was often a threat to Macedon

the Adriatic? Has he not set up the rulers he wished over all of Thrace? Don't you think that the man who has such great accomplishments will think that the one who sends him a book is a fool and conclude that the sender is quite confused about the power of his discourses and his own wisdom?" [22] When I heard this, I was distraught at first; but when I collected myself, I responded to each of the complaints in turn. I will pass over how this happened, so that I don't seem to anyone to be too pleased by how I neatly refuted them. When I gently rebuked (as I thought) each of those who dared to fault me, I finally promised to show the speech to them and no one else in the city, and I said that I would do with it only what they thought was right.[15] [23] When they heard this, they left. I do not know what they were thinking, except that a few days later, when the discourse was finished and was shown to them, they changed their minds so completely that they were ashamed about their former daring and regretted everything they had said; they confessed that they had never been so mistaken about a matter and that they were now even more eager than I that this discourse should be sent to you.[16] They also said they hoped that not only you and Athens would be grateful to me for what I say but all the rest of the Greeks too.

[24] I have gone through all this for you so that, even if something I say at the beginning should seem to you either unbelievable, or impossible, or inappropriate for you to do, you would not become angry and reject the rest of what I say. You should not react the way my pupils did, but you should be patient and keep your attitude calm

---

in the sixth to fourth centuries but was eventually controlled by Philip after the battle of Lyncus about 357 (Borza 1990: 201–202). In Hellenistic times, Illyria served as a buffer between the Roman world and Macedon.

[15] Isocrates describes such a discussion with his pupils in more detail toward the end of *Panathenaicus* (12.200–265).

[16] Isocrates knows that his suggestions are contrary to many Athenians' views, especially prominent Athenians such as Demosthenes; see the Introduction to this speech. He adds this interchange with his pupils as a model for those who read the discourse of a way to change their mind and agree with him. Offering an example as a model for behavior is characteristic of what has been called the "hypodeictic" discourse of Isocrates (Papillon 1995). This is in addition to his concerns about how Philip will receive the advice (24).

until you hear everything I am going to say right to the end. For I think I will say something necessary and also advantageous for you. [25] Still, I am not unaware of how much spoken discourses differ in their persuasive power from discourses that are read. I know that everyone assumes that spoken discourses concern serious and pressing matters, while written discourses are composed for display and for obtaining a commission. [26] And this view is not unreasonable. When a discourse lacks the authority of the speaker and his voice and the variations that occur in oral presentations (*rhētoreia*) as well as the crucial sense of timing (*kairos*) and the seriousness of the speaker toward the issue, when there is nothing to help the discourse present its case persuasively but it is empty and stripped of everything that I just mentioned, and when someone reads it unconvincingly and does not inject any personality into it, as if he were simply counting,[17] [27] then I think that the discourse would naturally seem worthless to the hearers. And just such a situation threatens to harm the discourse now being presented to you so that it might seem rather worthless, since I have not decorated it with any grace or adornment in its style. I used to employ such tools when I was younger, and I showed models to others so that they might make their discourses more pleasing and at the same time more persuasive.[18] [28] I am no longer able to accomplish such style because of my age, but I will be satisfied if I can simply set out only the actual situation. And I think that it would be proper for you to ignore everything else and just pay attention to this. You would discover very accurately and clearly if I actually say anything of value, [29] should you put off your annoyance at sophists and speeches that are composed to be read, and take up each of the points individually and examine them, not making a casual task of it (*parergon*)[19] or doing it carelessly but pursuing it with reason and love of knowledge (*philosophia*), characteristics that people claim you pos-

---

[17] Written discourses would normally be read aloud.

[18] Isocrates makes a similar claim at the beginning of *Panathenaicus* (12.2).

[19] Isocrates may be alluding to Philip's ancestral connections with Heracles here. The word he uses for a casual task is *parergon,* the word often used to describe one of the minor side labors Heracles did. Philip should not take Isocrates' advice lightly but consider it one of his major tasks, just like his ancestor Heracles' twelve labors. The reward for the labors of Heracles was his immortality.

sess.[20] If you investigate with these tools rather than rely on the opinion of the mob, you would make better decisions about them.

[30] This is what I wanted to say by way of preface. I will now turn to the actual subject of my discourse. I claim that you should not ignore any of your own personal interests but should also try to reconcile the cities of Argos, Sparta, and Thebes and our own city, Athens.[21] If you can bring these together, you can easily make other cities agree to work together, [31] for all of them are dependent on those cities. Whenever they are afraid, they run for help to whichever city they happen to be allied with, and they receive aid from them. Thus if you just persuade these four cities to be sensible, you will save the others from many troubles as well.

[32] You should realize that it is inappropriate for you to slight any of these cities when you consider their behavior toward your ancestors. You will find that each has great friendship for your country and has done it great kindnesses. Argos, for one, is your ancestral home, and it is right that you have as much regard for it as you would for your own ancestors.[22] The Thebans honor the founder of your race with public expenditures and sacrifices more than any other god.[23] [33] The Spartans have bestowed kingship and leadership for all time on his descendants.[24] Finally, reliable authorities on ancient matters say that our city was partly responsible for Heracles' immortality—how this occurred you can easily discover, but now is not the right time (*kairos*) for me to explain—and also responsible for the safety of his offspring.[25] [34] Our city alone endured the greatest dangers posed by the

---

[20] Isocrates makes a similar claim about Philip's son, Alexander the Great (*Ep.* 5.2).

[21] Cf. *Ep.* 3.2.

[22] Herodotus tells the story (8.137–139) of the Macedonian king Perdiccas, who came as an exile from Argos. Isocrates mentions the connection with Argos in *Archidamus* as well (6.17–18).

[23] This refers to Heracles, whom Isocrates considered to be Philip's mythic ancestor and who was especially honored at Thebes.

[24] Cf. 6.18.

[25] Isocrates describes Athens' aid to the children of Heracles against Eurystheus in *Panegyricus* (4.54–60) and *Panathenaicus* (12.194). Pausanias reports (1.32.4) that those at Marathon, located in Attica, first worshiped Heracles as a divinity.

power of Eurystheus, put an end to his arrogance, and freed Heracles' children from the fears that always hung over them.[26] As a result, we rightly deserve the gratitude not only of those who were saved then but also of those living now, for it is through us that they are living and enjoy their present blessings. If their ancestors had not been saved, they would never even have been born.

[35] Therefore, since all these cities have acted in this way, you should never have had a dispute with any of them. Nevertheless, we all are naturally more prone to do wrong than to do right, and thus we can rightly ascribe prior mistakes to a common failing, but from now on, you must be on your guard that nothing like it happens to you again. You must also consider what good you can accomplish for them to make it clear that you have done things that are both worthy of yourself and a worthy response to their prior actions. [36] You now have a prime opportunity (*kairos*): although you are paying back only what you owe to them, because it has been such a long time, they will assume that you are taking the initiative in good deeds. It is a fine thing to appear to be treating the greatest cities well while you aid yourself no less. [37] Apart from this, if there has ever been any difficulty with these cities, you can eliminate all of it, for good deeds done in the present cause people to forget past offenses against each other. This too is clear, that all people remember best those benefits they have received in times of trouble. [38] You see now how they have suffered because of war and how they are acting as if they had a private quarrel: as long as their anger is increasing, no one could reconcile them. But after they have beaten each other down miserably, they separate of their own accord without needing any mediation. This is what they will do, I think, if you do not do something about them first.

[39] Someone might perhaps venture to object to what I have said, asserting that I am trying to persuade you to attempt the impossible, for the Argives would never become friends with the Spartans, nor the Spartans with the Thebans, and generally those who have always been

---

[26] It is odd that Isocrates does not take this opportunity to digress on Athens' contributions here more fully, as he does in *Panegyricus* (4.54–60). This may demonstrate the change in the political landscape from the time when he wrote *Panegyricus* (380); he had larger hopes for Athenian prominence in his early writings.

accustomed to looking at their own advantage would never agree to share equally with one another.[27] [40] Now do not think that such a thing would have happened when either Athens or Sparta held supreme power. For either of these cities would have easily blocked the other if it tried to do this. But now I think that things are different, for I know that everyone has been put on equal footing now because of their troubles. As a result, I think they would much prefer the gains of an alliance to the advantages that came from past actions. [41] Also, although I agree that no one else could reconcile these cities, something like this is not difficult for you, since I see that you have accomplished many things that others thought were hopeless or beyond expectation. Thus it would not be strange if you were the only one who could accomplish this. Those who have high ambitions and superior talents must not attempt to accomplish things that any average person might do but only those that no one else would attempt, except those who are your equal in natural ability and power.

[42] I am amazed at those who think this sort of thing cannot be done; they apparently do not know and have not heard from others that in fact there have been many terrible wars after which, once the participants put an end to them, they produced many benefits for both sides. What hatred, for example, would be greater than that of the Greeks against Xerxes? Yet everyone knows that we and the Spartans both esteem our friendship with Persia more than with anyone else who helped either of us establish our empires.[28] [43] But why must we speak of ancient history or foreign affairs? If someone were to investigate closely the misfortunes of the Greeks, these would seem like nothing in comparison with what we suffered through the Thebans and the Spartans.[29] Even so, when the Spartans were campaigning against Boeotia and planning to devastate it and to break up its

---

[27] The hostility of these cities toward each other is legendary in the fourth century. Note how Isocrates strategically leaves Athens out of the list of unreasonable cities.

[28] Though the Greeks and Persians were hostile in the fifth century, they worked together on some occasions in the fourth, such as the Peace of Antalcidas in 387/6.

[29] At the end of the Peloponnesian War, which ended in 404 with Athens subject to Sparta.

league, we gave help and thwarted the Spartans' plans.[30] [44] Again, when fortune changed, and the Thebans and all the Peloponnesians were trying to destroy Sparta, we alone of the Greeks allied with Sparta and were responsible in part for their survival.[31] [45] Therefore, anyone who sees such changes happening and sees that our cities give no thought for their previous hatred, oaths, or anything else, except what they take to be to their own advantage, and that they desire this alone and expend all their energy for this, would be a complete fool if he did not think that they will have this same attitude now, especially when you step in to organize their reconciliation, while their own self-interest persuades them and their present difficulties compel them. I believe that since these factors support you, everything will turn out appropriately.

[46] I think you will understand best whether these cities are peacefully or aggressively disposed toward each other if we consider, not in excessively general terms nor in too much detail, the most important factors affecting them. First, let us look at the Spartans' situation. [47] Although they ruled over Greece not too long ago by both land and sea,[32] they suffered such a reversal when they lost the battle at Leuctra that they were stripped of their empire over the Greeks and lost many of their men who chose to die rather than live after being defeated by those who used to be their subjects. [48] Furthermore, they saw that all the Peloponnesians, who used to follow Sparta in attacking others, now were invading their own territory in league with the Thebans. They were compelled to take their stand not out in the country in defense of their crops but in the middle of the city near their government offices in defense of their children and wives. The danger was such that they would die immediately if they did not succeed, [49] and even when they were victorious, they did not free them-

---

[30] After the end of the Peloponnesian War, Sparta asserted itself as a leader, became too aggressive toward Thebes and the Boeotian League, and was eventually defeated in 371 at the battle of Leuctra.

[31] After the battle of Leuctra in 371, Thebes asserted itself as leader, following the pattern of Athens and Sparta. It too became too aggressive and was defeated in 362 at the battle of Mantinea.

[32] From the end of the Peloponnesian War (404) until the battle of Leuctra (371).

selves from their troubles. They are being attacked by their neighbors, and they have lost the trust of all the Peloponnesians; they are hated by most of the Greeks, and they are harassed and pillaged night and day by their own servants;[33] there is no time when they are not campaigning, or fighting against someone, or rescuing citizens who are being destroyed. [50] The greatest of their problems, though, is that they are in constant fear that the Thebans will reconcile with Phocis, turn back again, and attack Sparta with even more disastrous results than before. How can you not see that people in such a situation would not gladly see someone presiding over the peace who has a good reputation and can put an end to the war that burdens them?

[51] As for the Argives, you can see that their situation is in some ways the same as the Spartans' situation and in other ways worse. Like the Spartans, they have been at war with their neighbors ever since the foundation of their city, but they differ in that the Spartans fight against weaker forces, while the Argives' opponents are stronger. All would agree that this is the worst situation. They are doing so badly in the war that they see their own land almost completely wasted and sacked during each year's campaign. [52] Most shocking of all, whenever the enemy stops causing them trouble, they themselves destroy the best and wealthiest of their citizens, and while doing this they celebrate more than anyone else does when killing the enemy.[34] The reason for their living in such turbulence is nothing other than the war. If you put an end to this war, you will free them from these troubles but also cause them to make better decisions about other matters.

[53] As for the Thebans, you know their situation. Although they

---

[33] Spartan (and Messenian) society was supported by a servant class called the helots. The helots were a local ethnic group that the Dorian Spartans subjugated when they came into the region. The helots were owned by the state, not by individuals. They provided agricultural labor and served as soldiers in war. They tended to maintain family structures, unlike many slave populations, but were treated harshly by the Spartans and Messenians to keep them under control. It is certainly true that the Spartans were continually under pressure to control the helots, but Isocrates probably exaggerates the trouble they caused with his reference to troubles from them "night and day." See Demand 1996: 120–121.

[34] Argos was well known for its internal factional political fighting.

won a great victory and acquired the greatest fame as a result,³⁵ they
did not take advantage of their good fortune, and thus they fare no
better than those who had the bad fortune to lose. They had no sooner
defeated their enemies when they neglected all else and began annoying all the cities in the Peloponnese, tried to enslave Thessaly and
threatened their neighbors, the Megarians; they took a piece of our
land from us, sacked Euboea, and sent triremes to Byzantium, intent
on becoming the rulers over land and sea. [54] Finally, they brought
war against the Phocians;³⁶ their plan was to conquer the cities in a
short time, take control over the entire surrounding region, and gain
control of the funds deposited at Delphi by using their own re-
sources.³⁷ None of this turned out for them: instead of taking the
Phocians' cities, they lost their own, and in attacking the land of their
enemy, they inflicted less damage on them than they suffered while
retreating to their own land. [55] In Phocis, for example, they killed
some of the mercenaries, who are better off dead than alive, but when
retreating, they lost their most illustrious men, men who were very
willing to die for their country. They have reached the point where, although they once hoped to have all Greece in their control, now their
hopes for their own safety lie with you.³⁸ Thus I think that they would
quickly do whatever you order or advise.

[56] It would remain for us only to discuss Athens, if it had not already had the good sense to make peace before the others. I think it
will now join you in your undertakings, especially if it can see that you
are arranging these matters in preparation for a campaign against the
barbarian.

[57] I think it has become clear to you from what I have said that it
is not impossible for you to bring these cities together. Moreover, I
think I can make you understand from many examples that you will

---

³⁵They defeated Sparta in the battle of Leuctra in 371 and claimed superiority.
³⁶The so-called Sacred War of 356–346.
³⁷The Phocians took advantage of their control over Delphi to use funds from
the treasuries there for the war. The Thebans had to overcome this war chest with
only their own finances.
³⁸Philip helped bring the Sacred War to a close when Phocis was prevailing
over Thebes, thus rescuing the latter.

do this easily. For if it can be shown that some of our ancestors undertook to do things that are certainly no more noble or righteous than what we have advised, and have accomplished tasks that are greater and more difficult than these, what ground will be left for critics to say that you will not accomplish this easier task more quickly than they accomplished more difficult tasks?

[58] Consider first the case of Alcibiades, when he was an exile from our city.[39] He saw that others who had been in this trouble before him cowered in fear of the greatness of the city, but he did not share this view. Rather, he thought that he should try to return by force and thus chose to make war against the city. [59] Now, if someone should try to relate every event of the past, he could not recount each detail accurately, and for the present, such an account would perhaps be annoying. But Alcibiades created such turbulence not only for our city but for the Spartans and all other Greeks too, that we suffered reverses that are well known,[40] and others fell into such bad times [60] that the misfortunes caused by that war are not forgotten even today. The Spartans too, who back then enjoyed a reputation for success, were brought to their present sorry state because of Alcibiades, for they were convinced by him to covet naval supremacy and thus lost even their dominion on land.[41] [61] Thus if anyone should say that the beginning (archē) of their troubles came when they tried to achieve a naval

---

[39] Alcibiades was exiled from Athens in 415, during the Peloponnesian War, for allegedly taking part in the mutilation of the Herms and profaning the Eleusinian Mysteries. He then went over to aid anti-Athenian parties before returning to the Athenian side later in the war.

[40] After the Athenian defeat in Syracuse, Alcibiades assisted places such as Chios and Lesbos that wanted to revolt from Athens. He also was influential in the oligarchic coup and establishment of the Four Hundred at Athens in 411. He then worked for its collapse and was greeted as a leader in Athens after the reestablishment of democracy. On Alcibiades' career, see W. M. Ellis 1989.

[41] Alcibiades influenced Spartan policy at various points from 415 (after fleeing Athens) until his death in 404. The passage here is probably a reference to Sparta's attempt, at Alcibiades' encouragement, to emphasize a naval campaign in the Aegean Sea (instead of the Hellespont) in 412 and Alcibiades' machinations to get Persian aid for Sparta.

empire (*archē*),[42] they would not be convicted of lying. And Alcibiades, having caused so much trouble, returned to our city and gained a great reputation, though not everyone agreed.

Not many years later, Conon's career was the reverse of this. [62] When he lost the naval battle in the Hellespont[43]—not through his own actions but because of the other generals—he was too shamed to return home. Sailing to Cyprus, he spent some time attending to his own affairs, but then when he saw that Agesilaus had crossed over into Asia with a large army and was pillaging the area,[44] he was so inspired that [63] although he had no resources but his body and his mind, he hoped to conquer the Spartans, who were leaders of Greece on both land and sea, and Conon sent to the generals of the Persian King, promising to do this. What more need I say? He gathered a naval force near Rhodes, defeated the Spartans in a naval battle, removed them from their command, [64] and freed the Greeks. Then he rebuilt the walls of his city, but he also brought Athens back to the high repute from which it had fallen. Who would have expected that the fortune of Greece would be reversed by a man who was faring so poorly and that some Greek cities would lose all honor while others would rise to the top?

[65] Then there is Dionysius—for I want you to be persuaded by many examples that the task I am urging you to undertake is easy—he was far from the best of the Syracusans in birth, reputation, and everything else; nonetheless, he desired illogically and quite rashly to be ruler and dared to do anything that would contribute to this goal. He gained control of Syracuse, conquered all the Greek cities in Sicily, and then surrounded himself with a greater army both on land and sea than any man before him.[45]

---

[42] Isocrates invokes the common pun on the Greek word *archē,* which means both beginning and empire. Cf. 4.119 and 8.101.

[43] Athenian orators rarely mention the disastrous defeat at Aegospotami in 405 by name but use various euphemisms.

[44] At the battle of Cnidus in 394.

[45] This description contrasts with the much more positive view of Dionysius seen in the letter (1) written to the Syracusan tyrant in 368/7, when Isocrates appealed to him as a possible leader to unify Greece. Isocrates was unsuccessful

[66] There was also Cyrus—so that we recall the barbarians too—who was left out on the road by his mother and was rescued by a Persian woman, but whose fortune changed so completely that he became King of all Asia.[46]

[67] Therefore, since Alcibiades, who was an exile, Conon, who had such misfortune, Dionysius, who had no reputation, and Cyrus, whose life right from the beginning was so pitiable, all had so much success and did such amazing things, how can we not expect you to accomplish easily what I was recommending, since you are born from such noble ancestors and are king of Macedon and master of such a vast empire?

[68] Consider too how worthy it is to attempt those deeds in particular that, if accomplished, will establish your reputation as equal to the best of men, whereas if you fail in your goal, you will nevertheless have the goodwill of the Greeks. It is much better to gain this than to seize many Greek cities by force. Such acts promote envy and hostility and much abuse, but what I advise causes none of this. Still, if one of the gods should grant you a choice of what kind of concern or occupation you would wish to have as the focus of your life, you would choose nothing over this, if you take my advice. [69] For you not only will be envied by others but you also will consider yourself fortunate, for what could surpass the happiness that results when men of the highest reputation come from the greatest cities as delegates to your kingdom, when you consult with these men about your common good (for it will be clear that no one else is concerned with such matters), [70] when you see that all Greece is interested in what you propose, and when no one disparages what you have decided? Indeed, some ask how things stand, others pray that you not fall short of your goals, and others fear that something may happen to you before you can put a successful end to your projects. [71] Since this is the situation, how can you not naturally be very confident? How can you not spend your life very happily, knowing you have overseen such great ac-

---

with him, and now over twenty years later, the description of Dionysius is less complimentary.

[46] Cyrus the Great, who rose from very dangerous beginnings to be King of Persia and leader of its expansion in the sixth century; cf. Herod. 1.107–130. He was the topic of moralizing, as can be seen in Xenophon's *Cyropaedaea*.

complishments? What reasonable man would not encourage you to choose particularly those actions that can bear, so to speak, two fruits at the same time: abundant pleasure and unending honor?

[72] Now, what I have said about this would already suffice, if I had not omitted a point I think I should now reveal. Not that I forgot it, but I was hesitant to mention it. Now, however, I think that it would benefit you to hear about it, and it would be proper for me to speak candidly, as I am accustomed. [73] You see, I know that you are being slandered by those who are envious of you[47] and who also are in the habit of keeping their own cities in disarray, because they think that a common peace for all would be an attack on their own personal interests. These men disregard everything else and speak only of your power, saying that it grows simply for its own sake and not for the benefit of Greece and that you have been plotting against us for a long time now; [74] according to them, you say your intent in taking control of affairs in Phocis is to help the people of Messene, but in fact you want to put the Peloponnese under your control. They say that the Thessalians and the Thebans and all the members of the Amphictionic League[48] are ready to follow you; the Argives and the Messenians and the Megalopolitans and many of the others are ready to fight alongside you and destroy Sparta; and if you accomplish this, you will easily control the rest of the Greeks too. [75] By uttering such nonsense and pretending to know exactly what is happening, and quickly turning aside all objections with their cleverness, they persuade many people, especially those who desire the same evil gain as the speechmakers, who have no thought for the common good and are completely insensitive to it, who welcome those who pretend to be concerned but are afraid for their own sake, and who accept that you appear to be plotting against the Greeks but think that this is a worthwhile motive. [76] This last group is so foolish that they do not know now with the same words one might harm some and help others.

---

[47] Isocrates refers here to Athenian orators who present a more hostile view of Philip. Demosthenes' *Philippics* and *Olynthiacs* are the most famous examples.

[48] The Amphictionic League was a group of states joined in protection and administration of the holy precinct of the Temple of Apollo at Delphi. Philip would become involved with the league in 346 when elected a member in place of Phocis.

In this case, for example, if someone should say that the King of Persia is plotting against the Greeks and preparing to launch a campaign against us, he would not be saying anything disparaging, but he would be making himself seem more courageous and important than he really is. But if he brings this same charge against one of the descendants of Heracles, who is the benefactor of all Greece, he would be accusing himself of shameless conduct. [77] For who would not be upset and angry if he should be found to be plotting against those on whose behalf his own ancestor put himself at risk and was not trying to preserve the goodwill that Heracles left behind for his descendants, but ignored such concerns and sought instead evil and reprehensible actions?

[78] Considering all this, you should not overlook such rumors that are circulating about you. Your enemies seek to give you this reputation, while not one of your allies would speak in your defense. And yet, by considering the opinions of both groups, you can discern what truly is in your interest.

[79] Perhaps you think that it is beneath you to be concerned about these driveling, empty-headed babblers and those persuaded by them, especially when you know that you have done nothing wrong. But you must not look down on these people, and you must not consider your reputation among them unimportant. Rather, understand that you will have only a noble and great reputation, one fitting for you, your ancestors, and the deeds you all have accomplished [80] when you have made all the Greeks feel the same way about you as the Spartans feel about their kings, or your friends feel about you. It is not difficult to do this if you are willing to treat all the Greeks the same, and stop being friendly toward some cities and not others, and if you choose to do the sorts of things that will make the Greeks trust you and the barbarians fear you.

[81] And don't be amazed—as I also said in a letter to Dionysius, when he was tyrant of Syracuse[49]—that I am speaking to you more boldly than others do, even though I am not a general, or a politician, or in any other position of authority. For of all citizens, I was by nature the least suited to political activity. I did not have a strong enough

---

[49] *Ep.* 1.9.

voice or enough confidence to allow me to handle a crowd, to accept abuse, and to attack those who frequent the speaker's platform.[50] [82] But as far as being intelligent and well educated, even if someone says that I am uncouth to say so, I would disagree and would place myself not in the lower ranks but among the most prominent. Therefore, I try to give advice to the city, to the Greeks, and to men of the highest renown in the way in which I am by nature best able to do.

[83] You have probably heard enough about my own affairs and the way in which you ought to act toward the Greeks. As for the campaign against Asia, I will give my advice to the cities on how to fight against the barbarians when we see that they have been unified as I encouraged you to do. For now, I will address you, though not with the same attitude or energy as when I first wrote about this same thesis.[51] [84] Before I encouraged my listeners to laugh at me and criticize me if my work was not clearly worthy of the subject, of my reputation, and of the time I had spent in its composition.[52] Now, however, I fear that what I say will turn out to be far inferior to everything I said before. In addition to other things, my discourse *Panegyricus,* which made others who are engaged in learning (*philosophia*) more adept, leaves me in a dilemma: I do not want to say the same things as I wrote there, and I cannot find anything new to say. [85] I must not give up, however, but must choose whatever arguments in support of my thesis may help persuade you to do these things. And if I fall short in some way and cannot write in the same manner as I did before, I still think I will sketch out a pleasant discourse for those who can fill in the details and complete it.[53]

[86] I think that I have composed a beginning for the whole discourse that is fitting for those who argue for a campaign against Asia.

---

[50] That is, in the Assembly. He mentions his weak voice and lack of courage in *Ep.* 8.7 as well.

[51] In *Panegyricus* (380), when Isocrates was 56.

[52] He makes this claim at *Panegyricus* 14 but then backs away from it in section 187.

[53] Isocrates seems to think that his pupils will take the discourse as a model or outline and then work it out in more detail. Cf. 12. Or perhaps Isocrates shares Aristotle's notion that later generations will add to and improve his work.

One must do nothing more until he finds the Greeks giving one of
two responses, either joining the campaign or offering great support
for the plan. Agesilaus, who seemed to be the most intelligent of the
Spartans, ignored this rule not because he was evil but out of ambition.[54] [87] He had two desires, both noble, but incompatible with
each other and impossible to accomplish at the same time.[55] He decided to make war against the King[56] and to bring back his allies from
exile into their cities and have them regain control of public affairs. It
turned out, however, that his efforts to support his allies caused great
troubles and dangers for the Greeks, and because of the great turmoil
that resulted from this, he had no time or power to make war on the
barbarians. [88] Thus, from his ignorant mistakes at that time, it is
now easy to understand that those who plan well should not wage
war against the King before someone reconciles the Greeks and puts
an end to the madness that now possesses them. This is what I advise
for you.

[89] No one with any sense would dare to disagree on this issue.
But I think that if others should decide to advise you about a campaign against Asia, they would take the following approach, saying
that all those who undertook to make war against the King have risen
from anonymity to fame, from poverty to riches, and from low status
to become masters of a large realm and many cities. [90] I am not going to encourage you with such remarks but rather with the example
of those who seemed to have failed, specifically those who campaigned
with Cyrus and Clearchus.[57] It is reported that they won the battle
against the entire force of the King as soundly as if they had fought

---

[54] Isocrates uses the same example, with almost the exact same wording, in the
letter to Archidamus (9.13–14) in 356.

[55] Isocrates says almost the exact same thing in *Ep.* 9.13–14.

[56] Cf. 4.120n.

[57] This event is narrated in Xenophon's *Anabasis*. In 401 Cyrus hired Clearchus
to lead a troop of Greek mercenaries (Xenophon among them) into Persian territory to challenge the King. In the battle of Cunaxa, Cyrus foolishly ran ahead of
his army to pursue his brother Artaxerxes. When Cyrus and the other leaders were
dead, Cyrus by his folly, the others by the King's treachery, Xenophon had to lead
the Greek troops back to the coast. Isocrates also tells this story in *Panegyricus*
(4.145–149) and mentions it in 8.98, 12.104, and *Ep.* 2.8.

against their women. But just when they seemed to be in control of the situation, their fortune changed because of Cyrus' rashness. Cyrus celebrated too much and pursued the enemy far in front of the rest of his men; thus, he found himself in the middle of the enemy and was killed. [91] Still, even though such a disaster struck his enemy, the King thought so little of the force around him that he summoned Clearchus and the other opposition leaders to come into a meeting. He promised to give them great gifts and to give the rest of the troops their full salary and then let them go. But after leading them on with such hopes and offering them pledges that in Asia were considered the most binding, he arrested them all and killed them, preferring to offend the gods rather than enter battle against soldiers who were so isolated without Cyrus. [92] What appeal then would be more attractive or convincing than this? It is clear that if it had not been for Cyrus, those men would have defeated the King. It will not be difficult for you to guard against the trouble that happened then and to prepare a force much stronger than the force that defeated the King's army. And since you have both these advantages, how can you not be quite confident of succeeding in such a campaign?

[93] No one should think that I want to hide my expressing some of these points in the same way as I did before. Since I have stayed with the same ideas, I chose not to take the trouble to say things that have been expressed well elsewhere. Now if I were making a display speech (*epideixis*), I would have tried to avoid such repetitions, [94] but since I am advising you (*symbouleuein*), I would be a fool if I spent more time on the presentation (*lexis*) than on the ideas (*praxis*) or if I alone avoided the words I had used before when I see everyone else using them.[58] Therefore, I might happen to use my own words, if I am pressed and it is appropriate, but I would never borrow the words of other people, any more than I have done in the past.

[95] This is the situation then. It seems to me that after this, we must talk about the preparations you will undertake and the resources

---

[58] Isocrates makes a contrast here between what Aristotle would later call epideictic or display discourse and symbouleutic or deliberative discourse. He also contrasts style (*lexis*) with content (*praxis*). On Aristotle's distinctions, see his *Rhetoric;* on the discussion of the relationship of Isocrates and later theoretical categories, see Schiappa 1996 and 1999: chap. 7.

Cyrus and Clearchus had. Now the greatest thing is that you will have the goodwill of the Greeks if you are willing to follow the advice I have given, whereas they faced extreme hostility because of the decarchies established by the Spartans;[59] the Greek cities thought that they would continue to be slaves if Cyrus and Clearchus were successful, but if the King won, they would be freed from their present troubles, which ended up happening to them. [96] Moreover, you will find as many soldiers available for you as you wish, for affairs in Greece are such that it is easier to establish a large and strong army from exiled mercenaries than from citizens. In Cyrus' time there was no mercenary force, and so they were forced to recruit soldiers from the cities, and they spent more for the rewards to those who recruited the soldiers than for wages for the soldiers themselves. [97] And indeed, if we wished to examine and compare you, who will lead the force and will make all the decisions, with Clearchus, who was in charge of the situation then, we will find that he had not led any previous forces, land or sea, but became famous only as a result of the misfortune he experienced in Asia,[60] [98] whereas you have accomplished a great many and outstanding tasks, which it would be appropriate to describe if I were addressing this discourse to others; but since I am talking with you, you would rightly think me both stupid and verbose if I should narrate your own actions to you.

[99] It is also worth considering each of the two Kings, the one I am advising you to attack and the one Clearchus fought against, so that you understand the character and the power of each. The father of the current King overcame our city and the city of the Spartans, but this King never defeated any armies that ravaged his land.[61]

---

[59] In the years after the Peloponnesian War, Sparta set up "decarchies" or ten-member governing boards in many cities. This often led to resentment, partially because they were protected by a Spartan force in each city.

[60] We know nothing about Clearchus except in connection with the disastrous expedition Isocrates just narrated.

[61] Artaxerxes II (405/4–359/8), who ruled when Cyrus and Clearchus made their campaign, had a hand in the defeat of Athens at the end of the Peloponnesian War and the defeat of Sparta in the early fourth century. His son Artaxerxes III (359/8–338) was King at the time of this discourse and later regained Egypt. Isocrates perhaps overstates the strength of the former, but his assessment of the weakness of the latter may be fair, since in 346, when Isocrates wrote this dis-

[100] Moreover, the earlier King obtained all Asia from the Greeks in a treaty,[62] whereas this King, far from ruling over others, does not control even the cities that were handed down to him. Anyone would have to wonder whether he lost these cities through cowardice or whether they simply despised him and thought nothing of his royal power.

[101] Furthermore, how would anyone not be provoked to attack him if he heard about the conditions in his territory? Egypt was in revolt from him at that earlier time,[63] but they were still afraid that the King himself would make a campaign and would overcome the difficult natural barrier that the Nile offered and all the rest of their preparations. But this King has now freed them from such fear; although he prepared the largest possible force and campaigned against them, he left Egypt not just defeated but also humiliated and with a reputation for being unworthy of both kingship and military command. [102] Consider also the regions of Cyprus, Phoenicia, Cilicia, and that region from which they used to get naval forces.[64] Formerly, they belonged to the King, but now some have revolted; others are mired in wars and other troubles such that none of them is at all useful to him; if you are willing to campaign against him, however, they could be very helpful to you. [103] Further, it is fitting that Idreus, the richest king of those in the mainland,[65] is more hostile to the affairs of the King than any of those now fighting him. Indeed he would be the most wretched of all men if he did not wish to break up this kingdom, which torments his brother,[66] makes war against himself, and spends all its time plotting and wishing to gain control over him and his resources. [104] His fear of these things compels him to serve the King and to send a large amount of money as tribute each year. But if you were to cross over to the mainland, he would gladly greet you, thinking you had come to help him. You will also draw many other satraps

---

course, Artaxerxes III had not yet recovered Egypt and, in fact, had failed in his early attempts.

[62] The Peace of Antalcidas of 387/6.

[63] During the time of Artaxerxes II.

[64] That is, the coast of the Holy Land, including Tyre and Sidon. These would also be regained by Artaxerxes III after 346.

[65] By "the mainland" Isocrates means here Asia Minor, or modern-day Turkey. Idreus was satrap, or governor, of the Persian province of Caria.

[66] King Mausolus of Caria.

away if you promise them freedom and spread this word throughout Asia, for when this word came to Greece, it brought the downfall of our empire and Sparta's.[67]

[105] I would try to speak more about the military strategy that would most quickly give you victory over the King's empire, but I fear that some would fault me if I dared to give you advice when you have achieved the most and greatest successes in war, while I have never experienced it at all. So I think that I should say no more about these matters.

Concerning the rest, however, I think that your father, and he who founded this dynasty, and the founder of your people[68]—if it were allowed for the latter to speak and if the other two had the ability to speak from the grave—would make these same recommendations. [106] I find evidence for this in their own actions. Your father was on good terms with all the cities that I am encouraging you to favor. The founder of your kingdom, Perdiccas, had greater plans than his fellow citizens and aspired at monarchy, but he did not plan in the same way as others who have such ambitions. [107] Others arouse factions and turmoil and assassinations in their own cities to gain this status, but he kept away from Greek territory and set his heart on taking control of the kingship in Macedon. He knew that the Greeks were not used to allowing a monarchy, while other people could not manage their own lives without such a form of government. [108] And, in fact, because of his particular understanding of these things, it turned out that his rule was very different from that of others. For since he alone of the Greeks did not think he should rule over a people of the same race, he was also the only one able to avoid the dangers that arise in a monarchy.

---

[67] Isocrates here refers to the desire for freedom during and after the Peloponnesian War. During that war, Sparta and its allies fought for freedom from the tyranny of the so-called Athenian Empire. After defeating Athens, Sparta's subsequent attempt to control the Greeks moved the Thebans to lead a revolt that ended in Spartan defeat at Leuctra in 371.

[68] Philip's father was Amyntas III, who ruled from 393 to 370. Perdiccas I is said by Herodotus (8.137–139) to have founded Macedon when an exile from Argos. Heracles is said to be the founder of the race (see above, 32n). Heracles was said to have been deified after his death and was therefore able (theoretically) to speak; the other two were mortals, of course, and therefore dead.

For we would find that those who have done this among the Greeks have not only perished themselves but also have made their own race disappear from the face of the earth, whereas that man lived his life in happiness and left the same honors for his family as he himself had.

[109] As far as Heracles is concerned, others continually praise his strength and enumerate his labors, but you will find none of the poets or prose writers making any mention of the other virtues in his soul. I, on the other hand, see a special topic that is completely unworked—not a small or fruitless topic but one brimming with many praiseworthy and noble deeds, a topic in need of someone who could describe them in a worthy manner. [110] Now, if I had encountered this topic when I was younger, I would have easily shown that your ancestor surpassed all those who went before him, even more in his wisdom, ambition, and justice than in the strength of his body. But coming to this topic now, and seeing how much there is to be said about it, I lamented how little strength I had left, and I realized that the discourse would become twice as long as the one now being read to you.[69] As a result, I have avoided all the other topics and have taken up just this one deed of his—one that is appropriate and in keeping with what I have already said and also has a special timeliness (*kairos*) in view of what I am now saying.

[111] When Heracles saw that Greece was beset by wars and factional strife and many other evils, he put an end to these and reconciled the cities with one another and then, as an example to future generations, revealed which cities one should have as allies and which as enemies when making war. For he launched an expedition against Troy,[70] which at that time had the greatest force in all Asia, and as a

---

[69] An example of his choice to include such a digression is his praise of Agamemnon in *Panathenaicus* (12.74–89).

[70] The so-called first Trojan War, less famous than the Trojan War of Priam, Hector, Agamemnon, and Achilles. Apollodorus (*Library of Greek Mythology* 2.5.9 and 2.6.4) tells the story: Heracles stopped at Troy on the way back from his ninth labor, obtaining the girdle of Hippolyta. Laomedon, king of Troy, had offered his daughter Hesione as a sacrifice to a sea monster to appease an angered Poseidon. Heracles promised to rescue the king and his daughter for a prize; Laomedon agreed, was saved, but then went back on the agreement. Heracles swore revenge and later sacked the city with the help of Telamon.

military strategist, he was so superior to those who later made the same campaign that [112] although it was difficult for them with a Greek army to capture the city in ten years, he, with just a few men, easily took it by force in less than ten days. After this he killed all the kings of the peoples who lived on the shore of either continent,[71] and could never have done this if he had not also overcome their armies. After these successes, he built the so-called Pillars of Heracles, a sign of victory over the barbarians, a monument to his own excellence and the dangers he undertook and a marker of the limit of the Greek world.[72]

[113] I have related these events so that you might know that I am urging you by this discourse to undertake great deeds like those that your ancestors by their actions clearly judged the best. Therefore, although all men of good sense must set for themselves the finest example and then try to become like it, this is especially fitting for you. You do not need to use external examples but have one in your own family, so how can you not naturally be inspired by Heracles, with the ambition to show yourself equal to your ancestor? [114] I say this not because I think that you will be able to mimic all Heracles' deeds— for even some of the gods would be unable to do that—but rather in keeping with his character and his love of humanity and his goodwill toward all the Greeks, you might be able to accomplish a similar mission. It is up to you, if you heed my words, to get whatever glory you wish, [115] for it is easier for you in your present situation to gain the finest reputation than it was to achieve the glory that is now yours from where you started. And notice that I am not urging you to assemble an army of barbarians for a campaign against enemies who would be unjustly attacked but rather to campaign with Greeks against the sort of enemy that those sprung from Heracles ought to attack.

[116] And don't be surprised if throughout this discourse I try to encourage you toward gentleness and humanity and service to the Greeks.

---

[71] That is, Europe or Asia. The two continents face each other at the Hellespont, with Troy on the Asian side.

[72] When Heracles was on his tenth labor, to capture the cattle of Geryon, he had to go to the island of Erytheia, west of Spain. Since he had to go beyond the borders of the known earth, he set up two pillars as a memorial of his voyage. These came to be known as the Pillars of Heracles and are now called the straits of Gibraltar or Gibraltar and Ceuta.

For I see that severity is painful to those who use it and to those who experience it, whereas gentleness is revered, and not just among humans and all other animals. [117] For the gods who bring us good things are called Olympians, while those whose task is to bring troubles and punishments have more unpleasant names.[73] Moreover, both private citizens and states build temples and altars for the first group, while the second group receives no honor, either in prayers or in sacrifices, but instead we perform rituals to keep them away. [118] Considering this, you must get in the habit of working to ensure that all people have an even higher opinion of you than they do now. Those who seek a better reputation than others should commit themselves in their minds to deeds that are both practical and in agreement with their ideal and also seek to accomplish them whenever the opportunity (*kairos*) allows.

[119] You could understand from many examples that you must act in this way, but especially from the experience of Jason of Pherae.[74] His accomplishments were nothing like yours, but he gained the highest reputation not from what he had done but from what he had said, for he kept saying that he was going to cross over to Asia and make war on the King. [120] Now, if Jason increased his reputation so greatly just by his claims, what opinion do you think people will have of you if you actually accomplish these things? This is especially true if you try to capture his entire kingdom, but it will also be true even if you do not, if you try to take only as much of his territory as possible and gain control of Asia "from Cilicia to Sinope," as they say,[75] and then found cities in this territory and settle there those who are homeless from lack of daily necessities and cause trouble for anyone

---

[73] The contrast is between the main Olympian gods (so-called because they live on Mt. Olympus in northern Greece) and the underworld gods such as the Furies in Aeschylus' *Eumenides*. We should note, however, that the Olympians frequently punished and otherwise brought troubles to mortals.

[74] Jason was the king of Thessaly who at least temporarily unified that region. He was quite formidable, accomplished a great deal, and would have rivaled Philip's fame if he had not died prematurely. See further Laistner 1927: *ad loc.*

[75] That is, the whole of Asia Minor, modern Turkey. Cilicia is on the west side, and Sinope is on the east. The whole of Asia Minor would still only be a small portion of the Persian kingdom.

they meet.[76] [121] If we do not give this group enough to live on and stop them from gathering together, without our noticing it, they will suddenly become such a large group that they will become a terrible threat to the Greeks no less than the barbarians. But we pay no attention to this and ignore this increasing force that poses fearful danger to all of us alike. [122] Therefore, it is the job of a man with high ambition, with a concern for Greece, and with a more accomplished intellect than other men to use men such as these against the barbarians, to cut away that portion of the territory we just mentioned, and to free the mercenaries of the troubles they now have and which they also cause for others, to found cities with these men, to give a boundary to Greece, and to make these cities into a buffer zone for us all. [123] If you do this, you will not only make the mercenaries happy but you will give all of us greater security. Even if you miss the chance to help the mercenaries, you will still easily free the cities of Asia that are inhabited by Greeks.

Whatever part of this you are able to accomplish, or even if you just make the attempt, there is no way that you will not gain a greater reputation than others, and quite justly, if you set out to do this and rouse the Greeks to it as well. [124] For as things are now, who would not naturally be amazed at what has happened and feel contempt for us, seeing how among the barbarians, whom we assume to be soft and inexperienced in wars and corrupted by luxury, there have risen men who think they deserve to rule over Greeks, while none of the Greeks is ambitious enough to try to make us lords of Asia. [125] We are so far from such thoughts that the barbarians did not hesitate to begin hostilities against the Greeks, whereas we do not even dare to avenge ourselves against them for injuries we have suffered. Instead, while they admit that they have neither soldiers nor generals nor anything else that might help combat dangers, [126] and request these things from us, we are so eager to do ourselves wrong, that though it is possible for us to have their possessions without trouble, instead we make war against ourselves over minor issues. We help the King subdue those revolting from him, and we do not notice that by allying our-

[76] Isocrates frequently mentions the problem of homeless mercenaries. Cf. 4.168; 8.24 and *Ep.* 9.9.

selves with our ancestral enemies, we are trying to destroy those who share our heritage.

[127] Therefore, I think that it will be advantageous for you, since everyone else is so cowardly, to take the lead in this war against the King. And just as it is fitting for all the other descendants of Heracles and those who are tied to a particular government and its laws to love that city in which they live, so it is fitting for you, who were born free of worldly concerns to think of all Greece as your homeland, as did your ancestor, Heracles, and to take risks on its behalf, just as you would for everything that is especially important to you.

[128] Some men, who can do nothing but complain, might perhaps venture to fault me because I chose to urge you to campaign against the barbarians and to care for the Greeks but neglected my own city. [129] Now, if I had undertaken to discuss these things with anyone else before approaching my own country, which has freed Greece on three occasions, twice from the barbarians and once from the Spartans, I would admit that I had made a mistake. But it will be clear that I encouraged Athens first with all the energy I could, but when I saw that the city thought less of my advice than the opinions of those who rant and rave in the Assembly, I gave up on Athens but would not give up on my plan.[77] [130] Therefore, all might justly praise me because I have used whatever power I have and have spent all my time fighting the barbarians, criticizing those who do not share my views and trying to encourage those whom I thought had the greatest power to do something particularly good for the Greeks and take from the barbarians their present prosperity. [131] So I address my words to you now, not unaware that many will be angry at what I am saying but knowing also that they will all be pleased by these same things, once you accomplish them. For though no one has shared in the advice I have given, everyone will think he has a share in the benefits when they are achieved.

[132] Consider how disgraceful it is to overlook that Asia is doing better than Europe and that the barbarians are more prosperous than the Greeks. Consider, too, that those who have inherited their

---

[77] Isocrates probably refers to his *Panegyricus* of 380, in which he tried to encourage Athens to lead the Greeks against Persia.

kingdom from Cyrus—a man whose mother threw him into the
street!⁷⁸—are called the "Great King," while those who are born from
Heracles—whose father (Zeus) raised him to be with the gods because
of his excellence (*aretē*)⁷⁹—are addressed by a lesser title than they.⁸⁰
None of this should be allowed to continue, but rather the whole situation should be reversed and changed.

[133] Know well that I would not have tried to persuade you to try
any of this if I saw that only empire and wealth would come of it. I
think you already have more than enough of these and that anyone
who chooses to risk either gaining these things or dying has an insatiable desire. [134] So, I did not compose this discourse with the ac-
quisition of these things in mind but with the idea that you could
gain the greatest and finest reputation from them. Keep in mind that
we all have a body that is mortal, but we partake of immortality according to others' goodwill and the praise we receive and the reports
that circulate about us and the memory we leave that lasts through
time. This is what we should desire, no matter what we suffer to obtain it. [135] You may notice that even the best private citizens would
not give up their lives for anything else but are willing to die in battle
to gain glory. In general, those who always desire greater honor than
they have are praised by all, whereas those who are insatiable for anything else are considered undisciplined and base. [136] My most important point, however, is that often our enemies gain control of our
wealth or our power, but no one except our children can inherit the
goodwill of fellow citizens and the other things I have discussed. Thus,
I would be ashamed if it were not for the sake of these things that I
am advising you to undertake this campaign and wage a dangerous war.

[137] As a result, you will make the best decision about this if you
assume that you are summoned not only by this discourse but also by
your ancestors, the cowardice of the barbarians, and those who have

---

⁷⁸ Cf. 66n. Herodotus (1.107–130) does not include this incident. Cf. Laistner
1927: 147.

⁷⁹ Isocrates makes the same claim about Heracles in his discourse *Helen*
(10.16–17).

⁸⁰ The Persian King was traditionally referred to as the "Great King" (*basileus megas*), while Greek kings were simply "king" (*basileus*).

become famous and are considered demigods because of their campaigns against these people, and above all by the present opportunity (*kairos*) in which you have acquired a force of such strength as no other European before you and that the man against whom you will fight is universally hated and despised as no king before ever was.

[138] I would give a great deal to be able to mix together all the speeches I have given on this topic; then this speech would seem more worthy of the topic at hand. In any case, you should consider out of all of them which points especially support and encourage this war, for in this way you would make the best plans.

[139] I am not unaware that many Greeks think the King's power is unbeatable. One should rightly be amazed at such people, however, if they really think that power gained by a man who is barbarian and poorly raised and based on slavery cannot be destroyed in the name of freedom by a man who is both Greek and experienced in war; they hold their opinion knowing that it is difficult to create anything but easy to destroy it.

[140] Keep in mind that all men honor and admire particularly those who are able to lead both a state and an army. Therefore, when you see that those who have this natural ability in one city are famous, what sort of praises must you think will be sung about you when people see you acting as a statesman, bringing benefits to all the Greeks, and acting as a general, defeating the barbarians? [141] I think that this will be the ultimate accomplishment, for no one else will ever be able to surpass it. There will never be another task such as this for the Greeks, to lead us all out of our present hostilities into an alliance. Also the barbarians are unlikely ever to raise another power like theirs if you destroy the present one. [142] Thus even if someone in the future might surpass everyone in natural ability, he will still not be able to accomplish such a task. I can rank even the deeds of your ancestors below what you have already accomplished; I am not quibbling but speaking the truth. Since you have conquered more nations than anyone else has conquered cities, how could I not easily demonstrate by comparison that you have accomplished more than they have? [143] Still, I chose to avoid such an argument for two reasons: because some people use it in the wrong circumstances (*akairos*) and because I do not want to make those who are regarded as demigods seem less than those alive today.

[144] Keep in mind—if I can speak about ancient people—that no poet or prose writer would praise the wealth of Tantalus or the rule of Pelops or the power of Eurystheus,[81] but all would praise, after the greatness of Heracles and the excellence of Theseus, those who campaigned against Troy and others like them. [145] Yet we know that the most famous and the best of them ruled over small cities and islands. Nevertheless, they left behind a reputation that was almost divine and was celebrated by all, for everyone loves not those who acquire the greatest power for themselves but those who bring about the most good for the Greeks. [146] You will see that people have this opinion not just about these men but about all who are like them. For instance, no one would praise our city because we ruled the sea or because we took a great sum of money from our allies and deposited it in the Acropolis,[82] and certainly not because we had power over many cities and could destroy some, expand others, and treat others however we pleased. [147] All these options were open to us, but they caused many accusations. Because of the battle of Marathon, however, and the naval battle at Salamis, and especially because we abandoned our own city to ensure Greek freedom, all sing Athens' praises.[83] They have this same opinion about the Spartans, [148] for they are admired more for their defeat at Thermopylae than for their other victories.[84] People admire and gaze fondly at the trophy set up by the barbarians against

---

[81] Tantalus offended Zeus and was punished by being tormented forever with hunger and thirst. Pelops offended the gods by violating a pledge and cheating to win the chariot race for his wife's hand. Eurystheus was the evil king who gave Heracles the twelve labors, hoping Heracles would die in the process.

[82] Athens' leadership of the Delian League in the fifth century slowly changed into an empire; tribute that was collected from the members became less voluntary and more coerced. Athens transferred the treasury of the league from Delos to Athens in 454 and soon after began a massive building program.

[83] In 480 the Persians marched against mainland Greece, as Herodotus describes (8.1–99). On Themistocles' advice, the Athenians abandoned their city and trusted in the ships of their navy. The Persians swept through the city and razed it to the ground. In the straits off Salamis, however, the smaller and more maneuverable Greek ships were able to defeat the Persian army and force the Persian retreat from Greece.

[84] On the battle of Thermopylae, see 4.90.

them,[85] but they do not praise the trophies set up by the Spartans against other Greeks; they look upon these with disgust, for they consider the one a sign of virtue (*aretē*), but the other a sign of greed.

[149] Therefore, examine all these things carefully and consider in your own mind whether any of these points is too weak or inadequate. If so, I ascribe this to my age, which should be treated with compassion by all.[86] But if the argument is up to the same standards as what I have circulated before, you should not think that my age discovered it but that some divine force brought it forth, not out of consideration for me but from concern for Greece and its desire to deliver this country from its present evils and to give you a greater glory than you already have. [150] I think that you are well aware how the gods tend to human affairs. They do not themselves cause the goods or ills that come upon us. Rather, they give each person the sort of disposition [151] that makes each of these things happen to us through our interaction with others. Perhaps, for example, they have assigned this discourse to me but have sent you to accomplish the actual deeds, for they realize that you are the best one to take charge of the actions and that a speech that comes from me will be the least annoying to those who hear it. I also think your previous accomplishments would not have been so great if some divinity had not helped out. [152] The divine purpose, I think, was not that you would spend your life fighting only against barbarians who live in Europe but rather that you would get training and experience in these battles and come to understand

---

[85] Herodotus (7.228) points out that the Greeks set up a trophy where the Spartans fell; neither he nor any other historian says anything about a trophy set up by the Persians. Norlin (1928: 334) says that this is a reference to the spot, not the later Greek trophy, but this seems unlikely. To quote Laistner in his commentary (1927: 168) on this section: "It is strange that the historical writers do not mention such a trophy, but the only alternative to believing in its existence on the sole authority of Isocrates is to suppose that our author, for rhetorical emphasis, invented the detail." Laistner does not speculate on what the rhetorical motive or emphasis might be in such a statement, especially when a Greek reading this discourse would know well that the Persians did not set up any trophy against the defeated Spartans. Perhaps Isocrates passes on some oral tradition about the arrogant boasting of the Persians after their victory, but this is unprovable.

[86] Isocrates denied that age was a problem in section 1.

your role and set your mind on the goals I have been advising. It would be shameful, then, when fate is so nobly leading, to be left behind and not dedicate yourself to go where it wishes to lead you.

[153] I think you should honor all who say something good about your past accomplishments, but you should realize that the finest praise comes from those who think your nature is capable of even greater accomplishments and from those who not only speak favorably about the present but will make those who come after you marvel at what you have done more than anyone else before now. I would like to say many such things, but I cannot, for the reason I have stated more often than I should.[87]

[154] There remains, then, only to summarize what I have said, so you can see briefly the topics of my advice. I say that you should be a benefactor for the Greeks, a king for the Macedonians, and master over as many barbarians as possible. If you do this, all will be grateful to you; the Greeks for the benefits they will receive, the Macedonians if you act like a king and not a tyrant, and the other group, if through you they put off the despotic rule of the barbarian and gain protection from the Greeks.

[155] It is right for me to learn from you, my audience, whether these things have been written with timeliness (*kairos*) and accuracy (*akribeia*).[88] I think I am confident, however, that no one would give you advice that is better or more fitting, given the situation.[89]

---

[87] That is, his old age.

[88] On *akribeia*, see O'Sullivan 1992: 42–47.

[89] This is an odd concluding paragraph; it refers to an audience beyond Philip and addresses issues of style and composition. This may serve as evidence of its nature, not as an actual discourse addressed to Philip, but as a political pamphlet distributed to a reading audience and/or a teaching tool given to his students. Cf. 12 and 85n.

6. ARCHIDAMUS

〰〰〰

INTRODUCTION

This discourse is written in the voice of Archidamus, the 24-year-
old son of Agesilaus, one of the two Spartan kings. Its dramatic date
of 366 is a dark time in Spartan history. Sparta's hopes for hegemony
were dashed at the battle of Leuctra in 371, where it was defeated by
Thebes and its famous general Epaminondas. After this, the Thebans
continued to harass Sparta in a variety of ways: they encouraged the
helots, a serf population controlled by Sparta; in 369 they began set-
tling the city of Messene in nearby Messenia to be a rival of Sparta;
and they continued to invade Spartan territory in the summers following 371. The cities near Sparta suffered under Theban invasions
and, led by Corinth, negotiated with Thebes for peace. At a crucial
assembly held in Sparta in 366 to discuss the peace, Thebes demanded that one of the conditions must be the independent status
of Messene; Thebes thought that this city would serve as an effective counterweight to Spartan influence in the Peloponnese. Corinth then urged Sparta to agree to the Theban proposal. The speech
translated here is a Spartan reply to the Corinthian speech. Archidamus urges Sparta to reject such a peace and says that Sparta should
fight to maintain its claim of leadership in the Peloponnese and its
hereditary control of Messene, a view that reflects Spartan attitudes at
the time.

It is unclear whether this discourse was actually written for Archidamus to present to the Spartan assembly or whether it was an exercise for Isocrates' school. If it was written on the actual occasion of the
peace negotiations (whether or not it was really written for Archida-

mus), its date would be 366.[1] If the speech was a rhetorical exercise for his school, it would have to be dated sometime after 366, but further precision would be difficult. One could argue that Isocrates would choose subjects for his example speeches from recent events and thus date the speech close to 366. One could also argue, however, that Isocrates chose this particular occasion because of its crucial moment in history to demonstrate how to make a plea in a deliberative context at a critical time.[2] The date could then be much later, and the work has been seen as a companion piece to the discourse *On the Peace* (8), which has a dramatic date of 355 (Harding 1973). The latter argues for a peace treaty and abuses those who use patriotic themes to argue for war, as *Archidamus* does.[3]

The speech shows a pro-Spartan flavor that is unusual in the works of Isocrates.[4] Isocrates, however, viewed Archidamus favorably and sent him a flattering letter about 356 after Archidamus replaced his father as king (*Ep.* 9). Thus there are again two possibilities: the pro-Spartan sentiment could argue for its status as a rhetorical exercise. The rhetor must learn to take on the character of his client. This skill was called *ēthopoiïa* and was most notably demonstrated in ancient Greece by the works of Lysias. The pro-Spartan sentiment, however, might also be a result of Isocrates' actual admiration of Archidamus (and his father Agesilaus) and his hopes for what could be accomplished by a benevolent monarch.

6. ARCHIDAMUS

[In the voice of Archidamus, prince of Sparta, to the Spartan assembly:]

---

[1] This is the dating provided by Norlin 1928: 345.

[2] Thus Brémond (in Mathieu and Brémond II 1938) does not feel bound to 366 and using other internal evidence, dates the speech to 362. If we entertain the idea that Isocrates looked back to 366 as a source for a teaching text, then he might be seen as an antecedent to the ancient educational tool *suasoria*, the deliberative example of a declamation. On declamation, see Kennedy 1994: 83–84 and Russell 1983.

[3] Cf. 8.36 to 6.57, 82, 94.

[4] Though not unprecedented. The speech *On the Peace* closes with a praise of the Spartan kingship (8.142–144).

[1] Perhaps some of you might be surprised that although as far as I know I have followed the customs of my city better than anyone else my age, I have made such a drastic change in my behavior now and have come forward, in spite of my youth, to give advice on matters that even the elderly hesitate to address. [2] Indeed, I would have kept quiet if any of those who regularly addresses you in the Assembly had given advice worthy of the city;[5] but seeing that some agree with our enemies' demands, others oppose them only weakly, and still others are entirely silent, I have risen to set out what I know about this issue, for I think it would be a shame if I were to preserve the proper conduct of my own life but allow the city to vote against its interests. [3] I think that even though it is proper in other matters for men of my age to keep silent, it is particularly appropriate that we offer advice in matters of war and peace, since we are the ones who will bear the largest share of the dangers, especially since it is for us all to decide what is the common good. [4] If it had been demonstrated that the elders had the best advice in all matters and that the youth knew nothing about anything, it would be right to keep us from offering advice. But since we do not clearly differ from one another in practical intelligence (*phronēsis*) on the basis of our age but on the basis of our nature (*physis*) and diligent attention (*epimeleia*), why not use the experience of people of both age groups so that you can take the most helpful advice from all that is given to you?[6] [5] I'm amazed at how many people think we can lead triremes or command armies, where we could cause many great troubles for the city if we do not plan well, while they do not think we should say what we know on matters where you are about to make a decision, since if our advice is right, we will help you all, but if we do not win your agreement, we will perhaps seem foolish, though we would not cause harm to the state.

[6] I have spoken in this way not because I wanted to speak, and not because I am preparing to change my life from what it has been,[7]

---

[5]This argument is a rhetorical commonplace. Demosthenes also uses it in the *First Philippic* (4.1), and it appears in the Demosthenic *Prooemia* (1).

[6]On *phronēsis,* cf. *Ep.* 7.1n.

[7]Archidamus refers to the distinction between a general (*stratēgos*) and an orator or politician (*rhētor*). Archidamus is not leaving his military interests behind to become a politician.

but because I wanted to urge you not to reject anyone because of his age, and instead to look in all age groups to see if there is someone who can speak well about the current situation. [7] From the time our city was first founded,[8] we have never faced any danger or war of such great importance as we have now gathered to consider. Before now we always debated about claiming leadership over others, but now the issue is how we can avoid doing what others command. This is a sign of freedom, for which we should endure every possible threat, as should others who are not too cowardly and make even a small claim to courage (*aretē*). [8] So if I must state my personal opinion, I would prefer to die right now and not follow this order rather than live many times longer than is set for me because I voted for what the Thebans demand.[9] For I would be ashamed if, coming from the stock of Heracles, with a father who is king and myself likely to attain to this position, I allowed our slaves[10] to take over the land that our ancestors left to us. [9] I think you will agree with me if you consider that while we have always seemed to have bad luck in our battle against Thebes and have been defeated in body through the bad planning of the general,[11] in soul we are still unconquered. [10] If, however, out of fear of the dangers that beset us, we give up any of our own interests, we will simply strengthen the Thebans' arrogance and will set up a trophy in honor of our own defeat much more impressive and conspicuous than the one at Leuctra. The trophy at Leuctra commemorates our bad luck, but this one commemorates our character. Therefore, let no one persuade you to place such disgrace on our city.

---

[8] Archaeological and historical evidence suggests that Sparta was founded in the twelfth or tenth century by invaders from the north during the so-called Dorian invasion. The local population was subjected by these invaders and became what we now call the helots (cf. 5.49n).

[9] Isocrates will return to this theme in his conclusion (109). On the Spartan code of honor, see *Ep.* 2.6n.

[10] A derogatory reference to the Messenians, who would have great influence under the Theban plan and whom Sparta always viewed as inferior to itself because it saw the Messenians as the source of the helots. He will return to this point more explicitly in sections 28 and 87.

[11] Cleombrotus, the Spartan general who died in 371 at the battle of Leuctra. The defeat at the hands of the Thebans insured the collapse of Spartan power.

[11] The allies have been advising you much too zealously that you must give up Messene and make peace. You should quite rightly be much more angry with them than with those who revolted from you in the beginning. For those cities rejected your friendship and thus destroyed their own cities, throwing them into factional squabbles, butchery, and base forms of government. Our allies, however, have come here to do you harm, [12] for they want to persuade you to throw away in a moment the fame that our ancestors left to us after acquiring it at much cost seven hundred years ago.[12] Our ancestors couldn't find any calamity less fitting for Sparta or more shocking than this. [13] Our allies have gotten so greedy and decided we are such cowards that although they often think we should fight on behalf of their land, they do not think we should run the same risk to keep Messene. In order that they can enjoy their own land securely, they try to teach us that we must give up part of ours to our enemies, and on top of this, they threaten that if we do not yield in this, they will make their own peace treaty. [14] I do not think that the risk we run without them will be any more serious than the glory, fame, and reputation we will get among all people, for to try to preserve our own security and prevail over our enemies on our own without the help of others fits with the previous actions of our city.

[15] I have never favored speech and have always thought that those who spend their time on it are rather reluctant to take action, but at the moment, I would value nothing more highly than to be able to explain my recommendations about the current situation, for in the present situation, I would hope that through speech I could achieve the greatest benefits for the city. [16] First, then, I think that I should explain to you how we gained Messene and why you settled in the Peloponnese, when you were Dorians from ancient times. And I will go back even further so that you will know that they are trying to steal from us this land that you gained justly, just like the rest of Lacedaimon.[13]

---

[12] The mythic account, as opposed to the historical one mentioned above (7n), says that the children of Heracles, the *Heracleidae,* migrated to Greece in 1104 and became what we now call the Dorians.

[13] Lacedaimon (or Laconia) is the title of the region in the southern Peloponnese controlled through the Classical period by the Spartans. The Spartans often referred to themselves as Lacedaemonians.

[17] When Heracles ended his life and became a god instead of a mortal, from the beginning his children were forced to wander and face dangers continually because of the power of their enemies.[14] But when Eurystheus died,[15] they settled among the Dorians. In the third generation they came to Delphi, wishing to consult the oracle about certain matters. The god did not respond to their question, however, but commanded them to go to their ancestral land. [18] Studying the oracle, they discovered that Argos was theirs because of the right of kinship, since they were the only remaining descendants of Perseus, now that Eurystheus was dead.[16] Lacedaimon was theirs too by gift, for after Tyndareus was driven from power and Castor and Polydeuces had vanished from mortal life, Heracles restored Tyndareus to his throne and then was given the region by the king because of this kind deed and because of Heracles' relation to his sons.[17] [19] And Messene too was theirs (they discovered) as a war prize, for Heracles had been robbed of the cattle from Erytheia[18] by Neleus and his sons (except for Nestor) and so he took the land captive, killed those who treated him wrongly, and entrusted the city to Nestor. He thought Nestor had good sense, since he did not join in his brothers' crimes in spite of being the youngest. [20] Deciding that this is what the oracle meant, the Heraclidae joined with your ancestors, marshaled an army, and shared their own land with those who had joined them. In return,

---

[14] *Panegyricus* (4.54–60) gives another, quite different version of the Heracles and Eurystheus tale.

[15] Isocrates describes the end of Eurystheus' life in *Panegyricus* (4.59–60).

[16] Spartans traced their line back to Heracles, who was descended from the hero Perseus. Perseus' son was Sthenelus, the father of Eurystheus. Eurystheus was Heracles' cousin.

[17] Castor and Polydeuces (whom the Romans called Pollux) were the twin sons of Leda (brothers to Helen and Clytemnestra). Castor was fathered by Tyndareus, but Polydeuces was a child of Zeus, so the former was mortal and the latter, immortal. Polydeuces gave up his own immortality to save his brother from death. Now the two share the immortality of one: the two spend half their time in Hades and half on Olympus. Since both Heracles and Polydeuces were children of Zeus, Isocrates can call them relatives.

[18] Heracles' tenth labor was to capture the cattle of Geryon from Erytheia, an island west of Spain. On his way back to Greece, Neleus stole them but was killed by Heracles.

these people gave them the kingship, which is reserved for them;[19] they then made pledges affirming this and began their campaign. [21] I need not go into the dangers they encountered on the journey or other actions not directly relevant. But when they defeated those who lived in the regions I mentioned, they divided the kingdom into three parts.

You have lived by the agreements and oaths you swore to our ancestors up to this very day, [22] and for this reason you have fared better in the past than anyone else, and you must assume that in the future you will fare better than you do now if you do not change. The Messenians, however, became so impious that they ambushed and killed Cresphontes, the founder of their city and master of their land, a descendant of Heracles, and the commander of their army. [23] His children, in flight from these troubles, came to our city as suppliants, asked for revenge for their dead father, and gave their land over to us.[20] After consulting the god, who replied that you should receive these supplications and avenge those who had been wronged, you besieged Messene and took control of the land.

[24] I have not gone into great detail about what was yours from the beginning, for the present occasion does not allow for a lengthy narrative but rather required me to speak concisely more than clearly about this. Nevertheless, I think it is apparent to all from what I have said that we came to have this land, which is acknowledged to be ours, no differently than the land that is contested. For we inhabit Lacedaimon because the sons of Heracles gave it to us, the god's oracle commanded it, and we defeated the native peoples in war. We took Messene from the same people, in the same way, after consulting the same oracle. [25] If we are not likely to argue, even if they order us to abandon Sparta itself, then it is superfluous to worry about Messene. But if none of you thinks he could live if our homeland is taken from us, then you must also have the same conviction about Messene, for in

---

[19] This explains the origin of the peculiar nature of dual Spartan kingship, two men who had broad military authority from two families descended from Heracles.

[20] This is the first instance of the sons seeking aid from Sparta. Earlier versions say that two of his sons were killed by the usurper Polyphontes. A third son, also named Cresphontes, was hidden in Aetolia and later returned to kill Polyphontes. See Gantz 1993: 2.735–736.

both cases we can find the same justifications and make the same arguments.

[26] You are all aware, moreover, how all people agree that if someone has possessed property for a long period of time, whether public or private, they are lawfully and traditionally its owners. In our case, we took Messene before the barbarians[21] got their kingdom and gained power over Asia and before other Greek cities were founded. [27] Even in these circumstances, the Thebans would give Asia back to the barbarian as if it were his ancestral claim, even though he has ruled it for less than two hundred years, and they would take Messene away from us, even though we have held it for more than twice that time.[22] They destroyed Thespiae and Plataea only very recently,[23] but they plan to resettle Messene, after four hundred years. In both these situations they violate their oaths and the treaty. [28] Also, if they were restoring people who were truly Messenians, they would be acting wrongly but would have a better reason to wrong us. As it is, however, they want to settle helots there as our neighbors, so the worst part is not that we are being robbed of our own land unjustly, but that we will see our own slaves become masters of that land.[24]

[29] From the following considerations you will understand more clearly both that we suffer terribly now and that we held Messene justly then. In the past, during the many dangers we faced, we were compelled to make peace in a far worse position than that of our enemies. Nonetheless, when treaties were made at those times when there was no chance for us to gain an advantage, [30] we had discussions about all sorts of matters, but never did the Persian King or the city of Athens ever accuse us of holding Messene unjustly. What decision could be more accurate regarding the justice of our case than one made by our enemies at a time that was unfavorable for us?

[31] The oracle of Apollo at Delphi, which all agree to be the old-

---

[21] That is, the Persians. On Isocrates' use of the general term "barbarian," see 4.3n.

[22] Cyrus became king of Persia in 559. Messene came under Spartan control in 724.

[23] Thespiae was seized by the Thebans in 373. Plataea was taken in 373 or shortly after. The situation with Plataea is dramatized in Isocrates' speech *Plataicus* (14).

[24] On the helots, see above, 7n and 8n as well as 5.49n.

est, most widely recognized, and most trustworthy, decided that Messene was ours not only when it commanded us to accept it as a gift from the children of Cresphontes and avenge those who had been wronged[25] but also from a later response: when the war was dragging on[26] and both sides sent embassies to Delphi in which the Messenians asked for security and we asked how we could most quickly conquer their city, the oracle made no response to them, since their request was improper,[27] but it told us which sacrifices we needed to make and whom we should ask for help.

[32] How could one provide a better or clearer testimony than this? It is clear, first, that we took this land from its owners (for there is nothing to prevent us from recalling these facts briefly here); second, we took it in war, which is the way most cities were established at that time; third, we expelled those who treated the children of Heracles impiously, men who rightly should have been exiled from every community; and in addition, we have properly held Messene for a long time, with the approval of our enemies and in accordance with the oracles of the god. [33] Any one of these would be sufficient proof to destroy the arguments of those who dare to accuse us of refusing to make peace now out of greed or making war against Messene in the past out of a desire for the land of others. So I think I have said enough about our possession of Messene, even though I could perhaps add more on the subject.

[34] Those who advise us to make peace say that intelligent people should not have the same approach to matters when they are faring well as they do when faring badly; they should always look to the pres-

---

[25] See above, sections 22–23.

[26] Sparta was involved in several so-called Messenian wars: the first Messenian war (740–720), the second (640–621), and the third (469–460). The dates are not certain; those given here follow Hammond 1986. See also Cartledge 1979. The first two wars are clouded by legend. Pausanias (4.12) describes an oracle during the first Messenian war, but it does not agree with Isocrates' account, and so it is unclear to which struggle Isocrates refers. On Isocrates' use of history, see Koch 1914; Laistner 1927: 24–25; Baynes 1955; Welles 1966; Hamilton 1979; Nouhaud 1982; and Nickel 1991.

[27] Pausanias (4.12) says that both sides sent to the oracle for information, and both got responses, though the Messenians did not understand theirs.

ent moment, adapt themselves to changing fortunes, not be more confident than their power warrants, and finally seek advantage (*to sympheron*) rather than justice (*to dikaion*) in such crucial situations.[28] [35] Now I agree with them on most of this, but no one could persuade me that we should value anything above justice. I see that laws are passed because of it, men are honored as noble based on it, cities that are governed well take it very seriously, [36] all wars up to now have ended not according to who is stronger but who is more just, and more generally speaking, human life is destroyed by vice (*kakia*) but preserved through virtue (*aretē*). Thus, it is not those who are going to face danger on behalf of justice who should lose heart, but those who are arrogant and those who do not know how to accept their good fortune in moderation. [37] Consider this next: all people now have the same opinion about justice, but they disagree about advantage. When two goods are offered and one is clearly so, while the other is unsure, would you not be foolish if you should reject the obvious good and decide to take the one that is unsure, especially when so much is at stake in the choice?[29] [38] My recommendation will not cause you to abandon any of your claims, nor will it bring shame upon the city, since those who face danger on behalf of justice can expect to have better luck fighting than their enemies. Their recommendations,

---

[28] In his *Histories,* Thucydides represents the Athenians having a debate over the fate of Mytilene in 427, where Cleon argues for severity based on the criterion of justice and Diodotus argues for leniency based on the criterion of advantage (3.35–50). Diodotus wins the day. Thucydides also has the Athenians make an argument about looking to advantage when they advise the Melians in 416 to give in to Athenian power and not fight a losing battle (5.84–116). The Melians prefer to look to justice and are destroyed.

[29] These sections, with a philosophic flavor to them, are reminiscent of Socrates' argument in Plato's *Apology* and *Crito* about avoiding death. Socrates argues that one should not choose to avoid death if one must commit a known injustice to do so. Since we do not know whether death is an evil or not—and Socrates is fairly sure that it is a good thing (*Apology* 41)—we should not choose something that is clearly unjust (our action to avoid death) when we do not know if the other option (death) is an evil or not. Isocrates' argument here is simpler and clearer, since it is cast in a positive argument—choosing between goods rather than choosing between evils—and has fewer immediate repercussions—the implications of bad public policy rather than death.

however, would cause you to give up Messene immediately, and by doing yourselves wrong in this way, you would perhaps lose what is advantageous, what is just, and everything else you hope for. [39] You do not know for sure yet whether we will even have a secure peace if we do what they tell us; I think you are aware that everyone usually negotiates with those who staunchly defend themselves about a just settlement, while they always attach more demands than they had originally planned when they talk with those who are overly ready to give in to demands. Thus those who keep a hostile attitude tend to get a better peace settlement than those who easily agree to terms.

[40] So as not to seem to be spending too much time on these issues, I will set aside all similar kinds of arguments and turn to the simplest of my points.[30] If no people who have encountered bad luck had ever restored themselves and triumphed over their enemies, then it would not be likely (*eikos*) that we would have any hope of defeating our enemies. But if it has often happened that the stronger are defeated by the weaker and that those who besiege a city are destroyed by those who are trapped inside it, why would it be surprising if current circumstances also should experience a reversal? [41] I have no such precedent to cite in the history of our city, since up to this time no one stronger than us ever invaded our land. In the case of other cities, however, one can find many examples, and especially with Athens.[31] [42] We will find that this city had a bad reputation among the Greeks as long as it dictated to others, but when it was defending itself, it enjoyed a high reputation among all people. Now, if I were to recall the old threats they faced against the Amazons or the Thracians or the Peloponnesians who invaded their land under Eurystheus,[32]

---

[30] Part of Isocrates' *ēthopoiïa*, or character portrayal, here is to play on notions of Spartan brevity and practicality. Archidamus is uncomfortable with the philosophic argument that the previous sections have offered and turns back to more practical issues.

[31] Praise of Athens is unlikely in an actual speech by a Spartan. Thus, this may be an indication that this speech was not actually delivered to the Spartans, or at least not in this form. Given the contrast with Sparta, however, this story shows that there were powers stronger than Athens.

[32] Isocrates briefly discussed the Amazons and Thracians in *Panegyricus* (4.70). Theseus and Heracles made a joint campaign against the female warriors known as the Amazons, where Theseus captured the Amazon Antiope for a mate. As a re-

perhaps I might seem to bring up ancient events, far from our present concerns. But in the Persian Wars too, who doesn't know what height of fortune they came to after being so low? [43] They alone of all those living outside the Peloponnese[33] saw that the power of the barbarians was unstoppable and yet still did not think that they should consider what was being dictated to them. Rather, they immediately chose to let their city be destroyed rather than give in to slavery. They left their land, considering freedom their rightful homeland, and by joining with us to face the danger, they met with such a change of fortune that by giving up their own land for a few days, they became the masters of others for a long time.

[44] Athens is not the only example someone might show of how daring to ward off enemies could be the cause of many blessings. When Dionysius, the tyrant of Syracuse,[34] for example, was besieged by the Carthaginians with no apparent hope of rescue, under the pressure of war and facing the wrath of the citizens, he was about to escape by sea when one of his companions ventured to say, [45] "Tyranny is a noble burial shroud."[35] Embarrassed at his plans, he changed his mind and returned to the war again. He killed many Carthaginians, made the

---

sult, the Amazons invaded Attica and were defeated. The Thracians lived near the northern border of Greece and were driven back by the Greeks. The Amazons and the Thracians, as well as the Persians later on, were common examples of foreign barbarism that needed to be subdued.

After Heracles died, Eurystheus exiled his children. When they came to Athens for help, Eurystheus invaded and was killed by Hyllus, one of the sons of Heracles. Isocrates discusses this story in *Panegyricus* (4.56).

[33] Again Isocrates, wanting to praise Athens for its ability to restore itself but writing in the voice of a Spartan, carefully reminds the reader of the strength of those in the Peloponnese.

[34] Dionysius I was tyrant of Syracuse from 405 to 367. His son, Dionysius II, also ruled at Syracuse, from 367 to 357. A tyrant is a monarch who seizes control by force. Though the word is more often pejorative in the fourth century than in earlier centuries, Isocrates is not necessarily hostile to the idea. Many cities in Greece, especially in the sixth century, saw tyrants lead them to great prosperity. Isocrates addresses a number of tyrants respectfully. See *To Demonicus, To Nicocles, Nicocles (Cyprians), To Philip, Epistles* 1, 2, 3, and 9.

[35] His companion encourages him to stay and fight by advising that it is better to die as a king in battle than to live shamefully in exile.

people's authority stronger, and increased his own power beyond what he had before. He ended his life as a tyrant and left his son to be tyrant with the same position and powers as he had.

[46] Similar to these two was Amyntas, the king of Macedon.[36] When he had been defeated in battle by the barbarians who lived at his borders and had lost all Macedon, he first thought to leave the region and save his own life, but when he heard someone commending what had been said to Dionysius, he changed his mind like Dionysius, took back a small outpost, and sent for help from there. Within three months he recovered all Macedon and then remained king for the rest of his time until he died in old age.

[47] We would soon be exhausted, both you listening and I speaking, if we recounted all such stories. Even the experience of Thebes, though we would be pained at the outcome, would give us greater hope for the future. When they had the daring to withstand our attacks and threats, fortune caused such a change in their situation that although formerly we controlled them, now they think they can tell us what to do.

[48] So whoever sees that such changes of fortune have occurred but thinks that they will stop before reaching us is particularly foolish. We should, rather, take heart at the present situation and be encouraged about the future, knowing that cities repair such disasters by applying good government and their experience in war. No one would dare disagree that we have more experience than others and that we are the only ones who have the sort of government one should have. Since this is so, there is no way that we will not fare better than those who have paid little attention to either of these matters.

[49] Some people condemn war and go on about its fickleness, giving many examples, especially from events in our own history. They marvel that anyone would be willing to trust such a difficult and risky undertaking. I, however, know that many people have gained great prosperity through war, and many have lost what they have through peace. [50] Neither of these, war or peace, is entirely bad or good, but how each one turns out must always depend on how someone makes use of the situation (*pragmata*) and the opportunities (*kairoi*) it pre-

---

[36] King of Macedon from 393 to 370, father of Philip II, and grandfather of Alexander the Great.

sents. Certainly those who are well off desire peace, for in this condition they can maintain their present circumstances for the longest time. Those who are doing poorly, however, must turn their attention to war, for their situation could change more quickly as a result of confusion and upheaval. [51] I fear we seem to be doing the opposite; when we were able to live comfortably, we kept making more wars than we needed, but now that we have been forced into a dangerous situation, we desire peace and plan for our security. But those who want to be free must avoid agreements that are based on the orders of others as if they were akin to slavery and must make a treaty only when they are superior to the enemy or have made their own power equal to that of their enemy. Thus, what sort of peace each city will have depends on what sort of conclusion they make to the war.

[52] Considering this, you must not throw yourselves rashly into a shameful alliance, and you must not seem more negligent about your homeland than about other things. Remember that in the past, if just one Spartan citizen gave aid to an allied city under siege, everyone would agree that its rescue came through this man. You could hear about most of these men from the elders among us, but even I can describe the greatest of them. [53] Pedaritos sailed to Chios and saved their city;[37] Brasidas came to Amphipolis, assembled around him a few of those under siege, and defeated the enemy in battle, in spite of their numbers;[38] Gylippus helped the Syracusans and not only saved them but also captured Athens' force, which had held control over them on both land and sea.[39] [54] Is it not shameful, then, that on those occasions just one of us was able to protect others' cities, whereas now all of us together cannot and do not even try to preserve our own city, or that we have filled all Europe and Asia with victory trophies while fighting for others, but we clearly have not fought one single battle worthy of note for our own homeland, which is being so openly violated? [55] Other cities have endured extreme sieges in defense of

---

[37] Pedaritos helped the Chians revolt against Athens in 412 (Thuc. 8.55).

[38] Brasidas, the famous Spartan general, got Amphipolis from Athenian control in 422 but died in the process (Thuc. 4.102–108 and 5.6–11).

[39] Gylippus defeated Nicias in 413 in the harbor battle at Syracuse that was disastrous for Athens and turned the tide of the war in Sparta's favor (Thuc. 7.21–87).

our empire, but we ourselves do not think we should endure even a little hardship to avoid acting unjustly. Instead, we can now be seen feeding hungry teams of horses, acting rich and stable even though we are trying to make a peace as if we had fallen in the worst troubles and lacked our daily needs. [56] The most shocking thing of all would be if we, who have the reputation of being the hardest workers in Greece, are lazier than others when we consider this question. Do we know any people worth recalling who lost a single battle and experienced a single invasion, and then were so cowardly that they agreed to do everything they were told? How would such people hold out if they were to suffer for a long time? [57] Who would not fault us if we should leave Messenia so quickly in accordance with the treaty, when the Messenians endured twenty years of siege to defend it,[40] or if we should forget about our ancestors and instead be persuaded by words to abandon this land that our ancestors acquired for us through much toil and danger?

[58] Some think nothing of this, pay no attention to the issue of shame, and recommend to you policies that will bring the city into reproach. They are so eager to induce you to betray Messene that they even dare to describe our weakness and the enemy's strength, and they then ask those who oppose them to explain where we think help will come from when we encourage them to go to war. [59] In my view, the greatest and surest alliance is to do what is right—for it is likely that the goodwill of the gods will be on this side, if one can use the past as evidence for the future. Add to this a sound government, a moderate lifestyle, a willingness to fight to the death against your enemies, and the conviction that nothing is worse than to have a bad reputation among your fellow citizens. We have these qualities more than other people. [60] I would much rather fight with these qualities on my side than with many thousands of men, for I know that those of us who first came to this land did not conquer others through the size of our army but through the excellent qualities I have just described. Thus you should not fear our enemies just because they are many, but we should rather face them with confidence when we see that we have endured our misfortunes as no one else ever has [61] and have abided by the laws and customs that we established at the beginning. They,

---

[40] During the first Messenian war, 740–720.

on the other hand, are unable to handle their good fortune but have been thrown into confusion by it; some have tried to seize allied cities, others have done the opposite, still others argue with their neighbors about borderlands, and others are more envious of each other than they are hostile toward us.⁴¹ I am amazed as a result at those who seek a greater ally than our enemies' mistakes.

[62] If I must speak about external aid, I think that there will be many who will want to help us.⁴² I know first that the Athenians, even if they are not always on our side, will certainly do anything to insure our security. Second, there are a number of other cities that will make plans with the same regard for our interests as for their own. [63] Third, Dionysius the tyrant and the Egyptian king and other rulers in Asia will readily come to our aid to the extent that each is able. Finally, in addition to these, the Greeks who have the most wealth and the leading reputation and value the best governments,⁴³ even if they have not joined with us yet, nevertheless are well disposed toward us, and so it would be reasonable to hope for their aid in the future.

[64] I think that the rest of the people in the Peloponnese in general, especially the democratic faction, whom we assume are particularly hostile to us, long for our protection now; they gained nothing that they had hoped for when they revolted, but instead of freedom, they got just the opposite. They lost the best men they had and are now ruled by the worst citizens, and instead of autonomy, they have fallen into widespread and fearsome lawlessness. [65] In the past they

---

⁴¹ This section is probably meant to criticize the Thebans and their behavior toward other cities of the Boeotian League, as described by Xenophon (*Hellenica* 7).

⁴² After the battle of Leuctra in 371, Thebes wielded a powerful influence in Greece, and Archidamus is correct that many cities, Athens included, would join with them to insure that Thebes did not become stronger. Xenophon describes this in *Hellenica* 7.4.

⁴³ Archidamus refers here to an oligarchy (or monarchy). "The Best" (*beltistoi*) is the standard way of referring to oligarchic leadership. Isocrates will contrast this with democracy, which Archidamus views as dangerous (64). Cities led by an oligarchy might include those hostile to the Arcadian league, such as Orchomenus, Heraea, Lepreae (Xen., *Hellenica* 6.5.11 and 22), or Phlius (*Hellenica* 7.2.1–2).

were accustomed to making campaigns with us against others, but now they see others marching against them. Finally, the factionalism that in the past they used to see in other states, they now see breaking out almost daily in their own communities. Their troubles have made them all so equal that no one can tell who is the worst off. [66] No city is unharmed, and no city is without neighbors who would do it harm. Thus, their land has been ravaged; their cities have been sacked; their private homes have been razed to the ground; their governments have been overthrown; and their laws, which had made their lives the most prosperous of the Greeks, have been abolished. [67] They have so little trust and so much hostility toward one another that they fear their fellow citizens more than their enemies. Instead of the unity of spirit they had during our rule and the prosperity they had from one another, they have become so inhospitable that those who have wealth would rather throw it into the sea than give help to someone in need, while those who are in need would prefer not to find some money by chance but to steal it from the rich. [68] Abandoning sacrifices of animals on their altars, they now slaughter one another. There are more exiles now from one city than there used to be from all the Peloponnese. And for all the troubles I have listed, I have passed over many more than those I have mentioned, since there are no disasters or difficulties that have not rushed together into this place. [69] Some cities are already full of such difficulties; others will soon be filled to overflowing, and they will seek some relief from their current distress. Do not think that they will last in this condition, for how can those who grow weary even when flourishing hold out for long when they are suffering? Thus, we do not have to defeat them in battle, for even if we take no action and remain as we are, you will see them change their mind and realize that an alliance with us is their own salvation. Such then are the hopes I have.

[70] I am so opposed to what they demand that even if none of what I have projected happens and we get aid from nowhere, but instead some Greeks mistreat us badly and others simply ignore us, I still would not change my mind but would endure all the dangers that the war might bring before I would make this pact. I would be ashamed in any case, either because I would be condemning our ancestors for taking Messene unjustly or because, even though they acquired this land justly and properly, we would be unjustly compromising our in-

terests in it. [71] We should do neither of these. Instead, we should consider how we will fight in a manner worthy of our name, how we will show that those who usually praise our city are not liars, and how we will present ourselves to be such men that they have not praised us highly enough. [72] In my view, nothing more terrible will happen than what we are experiencing now, but our enemies will plan and act in ways that they will actually help us recover. Still, should we be deceived in our hopes and be harassed from every direction and not be able to defend our city any longer, then what I have to say is difficult, but nevertheless, I will not hesitate to speak honestly to you about it, for it is a finer plan to be made known to the Greeks and more in accord with our own spirit than what some are recommending to you.

[73] For I think that we must send our own parents, our children, our wives, and the rest of the people away from the city, some to Sicily, others to Cyrene, still others to Asia (all these will gladly help us receive them because of the abundance of their land and other necessities of life, some out of thanks for when they were treated well, others expecting to gain from what they do first).[44] [74] The rest of us who are willing and able to endure the dangers of war will abandon the city and our possessions, save what we can carry ourselves, occupy a small outpost that is very secure and well suited for war, and then harass and plunder our enemies by both land and sea until they stop laying claim to what is ours.[45] [75] If we dare to do this and not shrink from the task, you will see those who are now trying to dictate to us become suppliants and beg us to take back Messene and make peace.

What city in the Peloponnese could endure the kind of war that is likely to happen if we plan this way? Who would not be terrified and afraid of an army assembled like this and acting as I describe, justly angry at those responsible for their plight, with a desperately careless attitude toward life, [76] which in its lack of other distractions and its focus on nothing other than war is very similar to a mercenary army

---

[44] Isocrates has already said in section 63 that Dionysius (of Syracuse, in Sicily) and the kings of Asia Minor were favorably disposed to Sparta. He says in *To Philip* (5.5) that Cyrene is a Spartan colony.

[45] Although this sounds like an impractical plan, Archidamus had already mentioned an approach much like it that succeeded when he described the plans of Amyntas of Macedon in section 46.

but in its courage and discipline is an army such as no one ever levied before? It will no longer have a set government, will be able to live in the wild and go wherever it wants, locating itself next to any country wherever it wishes and considering its homeland to be whatever place is conducive to the war. [77] I think that if this proposal is simply announced and spread throughout the Greeks, it will send our enemies into considerable panic and even more if we should be forced in the end actually to carry this out. What opinion do we think they will have when they are suffering and can do nothing to us, [78] when they see their own cities under siege, while ours is organized in such a way that it will never again fall into such difficulty? Further, we will have sufficient food from our own resources and from the spoils of war, while it will be difficult for them to have enough, since providing for an army such as ours is not the same as feeding all the people in the cities. [79] What will hurt them the most, however, is when they find out that our family members have been living amid great abundance, while they see their own people lacking the daily necessities of life and cannot do anything to alleviate these troubles; if they till the soil, they will lose the seed, but if they leave it fallow, they will not be able to hold out very long. [80] Perhaps, however, they will join together and make a common army that will pursue us and keep us from hurting them. What more could we hope for than to find an army drawing close, set out against us and making camp in the same difficult place as we do, a disorderly and mixed group of soldiers with numerous generals? It would not require a great effort; we would quickly compel them to face battle at the time most favorable for us, not for them.

[81] The rest of the day would be too short if we tried to mention all the advantages that would result from this. It is clear to everyone that we surpass the Greeks not in the size of our city or the number of our men but because we have a government that resembles a well-run military camp that wants to be obedient to its leaders.[46] Thus, if we shall fully establish that from which we have gotten benefit when we only copied it, it is clear that we will easily overcome our enemies. [82] We know that the founders of this city came into the Peloponnese with only a small army and yet conquered many great cities. It would be good, therefore, to imitate our ancestors and, since we have

---

[46] On the military nature of Spartan society, see Demand 1996: 118–139.

had setbacks, go back to the beginning and try to regain the honor and authority we had before. [83] The most terrible thing we could do, however, would be if we, knowing that the Athenians had left their own land behind to insure the freedom of others,[47] were not bold enough ourselves to abandon our city for the sake of our own safety, or if, when we should be providing an example of such noble behavior to others, we were not willing to emulate the Athenians' actions. [84] And even more laughable than that would be if even the Phocians left Asia and moved to Massalia when they fled from the despotism of the Great King,[48] but we should be so small-minded that we endure the demands of people we have always ruled. [85] We must not burden our hearts thinking about that day when we would need to send our most beloved away from us; we should look instead to the time when we will defeat our enemies, reestablish our city, restore our own people, and show to all that although we have suffered unjustly now, in the past we justly deserved to have the advantage over others. [86] This is how it is: I have not said these things because we must do them right now or because in our situation there is no other way to save ourselves, but because I wanted to encourage you to understand that we ought to endure these and much more terrible calamities before we accept the treaty about Messene that they push us to make.

[87] I would not be urging you so strongly to go to war unless I saw that my proposals would lead to a noble and secure peace, whereas the proposals of others would result in a peace that would not only be disgraceful but would not last very long. If we settle the helots next to us in Messene[49] and watch as their city grows, who cannot see that we

---

[47] Cf. section 42. The Athenians allowed the Persians to sack Athens in 480, retreating to the "wooden walls" of their ships and setting up the battle of Salamis. On the battle of Salamis, see 5.147.

[48] Phocian settlers in Asia Minor were harassed in the sixth century by the Persian King. They left there in the mid sixth century and suffered difficulties in Chios and Corsica (Herod. 1.162–167). Tradition (Isocrates here and Thuc. 1.13) says that they eventually founded Massalia, modern Marseilles. How and Wells (note to 1.163–167), however, deny the founding of Massalia by the exiled Phocians.

[49] Isocrates here (in the mouth of Archidamus) says that the Spartans will settle the helots in Messene, using the verb *parakatoikizō* (cf. also 28), which represents a city intentionally bringing in other settlers. This hints at a Sparta still in control. In the actual peace, however, Sparta would not be "allowing" the helots to

will spend our whole lives in confusion and danger? Thus, those who talk about safety fail to see that they are creating a peace treaty for us that will last just a few days but setting up a war that will last for all time. [88] I would gladly learn from them for what cause they think we ought to fight and die. Apparently it is not when our enemies dictate unjust demands, cut off part of our land, free our slaves, and then settle them in the country that our ancestors left to us, not only depriving us of our possessions but in addition to all these troubles driving us to disgrace. [89] In contrast, I think that these are cause enough for us to endure not only war but also exile and death, for it is much better to die with our reputation intact than to live with the shame we will get if we obey their orders. In short, if I may speak frankly, it is preferable for us to be driven from our homes than to become the laughingstock of our enemies. Those who have lived with such a high reputation and such a great spirit must face one of two outcomes: either to be first among the Greeks or to be entirely destroyed while doing nothing base and achieving a noble end to their lives.

[90] We must reflect on all this and not be too enamored with life or follow the advice of allies we used to lead; rather, we need to examine the situation ourselves and choose not what is easiest for them but what is appropriate for Lacedaimon and our past achievements; there is no need for all people to make similar decisions about the same matters, but each must decide according to the way he has lived his life. [91] No one, for example, would fault the Epidaurians, the Corinthians, or the Phliasians if they valued nothing besides their own survival and security. But the Spartans cannot put their safety above all else. If we cannot combine security with nobility of action, then we must choose to die with honor, for those who seek the prize for excellence must above all else strive to do nothing shameful. [92] The cowardice of cities is demonstrated no less in deliberations such as these as in the dangers of war, for in war, things happen for the most part by chance, but the decision we make here is a clear sign of our character. Thus, we must strive for success equally in the votes we take here as in our armed struggles.

[93] I am amazed at those who are willing to die for personal glory

---

settle; the Spartans would have little to say in the matter if they agreed to the peace proposed.

but do not feel the same about our common glory; yet for this cause we should endure anything so that the city is not brought to shame and should not let the city desert its place, the place where our ancestors stationed it.[50] Although there are many terrible dangers we must try to escape, [94] we must especially guard against appearing to act with cowardice or yield to our enemies contrary to justice. For it would be shameful if those worthy of ruling over the Greeks[51] should now be seen following commands and falling so far short of our ancestors that while they were willing to die to command others, we will not risk anything to avoid following orders. [95] We would deserve to be ashamed at the Olympic games or other panhellenic festivals, where each of us used to be more envied and more marveled at than the athletes who won victories in the contests. Who would dare to attend one of these now, when instead of being honored, he would be looked down upon, and instead of being admired by all for his courage, he would be stared at by the same people for his cowardice? [96] In addition, he would see his slaves making larger offerings and sacrifices from the land that our fathers left to us than those that we make, and would hear them uttering such abuse as you would expect from those who once were enslaved and harshly treated, but who now make equal treaties with their masters. Each of us would be so pained by these things that no one alive could ever describe it. [97] We must consider this and must not wait until the future and get frustrated when you have nothing left, but think now how to prevent this from happening to us. It is particularly shameful that in the past we used to deny even free people an equal right to speech, but now we must openly endure the free talk of slaves. [98] It will also appear that we were pretenders in the past, no different in nature than others, and that the confidence and dignity we showed was not real, but a facade. So let us give no such satisfaction to those who always abuse us, but try to refute their accusations by acting in accord with our ancestors' achievements.

---

[50] The phrase "desert its place" is a military phrase for desertion. It is a nice bit of *ēthopoiïa* or character portrayal on the part of Isocrates to put this in the mouth of the general Archidamus.

[51] A grand overstatement on the part of Archidamus. Sparta "ruled over the Greeks" for only thirty-three years, from the end of the Peloponnesian War (404) to the battle of Leuctra (371), and this was not always uncontested.

[99] Remember those who fought at Dipaea against the Arcadians, whom they say in spite of massing only a single infantry line, raised a trophy over many thousands of the enemy,[52] and the three hundred who defeated all the Argives in battle at Thyreae,[53] and the thousand who resisted at Thermopylae[54] [100] who faced seven hundred thousand barbarians and did not flee or lose but gave their lives there where they were stationed, demonstrating such exceptional heroism that the most skilled eulogists could not find words to equal their achievements.[55] [101] So remember all these heroes and take up the war even more vigorously. Do not sit and wait for someone else to cure our present troubles, but since they have happened on our watch, let us try to put an end to them ourselves. In times like these, good men must show themselves superior. [102] Good fortune completely hides the baseness of inferior men, but bad luck quickly makes it clear what kind of person each turns out to be. In these circumstances, we must reveal whether our upbringing and our education are superior to those of others in fostering courage (arete).

[103] There is no lack of hope that we might gain something desirable from our present situation, for I think you are aware that there have been many such events in the past that everyone at first took to be calamities and sympathized with those affected but later recognized that these same events brought about the greatest benefits. [104] Why should I speak of distant events? Even now, we could note that the leading cities, namely, Athens and Thebes, did not make great progress in times of peace but by regaining territory they had lost during a previous war. In this way, one of them, Athens, became the leader of Greece, while the other, Thebes, has become more influential now than anyone ever expected. This is because fame and great reputation tend not to arise from keeping quiet but from struggles (agōnes).

---

[52] Ca. 473–470. This battle is an odd parallel to cite, since Herodotus makes it clear (9.34–35) that this victory came as a result of a treaty made in haste under bad terms, a dangerous parallel for Archidamus to bring up.

[53] In 546/5. Herodotus (1.82) narrates the story at some length. Isocrates conflates two stories. According to Herodotus, both sides agree to a battle of the three hundred best soldiers. Later, the full armies faced each other in a separate battle.

[54] In 480. Isocrates tells this important incident from the Persian Wars in more detail in Panegyricus (4.90–92).

[55] On the inadequacy of the speaker's words, cf. 4.74, 14.4, and Thuc. 2.35.

[105] Our duty is to strive for these qualities not sparing our bodies, our spirits, or anything else we have. If we succeed in this and can restore our city to where it was when it fell, we will be admired even more than our ancestors, we will make it impossible for descendants to rival our courage and will make even those who want to praise us at a loss for words worthy of our achievements. [106] You must not forget that all are paying close attention to this gathering and to the decision we make here. Therefore, let each of you prepare his thoughts as if he were giving a proof of his own nature in a theater attended by all Greeks.

[107] It is easy to make the right decision about this. If we are willing to die for justice, not only will we be esteemed but we will be able to live securely for the rest of time, but if we stand in fear of the dangers before us, we will cause ourselves many troubles. [108] So, let us encourage each other and repay our homeland for the upbringing it gave us, and let us not allow Sparta to be abused or belittled; let us not prove false the expectations of those who think well of us, and let us not be seen to value life more than a good reputation among all men. [109] Keep in mind that it is a more noble thing to exchange a mortal body for immortal glory and to purchase, with the life we will have for only a few more years, a fame that will last forever for our descendants. This is far preferable to grasping for a little more time for our life and thereby covering ourselves completely in shame.[56] [110] I think you would be especially roused to war if you imagined that our ancestors and our children were here; the ancestors encouraging you not to shame the name of Sparta, the laws by which you were raised, or the battles they fought, while the children ask for the land our ancestors left behind, the authority we once had among the Greeks, and the empire that we received from our fathers. We would have nothing to say to them, since both of their pleas would be just.[57]

---

[56] He makes this point more emphatically in the opening of the speech at section 8.

[57] This passage borders on *prosopopoieia,* the presentation of another character speaking. It is an elaborate figure, used here in the peroration in the reference to ancestors, laws, and children to rouse emotion before the end. For an example of the laws actually pictured speaking, see Plato's *Crito.*

[111] I do not think I need say any more, except for this: though this city has seen many wars and dangers, as long as there has been a king from my family, never has an enemy set up a victory trophy over us. Thoughtful men, if they have had success with their leaders in war, should also trust these leaders more than other advisors when they deliberate about future threats.[58]

---

[58] Isocrates creates an ending that is abrupt, perhaps imitating the Spartan manner.

8. ON THE PEACE

INTRODUCTION

This discourse presents Isocrates' ideas about how Athens should handle its affairs in light of the so-called Social War.[1] The allies of Athens rebelled against its heavy-handed leadership in 357, and the war continued until 355, when Athens granted many concessions to the allies about their autonomy. This is a difficult time for Athens, and Isocrates offers advice on how Athens can regain its strength and reputation. The dramatic date is 355, after the peace was set (15). There is no way of knowing, however, whether this discourse was written at that time or later. As with many of Isocrates' discourses, we do not know if it was meant to address the real situation or whether it is a rhetorical exercise using a historical situation as the starting point.[2] If it was written at that time, there is still the question of whether it was presented by someone at an assembly or was only distributed for public reading.

Isocrates' point is quite broad: the peace that has been agreed upon does not go far enough. Athens should make peace not only with the disgruntled allies but with the whole of Greece (16). If Athens leads in promoting peace, it will win back respect from the rest of the Greeks and very likely will regain its empire. Furthermore, Athens should carry out this policy by returning to the notions of democracy fostered

---

[1] The Latin word for ally is *socius,* and so historians traditionally gave the name "Social War" ("war against the allies") to this conflict.

[2] See the Introduction to *Archidamus* above; Harding 1973; Moysey 1982; Davidson 1990; and Michelini 1998.

by the Athenians of the early fifth century rather than the later fifth century. Isocrates praises the Athenians of the Persian Wars and the early Delian League while criticizing the imperialistic policies of the Athenians of the Peloponnesian War. This contrast between the early and late fifth century runs as a leitmotif through the discourse.

In the opening sections, Isocrates asserts the need for good advisors (3–14); he will serve that function. He then states clearly that a broad peace is what is needed (15–16). Much of the discourse treats the notions of true advantage, that peace is preferable to war (17–40).[3] Isocrates then presents the idea that Athens must look to its distant past, not the recent events of the Peloponnesian War, for its models of behavior (41–94). The fourth century is no better as a model than the later fifth century; Isocrates analyzes Athens' actions in parallel with Sparta to show that both cities encountered difficulties because of their misguided notions of empire (95–131). Included in this damning accusation of recent policy is a condemnation, somewhat traditional in the fourth century, of the city's greedy and morally corrupt leaders, with particular emphasis here on their sykophantic tendencies. Isocrates then summarizes before closing with a stunning tribute to Spartan government (132–144).

The discourse is an important document for historical and political information about the years 360–350. M. L. W. Laistner (1921: 78) has said, "Among the writings of Isocrates the discourse 'On The Peace' ranks second only to *Panegyricus.*" He cites, among other aspects, its literary merits and historical importance. The speech gives additional and alternative evidence to the historical record of Xenophon and Diodorus Siculus. It must be approached with caution, however, since Isocrates sometimes adjusts history for the sake of rhetorical argument. I have made some references in the notes below to issues of history and how Isocrates uses history in his discourses.

There are two titles available for this discourse: *On the Peace* appears in the best manuscripts and in references from Dionysius of Hal-

---

[3] This is in stark contrast to the ideas presented by the Spartan prince Archidamus in Isocrates' *Archidamus* (6), where the speaker advocates war over the dangerous and disadvantageous peace being proposed in 366 by advocates of Thebes. Cf. Harding 1973.

icarnassus; *Alliance* (*Symmakikos*) appears in other manuscripts and in Aristotle's *Rhetoric* (3.17). Traditionally, the former has been used, even though the latter is more precise. The latter, in fact, may be a result of attempts to clarify the content of the discourse or to specify which peace, since the "Social War" was the war against the allies (*symmakoi*).

There is a commentary treating the speech by Laistner (1927) to which this translation is often indebted.[4] See also Gillis 1970.

8. ON THE PEACE

[1] All who come before you are accustomed to say that the matters they are about to advise you on are the most important and most worth the city's serious attention. Nonetheless, even if one might fittingly say this as a preface in some other situations, it seems right for me to begin my treatment of the present situation in just this way.[5] [2] For we have gathered in the Assembly to discuss war and peace; these matters have the greatest effect on human life, and people who plan well must necessarily do better than others. Such is the importance of the question about which we have come together.

[3] I see that you do not listen to speakers equally. You pay attention to some but cannot even endure the voice of others. That you do this is not surprising, for in the past you usually rejected all speakers except those who gave advice that matched your own desires. [4] Someone could rightly fault you for this, since even though you know that many great homes have been ruined by flatterers and you hate those who practice this art (*technē*) in private matters, you do not feel the same way about them in public affairs, where, despite condemning those who welcome such men and enjoy their company, you your-

---

[4] Laistner also discusses an important papyrus witness that clarifies some passages where the manuscripts are less helpful (1921). I have mentioned those that seem valuable in the notes.

[5] Isocrates must combat the notion that his opening is a commonplace in Greek oratory. Demosthenes uses a very similar argument in *Against Timocrates* (24.4). Evidence suggests that rhetorical education in the fourth century included memorization of generic opening paragraphs that could then be easily adapted to a specific situation. The *Prooemia* found in the Demosthenic corpus are a good example.

selves clearly trust them more than the rest of the citizens. [5] Indeed, you have made speakers practice and study not what will help the state but how they might say what pleases you. And even now, most of them have rushed to speak such words, for it is clear to everyone that you will be more pleased by those who urge you to war than by those who recommend peace. [6] Those who urge war lead you to expect that we will regain the property we had in other cities and recover the power we had before, whereas those who counsel peace offer nothing of the sort; they say rather that we must live in peace and not desire more than justice allows but be content with what we have at present, [7] which is the most difficult thing of all for most people. We depend so much on our hopes and are so greedy for what seems advantageous that even those with the greatest wealth are not willing to be content with that, but in their desire for more, they always risk what they now have. We too ought to fear getting caught up in such foolish thinking. [8] For some seem to me to be excessively eager for war, as if they had gotten advice not from ordinary advisors but from the gods them- selves that we will set everything right and will easily conquer our enemies. Intelligent people should not deliberate about what they al- ready know—that is a waste of time—but should do what they have decided; and when they deliberate about something, they should not assume that they know (*eidenai*) what will happen, but they should think about such matters aware that they are relying on their best judg- ment (*doxa*) and that the future depends on chance (*tychē*).[6] [9] You are doing neither of these but are behaving with as much confusion as possible. You came into the Assembly on the pretext that it was nec- essary to choose the best of all that was recommended, but as if you already know what needs to be done, you are not willing to listen to

---

[6]Isocrates introduces one of his fundamental epistemological ideas here, ex- pressed more fully in *Antidosis* (15.271). Exact knowledge (*epistēmē*) is not possible, therefore humans must use their best judgment (*doxa*) based on experience and training to make decisions. In contrast, Plato (cf. *Gorgias* 454 and *Theaetetus* 187) believes that knowledge (*epistēmē*) is the goal of intellectual activity, and has a low opinion of *doxa* ("what appears to someone"), which in Plato comes nearer to the sense of "mere opinion." Thus, the word *doxa* has very different connotations for the two philosophers. See Rummel 1979; Perkins 1984; Hutchinson 1988; and T. Poulakos 2001.

anyone except to those who say what pleases you. [10] Indeed, if you really want to find out what is most advantageous for the city, you should pay attention to those who oppose your views more than those who favor them, for you know that some of those who come here can easily trick you by telling you what you want to hear (for what is spoken to please you clouds your ability to see what is best), but you would have no such experience from advisors who are not seeking to please you, [11] for there is no way they could persuade you unless they make the advantages clear. And besides this, how could anyone either judge well about the past or plan well about the future unless he sets out the arguments on both sides and then examines them both equally? [12] Now, I am amazed at the elders if they no longer remember and at the young men if they have not heard from anyone that we have never suffered any harm because of those who advise us to cling to peace while we have already encountered many great troubles through those who blithely chose war. We make no mention of this, but are ready—without doing anything to help ourselves out—to fit out warships, to collect war levies, to assist and fight for whomever we chance upon, as if we were putting some other city at risk. [13] The reason for this is that although you should care about public affairs as much as private ones, you do not treat them the same way. Whenever you deliberate about your private affairs, you look for advisors who are wiser than you are, but when you hold an assembly to talk about the city's affairs, you distrust and are jealous of those people and cultivate instead the worst of those who rise to speak. You think there is more goodwill toward the people among those who are drunk than among those who are sober,[7] among the foolish more than among the wise, and among those who distribute the city's property more than among those who benefit the city at their own expense. It is amazing that anyone expects the city to prosper using advisors like that. [14] I know that it is dangerous to oppose your views and that even though we live in a democracy, there is still no freedom of speech,

---

[7] This may refer to Cleophon appearing drunk at an Athenian assembly after the battle of Arginusae. When given the chance to abandon Decelea and make peace, he convinced them to reject the option. Athens was destroyed at Aegospotami the next year. Cf. Arist., *Ath. Pol.* 34.

except here in the Assembly for those who are foolish and do not care about you, or in the theater for the comic poets.[8] What is the most shocking is that you feel gratitude to them when they drag our faults out in front of the rest of Greece such as you never show to those who help you; instead, you are as hostile to those who rebuke or admonish you as you are to those who actively harm the city.

[15] Nevertheless, even in these conditions, I would not back away from what I have been thinking. For I came here not to gratify you or to solicit your vote but to make clear what I actually think, first about the Prytaneis' proposal[9] and then about the remaining issues facing the city. We will derive no gain from what we now decide about the peace unless we also deliberate correctly about the rest of our affairs. [16] I assert, therefore, that we should make peace not only with the Chians, Rhodians, Byzantines, and Coans[10] but with all people and that we must use not the treaty that certain parties have just written but the one we made with the Persian King and the Spartans,[11] which

---

[8] The writers of Greek comedy, especially Old Comedy of the late fifth century, were quite free to bring up controversial subjects such as the current war, philosophical opportunism, or sex; they were also free to abuse openly the leading personalities of the day such as Cleon or Socrates. There seemed to be few limits on what such playwrights could present on the stage. Aristophanes' *Acharnians* and *Clouds* are good examples.

[9] Yearly, each of the ten tribes provided fifty men for their Prytany—the Prytaneis are the 50 members of the Prytany—and these ten groups form the five hundred men of the council (*boulē*). Each Prytany was charged with administrating the affairs of the state for a tenth of the year, setting Assembly times, announcing agendas, and making proposals for discussion.

[10] These are the cities that revolted during the Social War and asked for independence. Chios, Rhodes, and Cos lie off the coast of Asia Minor; Byzantium is on the north side of the Propontis as it enters the Euxine Sea. The manuscripts do not have Coans in the list, but a papyrus fragment (Laistner 1927: 83) supports including this name here. Dionysius of Halicarnassus (*Isocrates* 16) also includes the Coans in this list. The Coans are a natural group to mention in this context, but the Cnidians (also mentioned by an important papyrus text) are not, because the latter were not part of the *socii*.

[11] Isocrates does not argue against the independence of the named cities, but he argues for going beyond that. He does not like the limited peace that is cur-

directed that the Greeks be autonomous and that garrisons in other peoples' cities be sent home and that each city control its own land. We will find no agreement more just or more advantageous for our city than this.

[17] If I leave off my address here, I know that I will seem to have cheapened the state, since Thebes controls Thespiae, Plataea, and other cities it took in violation of its oaths, while we, under no compulsion, give up the cities we have.[12] But if you pay attention and hear me through to the end, I think you will all decide that people reveal great stupidity and madness if they think injustice is an advantage and if they control other peoples' cities by force and do not recognize the disasters that will come from such conduct. [18] Through the course of this entire discourse I will try to teach you this, but let us talk first about the peace and consider what outcome we want in the present situation, for if we determine this clearly and intelligently, then with this starting point in mind, we will deliberate better about the remaining issues. [19] Now, would we be satisfied if we could live in our city securely and have our daily needs well provided, if we are united in spirit within our city and have a good reputation among the other Greeks? In my opinion, if we have all this, I think our city will be completely prosperous. Now, the war has deprived us of all those things I just mentioned. It has made us poorer, has forced us to endure many dangers, has ruined our reputation among the Greeks, and has burdened us with every possible hardship. [20] If we make peace, on the other hand, and behave as the common peace requires us to,[13] we will

---

rently proposed. He would prefer to return to the King's Peace (called the Peace of Antalcidas) of 387/6, in which the autonomy of individual states was emphasized (cf. Thompson 1983). But that peace also gave cities in Asia Minor back to the Persian King and gave Sparta strong control. Thus, Isocrates is probably not advocating all details of that prior peace, only the issue of autonomy. In *Panegyricus* (4.115n), Isocrates is more critical of the King's Peace. On Isocrates' use of history, see Koch 1914; Laistner 1927: 24–25; Baynes 1955; Welles 1966; Hamilton 1979; Nouhaud 1982; and Nickel 1991. On a different view of the peace, see *Archidamus* (6), where Isocrates speaks in the voice of a Spartan.

[12] See his discussion of this in *Archidamus* (6.27) and the whole speech about the Plataean situation called *Plataicus* (14).

[13] A "common peace" (*koinē eirēnē*) occurred on several occasions in the fourth century and pertained to all independent Greek states—not just between two

govern our city with great security, we will be freed from the war, dangers, and confusion that now govern our relations with one another, we will make progress toward prosperity every day since we will be relieved of paying war taxes, fitting out triremes, or the other duties connected with war, and we will be able without fear to farm, to sail the sea, and to undertake all those other tasks that are suspended now because of the war. [21] We will see the city take in twice the revenues it does now and be filled with merchants, foreigners, and metics who have deserted it for now.[14] Most importantly, all men will be our allies not by force but through persuasion, and they will not just accept us in secure times because of our power and then leave us when we have troubles but will behave as true allies and friends. [22] In addition, what we cannot get now by war and great expense, we will easily obtain through negotiations. For do not think that Cersobleptes will fight for the Chersonese or Philip for Amphipolis when they see that we do not desire anyone else's property.[15] As things are now, they have reason to fear our city as a neighbor of their empires, [23] for they see us not content with what we have but always reaching for more. If we change this approach, however, and seek a better reputation, they will not only withdraw from our land but they will offer us some of their own, since it will be in their best interest to cultivate a friendship with our city to keep their own kingdom safe. [24] In fact, we will be able to cut off such a large area of Thrace that we will not only have plenty for ourselves but we can offer an adequate living to those Greeks who

---

contesting cities—and usually involved the Great King of Persia as well (cf. Sealey 1976: 397). The first was the Peace of Antalcidas, also known as the King's Peace, of 387/6; the last was the Peace of the League of Corinth after Philip's victory at the battle of Chaeronea in 338. Cf. Ryder 1965 and Jehne 1993.

[14] Merchants (*emporoi*) and foreigners (*xenoi*) are general terms. All foreigners had to pay taxes (*xenika telē*). Metics (*metoikoi*) were a special subclass of foreigners (*xenoi*) who set up permanent residence at Athens to run businesses and paid a metic tax (*metoikion*).

[15] Cersobleptes was in control of the Thracian Chersonese in 355. For more information, see Dem. 23 and Papillon 1998b. Philip's power in Macedon was growing at this time, and he was becoming a threat. He took Amphipolis in 357 without interference from Athens because of a bargain that he would trade it to Athens for Pydna. He never carried through, and in later years, Amphipolis became a source of great tension between Athens and Philip.

are destitute and homeless because of their poverty. If Athenodorus and Callistratus,[16] the former a private citizen, the latter an exile, were able to establish cities there, then surely we should be able to take many such places if we wish. Those who claim to be leaders of the Greeks should take leadership in activities like this much more than in war and in arranging mercenary armies, which we currently are fond of doing.

[25][17] This is enough about the advantages that negotiation promises, though someone might perhaps add much to this list. But I think we should not leave the Assembly having only voted on the peace; we should also decide how we will manage the peace. Let us not do what we usually do and fall back into the same confusion after a short time; let us not find just a delay but a real end to our present troubles. [26] None of this can happen until you are persuaded that advantage and profit will come more from peace than from meddling in others' affairs (*polypragmosynē*),[18] more from justice than from injustice, and more from tending one's own property than from a desire for others' property. None of the speakers has ever dared to say this to you, but I will devote most of my speech to these very issues, for I see that prosperity lies in them but not in what we are doing now. [27] Someone who tries to address you on subjects that are out of the ordinary and wants to change your view must touch on many different matters and make his argument rather lengthy, recalling certain things, criticizing others, commending others, and giving advice on still others, for even with all this, it is only with difficulty that someone might lead you to a better understanding.

[28] Here is the reason: it seems to me that all people desire their own advantage and want to have more than others, but they do not know (*eidenai*) what to do to achieve these goals, and they differ in

---

[16]Athenodorus was a private general and leader of mercenary troops who settled a colony in Thrace (cf. Dem. 23.170–174). Callistratus was important as an orator and politician in the Second Athenian League up to the battle of Leuctra (Xen., *Hellenica* 6.3); later he was exiled and settled in Thrace.

[17]Isocrates quotes this passage (25–56) as well as sections 132–145 in his speech *Antidosis* (15.66) as an example of encouraging Athens to behave justly.

[18]On Athenian distaste for "meddling" (*polypragmosynē*), see Carter 1986.

their judgment (*doxa*) about this.[19] Some have opinions that are reasonable and can figure out what they need, while others have opinions that completely miss their true advantage. [29] This is what has happened to the city,[20] for we think that if we sail the sea with many triremes and compel cities to pay contributions and send delegates here, we will get what we need; but we deceive ourselves completely. Nothing that we hoped for has come about; instead, we have hostility, wars, and huge expenses. And this is no surprise. [30] As a result of our meddling (*polypragmosynē*), we found ourselves in the gravest dangers before, whereas, by showing our city to be just, offering aid to those who were wronged, and not being greedy for others' property, we became the leader of the Greeks with their consent.[21] But now we scorn that kind of behavior and have for some time, both illogically and quite rashly. [31] Some have become so foolish that although they consider injustice to be reprehensible, they think it is profitable and useful for daily life; similarly, they consider justice to be praiseworthy but not profitable, more beneficial to others than to the just themselves. [32] They do not know that nothing contributes as strongly to material gain, to reputation, to whatever one must do, or to overall prosperity than excellence (*aretē*) and its parts.[22] Through the goods that we have in our soul we gain the other advantages that we find we need. Thus, those who neglect their minds do not realize that they are disregarding their ability both to think better and to act more nobly than others. [33] I am amazed if anyone thinks that those who cultivate piety and justice persist and persevere in them from a hope that they will have less than the wicked rather than with the thought that both among the gods and humans they will gain more than others. I am persuaded that these alone gain the advantage that they need, while

---

[19] On the tension between knowledge and opinion/judgment, see above, 8n.

[20] Isocrates moves from personal motives to state actions. This is akin to what Socrates does in Plato's *Republic,* where the question of individual justice is worked out on the analogy of the state.

[21] Isocrates probably refers both to the beginning of the Delian League in 478 and to the Second Athenian League in 378.

[22] See section 63, where he specifies the parts of *aretē* as piety (*eusebeia*), moderation (*sōphrosynē*), and justice (*dikaiosynē*).

others gain only what is worse, [34] for I see that those who prefer injustice and who think that taking others' property is the greatest good suffer a fate similar to animals trapped with bait: at first they enjoy what they have taken, but a little later they find themselves in the greatest trouble. Those who live piously and justly, however, lead a safe life in the present and have sweeter hopes for the future. [35] If this does not happen in all cases, at least in most cases, things turn out like this. Since we cannot always see clearly what will be to our advantage, those who are wise should make clear that they are choosing what is most often helpful. The most illogical behavior of all is when people consider justice a more noble pursuit and more loved by the gods than injustice but think that if they practice it, they will live a worse life than those who prefer wickedness.

[36] I wish it were as easy to persuade my audience to cultivate excellence (*aretē*), as it is fitting to praise it,[23] but I am afraid that I have spoken in vain on this subject. We have been corrupted for a long time now by men who can do nothing but lie to us and who think so little of the people that whenever they want to wage war against someone, they take bribes and then have the audacity to say that we must emulate our ancestors. We should not allow ourselves to be mocked or allow people to sail the sea if they refuse to pay us their contribution. [37] I would gladly learn from them which ancestors they want us to emulate, those of the time of the Persian Wars or those who lived here before the Decelean War.[24] If the latter, then they recommend nothing more than risking a return to slavery. [38] But if they refer to those who defeated the barbarian at Marathon and those earlier than this, how are they not the most shameless men, when they praise the statesmen of that time but persuade us to do just the opposite and to commit such huge mistakes that I am at a loss whether I should tell the truth, as I have elsewhere, or whether I should just keep silent, in fear

---

[23] There is a manuscript difficulty in this sentence. I follow the suggestion of Laistner 1921: 78–80.

[24] Athenians often looked back on the Persian Wars (490–479) with pride in the greatness of the citizens. The Decelean War refers to the last years of the Peloponnesian War, when Sparta controlled an outpost at Decelea in Attica in 413. From this point until the end of the war in 404, Athens' condition deteriorated; thus, a reference to this period is a reference to the defeat of Athens.

of incurring your hatred? It seems to me better to talk about these issues, but I also see that you are more hostile to those who criticize you than to those who are actually responsible for your troubles. [39] Yet I would be ashamed if I seemed to be more concerned about my own reputation than the security of the state.[25] Thus, it is my task and that of all others who care about the city to choose words that are not necessarily the most pleasant but those that are the most helpful. As for you, first you should know that for bodily illnesses many and varied remedies have been discovered by doctors, but for minds that are ignorant and full of evil desires, there is no other drug than discourse, a thing that dares to rebuke errors. [40] Furthermore, it is ridiculous that we will endure the cauteries and incisions of the doctors[26] so that we might be rid of greater pains, but we reject discourses before we know clearly if they have the power to help their audience.

[41] I have said these things at the beginning because I will not hold back during the rest of this discourse but plan to make my arguments to you with complete openness. For if someone came here from somewhere else who had not yet been corrupted by us and suddenly faced what was happening, would he not think we were raving mad, seeing that we pride ourselves on the deeds of our ancestors and think it right to praise the city for what they did in the past, but then we do nothing like what they did, but quite the opposite? [42] Our ancestors spent their lives fighting the barbarians for the sake of Greece, while we brought those who made their living in Asia over here and led them against Greeks.[27] Our ancestors, by freeing and helping Greek cities, were thought worthy of leadership, while we enslave them and do quite the opposite of our ancestors. Then we are upset if we do not get the same honors they had. [43] We fall so short of those who lived back then in our deeds and in our spirit that while they dared to leave

---

[25] An odd variation of this argument appears in *Panathenaicus* (12.86), where he says that he is more concerned about his literary topic than himself.

[26] Classical Greek medicine can best be seen in the corpus of works attributed to Hippocrates, which included treatises dealing with theoretical ideas about how the body worked, with observation of symptoms, and with therapeutic issues such as diet, drugs, and surgery.

[27] The Greek general Chares led Persian mercenaries into Greece as a result of the King's Peace of 387/6.

their own land for the sake of freedom for others and defeated the barbarians in battles on land and at sea,[28] we are not willing to risk anything even for our own advantage. [44] We want to rule over everyone, but we are not willing to send an army; we choose a war against—I might almost say—all men but do not equip ourselves for this, choosing rather men who are outlaws and deserters and have come from all other sorts of villainy, who will follow other leaders against us whenever they are offered more money. [45] Nonetheless, we love them so much that although we are not willing to take responsibility for our children if they do something wrong, we are not upset at the piracy, violence, and lawlessness of the mercenaries, even when the blame will come to us, but we even rejoice when we hear that they have committed some such crime. [46] Indeed, we have become so foolish that we are deprived of our daily needs, and yet we try to maintain mercenary troops; we maltreat each of our own allies separately and demand money from them so that we can pay the salaries of men who are the common enemies of everyone. [47] We are so much worse than our ancestors, not just those who were famous but even those who were hated, that if they voted to go to war against someone, even if their treasury on the Acropolis was full of gold and silver, they would still think they should risk their own lives for what they voted, whereas we employ mercenary soldiers just like the Great King, even though we are so poor and are ourselves so numerous. [48] Back then, if they were equipping triremes, they would put foreigners and slaves on the ships but send citizens as hoplites;[29] today, we use mercenaries as the hoplites and force our own citizens to row the ships, so that when they put to shore in the land of the enemy, those who claim to be leaders of the Greeks disembark carrying their cushions, while the others, whose character I described a little bit earlier, face the danger as hoplites.[30]

[49] If someone saw our domestic affairs being managed well, he

---

[28] References to the Athenians abandoning the city to the Persians just before the battles of Salamis and Plataea in 480–79. Cf. 5.147n.

[29] Hoplites are the heavily armed infantry soldiers.

[30] Isocrates makes it sound as if the citizens take their rowing cushions ashore to sit and watch the battle, leaving the fighting to the mercenaries. On the makeup of the rowers, see Morrison and Coates 1986: chap. 7 and Laistner 1927: 93.

might be encouraged about the rest; but as it is, would he not be particularly upset about this? Since we claim to be born of the land (*autochthones*)³¹ and to have founded our city before anyone else, we should be an example to others of a well-run government, but we run our own city worse and more chaotically than those who have just founded their cities. [50] We are haughty and arrogant about our superior birth, but we give out this noble birthright to whoever wants it more easily than the Triballoi or the Leucanians share their lowly lineage.³² We pass a great many laws, but we think so little of them—hearing one example you can judge the rest—that when death is the fixed punishment for anyone convicted of bribery, those who do this most blatantly we elect to be generals, and the one who can corrupt the most citizens we put in charge of the most important tasks. [51] We are no less serious about our government than about the security of our state, for we know that although democracy will flourish and endure in times of peace and security, it has already been destroyed twice now during war; and in spite of this, we are hostile to those who pursue peace as if they were oligarchs, but we treat those who instigate war as loyal citizens who care about democracy. [52] Although we are the most experienced at speech and action, we are behaving so illogically that we do not have the same opinion about the same situation even on the same day.³³ Rather, we condemn something before we get to the Assembly, and then once we get there, we vote for it; then a little later, after we leave the Assembly, we complain about the decisions we made there. We claim to be the wisest of the Greeks, but then we employ advisors whom no one could fail to treat with contempt; and we put these same men in charge of all our public affairs, when no one would entrust any of his own private affairs to them! [53] The most shocking of all is this: those whom we agree are the worst of the citi-

---

³¹ On autochthony, see 4.24n.

³² The Triballoi from Thrace were known for their rudeness and their violence toward those around them, mentioned by Isocrates in *Panathenaicus* (12.227). In Aristophanes' *Birds* (1529–1693), there is a Triballian god who is portrayed as barbaric in speech and dress. The Leucanians were from southern Italy and known for their violence.

³³ The repetition of "the same" in the Greek (*tōn autōn, tēs autēs, ta auta*) is emphatic.

zens we then think are the most trustworthy guardians of the government. We judge metics by the characters of sponsors (*prostatēs*) they choose, but we do not think that we will have the same reputation as those who lead us (*prostatēs*) in the Assembly.³⁴ [54] We also differ greatly from our ancestors in that they chose the same men as leaders of the city as they elected generals, for they realized that the one best able to advise them from the speaker's platform would also be the one who could make the best plans when by himself. We, however, do the exact opposite. [55] The men we take as advisors about the most important matters we do not think are intelligent enough to be voted generals; but those whom no one would consult on matters of private or public concern we send out with full powers, thinking that somehow they will be wiser out there and will more easily decide about the affairs of Greece than they do about issues proposed here in the Assembly. [56] Now, I am not saying this about everyone but about those who are to blame. What remains of the day would give out if I tried to examine all the mistakes that have been made in managing our affairs.

[57] Perhaps one of those who are to blame might get upset and ask, "How is it that we are secure and have power second to none, if our policies are so bad?" I would respond that our rivals are no wiser than we. [58] For example, after the battle in which the Thebans defeated the Spartans,³⁵ if they had remained at peace after freeing the Peloponnese and making the other Greeks independent, while we had committed the errors we actually did, then this man would not be able to ask such a question, and we would know how much better moderation (*to sōphronein*) is than meddlesomeness (*polypragmosynē*).³⁶ [59] The situation has come to this, that the Thebans save us, and then

³⁴ Isocrates puns on the word *prostatēs*, which is used as the technical term for both the official sponsor of a metic (who ensures the rights that the resident alien has in Athens) and the leader of the Assembly.

³⁵ In 371 at the battle of Leuctra, Thebes defeated Sparta and destroyed the claim to leadership Sparta had made since the end of the Peloponnesian War in 404. Thebes then claimed hegemony, but they maintained it only until 362, when they were defeated at the battle of Mantinea. Isocrates clearly thinks that Thebes could have maintained their leadership position longer if they had planned better.

³⁶ Cf. Davidson 1990.

we save them; they make allies for us, and we likewise make allies for them. Thus, if we were sensible, we would just provide money for each other's assemblies, for whoever gathers in assembly most often makes things better for its enemies. [60] Those who can reason even a little bit should not pin their hopes for security on the errors of their enemies but on their own actions and thoughts, for any good that comes to us through their ignorance might cease and even be reversed, but the good that comes through our own efforts would be stronger and more enduring for us.

[61] Therefore, it is not hard to refute those who rashly attack us. If someone more reasonable should stand up and grant that I am telling the truth and that my censure of what has happened is accurate, and would add that it is fair for well-meaning advisors not only to condemn what has been done [62] but also to advise us on what to avoid doing and what to try to do so that we will stop thinking in this way and making these sort of mistakes, then his argument would leave me at a loss not for an answer that was true and helpful but for an answer that would please you. Nonetheless, since I have risen to speak openly, I must not hesitate to state my opinion on this.

[63] I spoke a short time ago about the qualities people must have if they are going to flourish: piety, moderation, justice, and the rest of virtue.[37] How we are educated to acquire such qualities most quickly, however, I will speak about truthfully, though my words will perhaps seem frightening to you when you hear them and very different from the opinions of others. [64] I think that we will manage our city better, we will ourselves be better people, and we will prosper in all our affairs if we stop desiring a naval empire, for this is what now throws us into confusion, destroys that form of democracy under which our ancestors were the most prosperous of all Greeks, and is the cause of nearly all the troubles that we have ourselves and inflict on others. [65] I know that it is difficult for someone to seem to say anything tolerable when he condemns an empire that is desired by everyone and was acquired in great battles; nevertheless, since you have thus far put up with the rest of my words, which have been true but combative, I ask you to allow this too. [66] Do not judge that I am so mad that I

---

[37] See above, 31–35, where he focuses only on piety and justice.

would prefer to speak on topics so contrary to your views, if I did not have something true to say about them. I think I can now make it clear to everyone that the empire we desire is neither just nor possible nor in our own interest.[38]

[67] I can show you that the empire is not just, since I have learned this from you yourselves. When the Spartans had the power, how many speeches did we deliver condemning their empire and explaining how it is just for the Greeks to be independent? [68] What famous cities did we not invite into an alliance set up for this purpose?[39] How many delegations did we send to the Great King, explaining to him that it was not just or expedient for one city to control the Greeks?[40] We did not stop making war or risking other dangers on land and sea until the Spartans were willing to make a treaty granting independence. [69] We came to realize during those times that it is not just for the stronger to rule over the weaker, and now we acknowledge this in our own government too. I think I can quickly also show that we could not establish this empire again, for how could we acquire an empire in our current state of poverty when we could not preserve it even with thousands of talents, especially when our current way of life is the same as when we lost it and not when we acquired it?

[70] Furthermore, I think you will be able to understand most quickly from the following that it is not to the city's advantage to accept an empire even if it is given to us. But I prefer to digress a little first, for I fear that some will think that I have decided to accuse the city since I have leveled many criticisms. [71] If I were trying to explain this to anyone else, I could reasonably be open to this criticism. But I am addressing you not from any desire to slander you in the eyes

---

[38] Isocrates uses the topics of the three species of discourse and will treat each in the sections that follow: judicial discourse (67–68) treats what is just, epideictic discourse (69) treats what is possible (cf. J. Poulakos 1995), and deliberative discourse (70) treats what is advantageous. Treating advantage last of the three allows Isocrates to continue on with the topic, since interest is the focus of much of the rest of the speech.

[39] In 395 Thebes and Athens formed an alliance; they were joined later by Corinth and Argos.

[40] Persian money and ships assisted in weakening Spartan control at the battle of Cnidus in 394.

of others but because I want to stop you from carrying out such deeds and to get the city and the rest of the Greeks to make the kind of secure peace that is the subject of this discourse. [72] Of necessity, those who advise the state and those who attack it use similar words, even though their intentions are diametrically opposed. Thus, it is not always right for you to take the same attitude toward those who say the same things; you should hate those whose criticism is harmful, for they are hostile to the city, but you should praise those who give you helpful advice and think them the best citizens; [73] and among this latter group, you should praise especially that one who can most clearly show the wickedness of your actions and the troubles that result from them. For this man will most quickly make you hate what should be hated and desire better things. And so that is what I have to say to you about the harshness of the words I have spoken and what I am about to say.

I'll start again now from where I left off,[41] [74] for I was saying you would understand best that it is not to your advantage to acquire a naval empire if you examine the condition of the city before obtaining that power and its condition after you acquired it. If you think about the two situations in comparison with one another, you will understand how many evils the empire has caused our city. [75] Now, our government in the past was better and stronger than the one we established later on, in the same way that Aristides, Themistocles, and Miltiades were better men than Thrasybulus, Cleophon, and other current demagogues.[42] You will find that in the earlier period, the

---

[41] In section 70.

[42] Aristides "the just" was a prominent Athenian in the years surrounding the Persian Wars. He fought during the wars, was instrumental in the organization of the Delian League after the war and was viewed as an icon of aristocratic nobility. Themistocles was the famous general at Artemesium and Salamis in the Persian Wars and was the pro-democratic foil to Aristides. Miltiades was the Athenian leader during the Ionian Revolt before the Persian Wars and then led the Athenian forces at Marathon in 490. These three stand as examples of the excellence of the older generation, in contrast to the politicians of the late fifth and early fourth centuries. Thrasybulus led democratic forces during the reign of the Thirty in 411 and helped restore democracy after they were toppled. He then led the Athenian attempts to reassert their control in the early fourth century, for which

people ran the city without sloth, poverty, or empty hopes [76] but
were able to win battles over all those who invaded their land, were
awarded prizes for bravery during the dangers that threatened Greece,
and were so trusted that most of the cities willingly handed themselves
over to their leadership. [77] In spite of these conditions, this very
power of ours has brought us from a government esteemed by all to
such a lack of restraint that no one would praise it now. Instead of defeating those who march against us, we have educated our citizens so
poorly that they do not dare to go out and fight the enemy in front of
our walls.[43] [78] Instead of the goodwill they had from their allies and
their fame among the other Greeks, our city now endures such hatred
that it came close to being enslaved, if we had not found the Spartans
more favorable to us than our own former allies were, even though
they had fought against us from the beginning.[44] [79] And we could
not fairly fault those allies for being harsh toward us now, for they did
not begin hostilities but only defended themselves after they had suffered many terrible things and thus came to have their current opinion of us. And, in fact, who would have put up with the arrogance of
our fathers?[45] They brought together from all Greece men who were

---

Isocrates faults him here. Cleophon curried the favor of the people at the end of
the fifth century and stood as an example, with Cleon before him, of the corrupt
leadership existing in Athens after the death of Pericles.

[43] A reference to Pericles' policy in the Peloponnesian War of keeping the population of Attica within the walls of Athens while the Peloponnesians ravaged the
countryside (cf. Thuc. 1.139–145, 2.59–65). But, to quote Laistner (1927: 101):
"Isocrates is hardly stating the case fairly. It was Pericles' policy at the beginning
of the Peloponnesian war to restrain his countrymen from going out to meet the
Lacedaemonian army when it invaded Attica. His object was to keep strictly on
the defensive on land."

[44] After Athens' defeat in the Peloponnesian War, Sparta was considerably more
lenient toward the city than it might have been, and more so than many thought
it would be (cf. Xen., *Hellenica* 2.2; Sealey 1976: 375–379). Instead of the destruction of the city, execution of all males, and enslavement of females and children, the Spartans required only that the Athenians destroy their own defensive
walls, give up most of their ships, and accept a Spartan-controlled governing body
in the city.

[45] That is, the more recent generation of demagogues, not the more distant
generation of noble Athenians.

the laziest and the worst in every way, and filling their triremes with these men, they made themselves hateful to the Greeks. They forced the best men from the other cities into exile and distributed their property to the worst of the Greeks. [80] If I dared to recount in detail what happened then, I might perhaps lead you to make better plans about our current situation, but I would myself be criticized, for your habit is to despise not those who are responsible for our errors but those who accuse them. [81] Since you have this tendency, then, I fear that by trying to bring you some benefit, I will get a poor reward. Still, I will not back off at all from what I had in mind, but I will leave out the most bitter points and those that might be especially painful for you, and I will recall only those points from which you will recognize the foolishness of the city's leaders at that time.

[82] They figured out what actions incur the most anger among people so carefully that they voted to divide the money that remained from the war tribute into talents and bring it into the orchestra during the festival of Dionysus when the theater was packed.[46] And when they did this, they also brought in the children of those who had died in the war, showing the allies the value of their own property that was brought in by workers (*misthōtoi*)[47] and showing the rest of the Greeks the number of orphans and the misfortunes caused by this desire for excess profit. [83] By doing this, they boasted of the city's prosperity, and many foolish people considered this a blessing, but they gave no thought to what would happen because of this. They admired and coveted only the wealth that came to the city unjustly and that would soon destroy what we had acquired justly. [84] For they took so little care for their own property and were so greedy for that of oth-

---

[46] The theater of Dionysus, one of the main gathering places for the people and the most venerated theater on the mainland, was on the south slope of the Athenian Acropolis. The festival of the Greater Dionysia was held in Athens during late winter, probably March, and drew spectators from all over the Greek world. It was thus a good place to make a dramatic statement.

[47] Norlin (1929: 58) and Laistner (1927: 103) point out the oddity of this phrase. It clearly says "that was brought in by workers," but the word for workers can also refer to mercenaries. Isocrates seems to imply that the money being carried into the theater by workers was also the money that was brought to Athens through mercenary actions such as are described in section 79.

ers that when the Spartans had invaded our land and had already set up an outpost at Decelea, they fitted out triremes for Sicily and felt no qualms about watching their fatherland being cut off and pillaged while they sent an army against people who had never done us wrong.[48] [85] They had become so foolish that they expected to take control of Italy, Sicily, and Carthage,[49] even though they did not have control of their possessions near the city.[50] In fact, they were so much more foolish than anyone else that though others are restrained by their misfortunes and learn from them, those men did not learn anything from theirs. [86] Indeed, the misfortunes they suffered during this empire were more numerous and more severe than those the city had experienced in its entire existence. Two hundred triremes sailing for Egypt were destroyed along with their crews; 150 near Cyprus; in the Decelean War[51] they lost 10,000 hoplites, both their own and those of the allies; in Sicily they lost 40,000 men and 240 triremes; and finally, 200 in the Hellespont.[52] [87] And who could count the

---

[48] The Sicilian Expedition (415) is described by Thucydides (Books 6–7). Isocrates may be a bit loose with his chronology, since the so-called Decelean War, when Spartans had the outpost at Decelea in Attica, began in 413 and went to the end of the war in 404 (cf. above, 37n). It is possible, as Laistner (1927: 103) points out, that Isocrates does not refer to the original expedition to Sicily in 415 but to a later force sent when Decelea was being fortified (Thuc. 7.20). See above, 16n, on Isocrates and history.

[49] Thucydides (6.15, 6.90) says that Alcibiades wanted to take control of these three areas.

[50] Attic territory was being harassed from as close as the post in Decelea, 14 miles from Athens (cf. above 37n).

[51] Laistner (1921: 81–82) suggests the reading "in the Decelean War." Though it is in none of the manuscripts, it appears in an important papyrus and is surely correct. Cf. Raubitschek 1941.

[52] Laistner (1921: 81) points out that this list is in chronological order. The Athenians had sent two hundred ships to Cyprus, then sent sixty of those down to Egypt to aid Inaros of Libya in 460 (Thuc. 1.104–110). After beginning with a victory and control of Egypt, the Athenian fleet was destroyed in 454. The remaining ships were destroyed at Cyprus (Thuc. 1.112). The Decelean War was a difficult time, emphasized here by the disastrous Sicilian expedition. Though the Sicilian expedition predates the opening of the Decelean War (415 vs. 413), Isocrates has conflated the two just before this (84) and does so again here; this does not negate Laistner's point about chronology (cf. 1927: 103 and above, 84n). The

ships lost in groups of 5 or 10 or more and the men who died, 1,000 here and 2,000 there? One of the recurring events was to have public funerals each year where many neighbors and other Greeks came not so much to share in our grief for the dead as to gloat over our catastrophes.[53] [88] In the end, they did not even notice that they were filling the public cemeteries with the bodies of our citizens and the phratries and deme registers with people who had no connection to the city.[54] One could understand the extent of these losses especially since we will find that the families of the most illustrious citizens and the greatest households, who managed to escape the tyrannical regimes and the Persian Wars, were all destroyed in this time of empire that we coveted. [89] And if someone wanted to determine the condition of the rest of us, taking this as an example, we might say that we have changed almost completely. Still, we must not think a city is prospering if it adds to its citizen roles randomly from all other people, but only if it preserves the stock of those who originally inhabited it more than others. And we should also not envy those who rule tyrannies or who have acquired a larger regime than is just, but rather those who are worthy of the greatest honor and position while content with what has been given them by the people. [90] No man or city could have a life more excellent or secure or valuable than this. Those who lived during the Persian War had such a life and thus did not live like pirates; sometimes they had more than they needed, and at other times they were faced with hunger or siege or other severe troubles, but they never had too little or too much for their daily needs, and they were honored for the justice of their government and their own

---

Athenians suffered a great defeat at the battle of Aegospotami in the Hellespont in 405 (Xen., *Hellenica* 2.1).

[53] Laistner (1921: 82–83) makes the point that the word for "gloat over" is preferable to "sympathize with," which is found in the best manuscripts (as well as both the Budé and Loeb editions).

[54] The region of Attica was broken into demes or counties, and every citizen was connected to a deme, originally based on geography. Once a family was connected to a deme, that connection became hereditary, regardless of where the citizen lived. Citizens were also enrolled in the phratries, groups organized by hereditary family connections and linked with legendary ancestors. Toward the end of the Peloponnesian War, the record of citizens in these groups became chaotic, and many noncitizens came onto the roles.

virtue. Thus, the life they led was more pleasant than that of other Greeks. [91] Those who came later paid no attention to this life and craved not to rule but to be tyrants. These may involve the same amount of power but are far different from each other; for it is the task of those who rule to care for those who are ruled and make them more prosperous, while it is the character of tyrants to give themselves pleasure through the labor and troubles of others. But those who set their hands upon tyrannical acts must also experience the troubles of a tyrant and suffer the same sort of evil as they inflict on others. [92] This happened to our city, for instead of stationing their forces on the acropolis of other cities, they saw their enemies in control of their own acropolis; instead of taking children as hostages, dragging them from their fathers and mothers, many citizens were forced to raise and educate their own children during the siege in worse fashion than they deserved; instead of farming the land of others, for many years they could not even see their own.[55] [93] Thus, if someone were to ask us if we would accept being rulers for that length of time, only to see the city suffer what it did, who would agree, unless he were completely out of his mind and thought nothing of temples, parents, children, or anything else except the extent of his own life? You must admire not the views of such people but rather the attitude of those who think ahead, strive for honor on behalf of the city's reputation no less than their own, and choose a moderate life with justice over great wealth with injustice. [94] Our ancestors displayed just those qualities, handed down to their descendants a city that was very prosperous, and thereby left behind an imperishable memorial of their own valor. We can easily learn two things from this: that our land is able to nourish better

---

[55] The Spartans took control of the Athenian Acropolis, placing a garrison there after Athens' surrender in 404. The reference to children is more general but describes the difficulties of the Athenians during the Peloponnesian War. The comparison pales, however: dragging children from their parents is a more painful experience than difficulty raising the children who are able to stay with their parents. The people of Attica were called within the walls of Athens by Pericles and had to endure seeing the Attic countryside ravaged by Spartan forces each spring and summer. This contrasts with clerouchies, where a city sent citizens to farm the land of captured territory.

men than other lands and that what we call our empire was in fact a disaster and by its very nature made all those who were part of it worse. [95] The greatest evidence of the danger of empire is that it destroyed not only us but the Spartan state too. Thus, those who always used to praise the valor of Sparta cannot make the claim that we mishandled our affairs because we were a democracy, whereas if Sparta had had that power, they would have made themselves and everyone else happy. Indeed, the empire showed its true nature much more quickly with the Spartans, for it caused their government in a short time to stagger and almost collapse, although no one had seen it bothered by dangers or troubles for seven hundred years. [96] Instead of their established customs, it filled the citizens with injustice, laziness, lawlessness, and greed, and the city's government with arrogance toward their allies, desire for the possessions of others, and disregard for their oaths and treaties. They were so much worse than us in their crimes against the Greeks that in addition to their earlier crimes, they fostered murder and faction in other cities, giving their citizens an eternal hatred toward one another. [97] They were so infatuated with war and danger that though up until that time they had guarded against such things better than anyone else, they did not spare even their allies or benefactors; for when the Great King provided more than five thousand talents for the war against us, and the Chians were the most eager of all the allies to join their endeavor with their fleet, [98] and the Thebans added their very large land force, they no sooner had established their rule than they immediately plotted against the Thebans, sent Clearchus with an army against the King, and forced Chios' leading citizens into exile as well as taking the Chian triremes, dragging them from the dockyards, and sailing back home.[56] [99] This crime was not enough for them. About this same time, they ravaged the coast of Asia, attacked the islands, toppled the governments in Italy and Sicily and established tyrannies there, and harassed the Pelo-

---

[56]Xenophon and Diodorus Siculus provide additional information on these events. Spartans took hold of the Theban Cadmea in 382 (Xen., *Hellenica* 5.2.25–36); they sent Clearchus to help Cyrus against the King in 404 (Isoc. 4.145–149, 5.90, 12.104; especially Xen., *Anabasis*); they exiled Chian democrats when establishing the oligarchy in 404 (Diodorus Siculus 13.65, 70).

ponnese, filling it with factions and wars. What city did they not campaign against? Whom did they not wrong? [100] Did they not take part of the territory of Elis, destroy Corinth's land, displace the Mantineans, besiege the Phliasians, invade the Argolid, and continue treating everyone else badly, thereby bringing about their own defeat at Leuctra? Some say that Leuctra was the cause of all their troubles, but they are wrong. They are not hated by their allies because of this; rather, they lost that battle and brought danger to their land because of their arrogance in earlier times. [101] We should locate the causes of this not in their later troubles but in their first mistakes that led them to this final state. Thus, someone would be quite accurate if he said that the beginning (*archē*) of their troubles came when they acquired their naval empire (*archē*), for they then had a power unlike what they had before.[57] [102] Through their hegemony on land and the discipline and endurance they learned from it, they easily gained control of power at sea too, but through the lack of restraint they acquired from this naval empire, they quickly lost even their former hegemony. For they were no longer observing the laws that were handed down from their ancestors, nor were they following former ways; [103] instead, assuming they could do whatever they wanted, they fell into great turmoil. They did not understand how hard it is to use the free rein that everyone wishes for, and how deranged it makes those who covet it, for it has a nature much like a prostitute, who makes people lust for her but destroys those who use her. [104] And it clearly has been shown to have this power, for anyone could see that those who acquire a completely free hand, beginning with the Spartans and ourselves, have fallen into the greatest troubles. These cities previously had the most sensible governments and the best reputations, but when they acquired this power and took over an empire, they were no different from each other but as is normal for those who are ravaged by the same desires and the same disease, they undertook the same tasks, made almost the same mistakes, and finally fell into similar troubles. [105] We were hated by our allies and were rescued from the threat of slavery by

---

[57] Isocrates also puns on the word *archē*, meaning "beginning" and "empire," at 4.119 and 5.61.

the Spartans,[58] and they fled to us when everyone else wanted to destroy them and were rescued through our efforts. So how can you praise this empire when it has such wretched results? Or how can you not loath and reject something that induces both cities to commit and compels them to suffer so many terrible wrongs?

[106] It is no wonder that up to now, no one noticed how empire causes so many troubles for those who have it and that we and the Spartans fought over it; you will find that most people make mistakes in choosing a course of action, that they have more desire for evil than good, and that their plans tend to help their enemies more than themselves. [107] This is clear in the most important examples, for when has it not turned out like this? Did we not choose to do things that made Sparta the rulers of the Greeks, and did they not as rulers manage things so badly that a few years later we rose back to the top and took control of their security? [108] Did not the meddlesomeness of Athens' supporters make cities go over to Sparta, and the arrogance of Sparta's supporters compel those same cities to go back to Athens? Was it not the wickedness of the demagogues that caused our people to desire the oligarchy of the Four Hundred,[59] and the madness of the Thirty caused everyone to become even more enamored with democracy than those who occupied Phyle?[60] [109] But even in lesser situations and in daily life, one could show that most people enjoy those foods and habits that harm both body and soul but consider the things that benefit both of these too much work and too difficult, and those

---

[58] See above, 78n.

[59] In 411 Alcibiades and others persuaded the Athenians to vote for a panel of four hundred leaders to restructure the government (Thuc. 8.67–71, 91–98). It lasted less than a year. Isocrates describes this period in his forensic speech *On the Team of Horses* (16.4–5); the speech defends Alcibiades' son, also named Alcibiades, and presents a very positive picture of the father.

[60] Oligarchy returned to Athens in 404 after its defeat, when Sparta set up a council of thirty to oversee the city, later known as the Thirty. This oligarchy, too, lasted less than a year. The reference to Phyle, northwest of Athens in Attica, refers to the exiled democrats during the reign of the Thirty who fled to Phyle and from there worked for the restoration of the democracy. Led by Thrasybulus, they eventually took Piraeus and brought about the collapse of the Thirty.

who keep good habits seem slavish to them. [110] Therefore, when some clearly always make the worst choices in daily affairs where they have more immediate concern, why should it be surprising if they are ignorant about the nature of a naval empire and fight with each other over something to which they have never given much thought?

[111] Look also at how many people covet monarchies[61] established in some cities and are ready to endure anything to get them. What wretched and difficult troubles do they not endure? As soon as people gain this power, are they not immediately beset by all sorts of troubles? [112] They are forced to make war against all their citizens, to hate those who have done them no wrong, to distrust their own friends and associates, to hand over their personal security to hirelings whom they have never seen, to fear those who guard them no less than those who plot against them, and to be so suspicious of everyone that they do not even get any joy from being close with their families. [113] This is only reasonable, since they are aware that some of those who were tyrants before them have been overthrown by their parents, others by their children, others by their brothers, still others by their wives, and their family has then disappeared from the world. But nonetheless they willingly throw themselves into such a multitude of troubles. When the best men with the greatest reputations lust for such evils, why should it surprise us that other people desire other things like these? [114] I am not unaware that you may accept my point about tyrannies but are irritated at hearing what I say about empire. Your condition is the most shameful and lazy of all, for what you see in others, you ignore in yourselves. Indeed, not the least indication of those who are prudent is if they show that they recognize the same course of action in all similar circumstances. [115] None of this ever concerned you, but you considered tyrannies both difficult and harmful not only for others but even for those who hold them, while you thought that a naval empire was the greatest good, although it is no different from monarchies in either the actions or the sufferings it causes. You suppose that Theban policy is bad because they maltreat their neighbors, but

---

[61] Isocrates uses the more general term, monarchies, here instead of tyrannies, but his discussion refers to tyrannies. Isocrates elsewhere is favorable to kingships. See especially his discourse *To Nicocles*.

you yourselves treat your allies no better than they treat Boeotia, and you still think that you are doing everything you should.

[116] If you trust me, then, you will stop your utterly random planning, turn your attention to yourselves and the city, and think carefully about what it is that made these two cities—I mean our own and Sparta—each rise from difficult situations to rule over the Greeks, but then, when they achieved this unmatched power, risk falling into slavery. [117] And why did the Thessalians, in spite of having great wealth and the best and largest territory, also end up impoverished,[62] while Megarians, whose property from the beginning was small and of no consequence—they had little land, no harbors, no silver mines, and farmed rocky soil—possess the greatest estates in Greece?[63] [118] The acropolis of the Thessalians was always in the hands of others, even though they had three thousand cavalry and countless peltasts,[64] but the Megarians, who had very little power, always ran their city as they wished. In addition, the Thessalians are always at war among themselves, but the Megarians, who live in between the Peloponnesians, Thebes, and our city, are continually at peace. [119] If you think hard about this and things like this, you will find that lack of restraint (*akolasia*) and arrogance (*hybris*) are the cause of troubles, while self-control (*sōphrosynē*) is the cause of good. Still, though you praise this virtue in private individuals and think that the citizens who live by it have the safest lives and are the best citizens, you do not think we

---

[62] The land of Thessaly, in northern Greece, is described positively elsewhere (Thuc. 1.2; Plato, *Meno* 70A). Laistner (1927: 117) points out the short-lived attempt by Jason of Pherae to take advantage of Thessaly's strength.

[63] In fact, Megara had two ports, one on the Saronic Gulf and one on the Corinthian Gulf. Isocrates exaggerates the situation here. Laistner (1927: 117) cites a scholiast on the meagerness of the Megarian land. The Megarians sent an embassy to Delphi to ask what Greek city was the most famous. The oracle replied that Argos had the best land, Sparta the best women, Thrace the best horses, Syracuse the best men. It then continues: "but you, O Megarians, are neither third, nor fourth, nor even twelfth in wisdom or in size." Laistner also notes that the Megarian colony Byzantium had a "longer and more illustrious record than any other Greek settlement."

[64] A *peltē* was a light shield and peltasts were light-armed troops (contrasted with heavily armed hoplites).

should cultivate it in the public matters. [120] And yet it is more proper for cities than for individuals to practice virtue (*aretē*) and avoid vice, for an impious and wicked man might perhaps die before paying for his crimes, but cities, since they do not die, endure punishments both from men and from the gods.

[121] Keeping this in mind, you should pay no attention to those who offer gratification for the present but have no concern for the future, nor to those who say that they love the *dēmos* but at the same time injure the state as a whole. It was the same in the past: when such men took control of the Assembly, they brought the city to such confusion that it suffered the sort of things I was describing a little earlier.[65] [122] What one might find most amazing of all is that you do not vote for demagogues who share the same ideas as those who made this city great but for those who say and do things like those who destroyed it. And you know that the noble are superior to the wicked not only in making the city prosperous [123] but also because under their leadership for many years, the democracy was not threatened or changed, whereas under these men, in a short time, it has already been overthrown twice. Also, those who were exiled by the tyrants and by the Thirty were able to return not because of the sykophants but because of people who detested these men and who had the greatest reputation for excellence. [124] Nevertheless, even though you have so many reminders of how the city fared under each kind of leader, we take such pleasure in the wickedness of the orators that even though we see that many citizens have lost their inheritance because of war and the confusion that these men created, while they themselves have gone from poverty to wealth, we are not upset or envious of their success; [125] we allow the city to endure the slander that it mistreats and demands tribute from the Greeks, while these men reap the profits, and the people, who are told by these men that they should rule over others, are worse off than those enslaved in an oligarchy. They started with nothing good, but as a result of our stupidity, they have risen from their poverty to prosperity. [126] Further, Pericles, who led the people before these men, took a city that was less sensible than before it acquired its empire (though still tolerably well run) and did not strive for personal gain—he left behind an estate that was worth less

---

[65] In 82–94.

than when he inherited it from his father—but brought eight thousand talents into the treasury of the Acropolis, aside from the sacred funds. [127] These men are so different from Pericles that they have the audacity to say it is because of their concern for the public good that they are unable to attend to their private affairs, whereas it is clear that these neglected affairs have brought them an amount of profit that they never would have dared ask the gods to grant, while our people, whom they claim to care for, are in such a state that none of them live pleasantly or easily, and the city is full of lamentation. [128] Some are compelled to recall and lament their poverty and want among themselves; others must bear the bulk of the duties, liturgies, and all the evils associated with tax levies (*symmoria*) and property exchanges (*antidosis*).[66] These put such strain on them that life is more painful for those with wealth than for those who are continually poor. [129] I am amazed you cannot grasp that there is no group more hostile to the people than the wicked orators and demagogues, for in addition to all the other troubles they cause, they especially want us to be in need of the daily necessities of life, since they see that those who can manage their own lives from their own resources are on the side of the city and the wisest orators, [130] but those who make a living from the lawcourts and assemblies and the income from these[67] are compelled by

---

[66] Liturgies were regular annual tasks or common periodic tasks that Athens asked the wealthiest citizens to finance; examples include financing a warship or funding the plays in the festival of Dionysus. Symmories were categories of Athens' wealthiest citizens. The wealthy citizens would be grouped into twenty symmories, and then one symmory would be asked to contribute in a time of special funding needs. An *antidosis* (exchange of property) was a peculiar legal case stemming from the responsibilities of the wealthy class. If someone were asked to perform a liturgy, but thought that another Athenian was richer and had not completed a liturgy recently, the former could challenge the request. He would try to transfer the responsibility to the second person. The latter then had the choice of performing the liturgy or exchanging estates (thus the name *antidosis,* exchange) with the first man. This process goes on the assumption that the second man would refuse the liturgy only if he had a smaller estate and would then gladly choose to trade estates with the original man. Actual exchanges were rare; Isocrates wrote a speech, *Antidosis* (15), for a fictitious case of this sort (see *Isocrates I* in this series).

[67] Citizens received three obols per day to serve on the juries or attend the Assembly.

their need to be under the orators' control and to show their gratitude for the impeachments and indictments and other sykophantic activities that the orators are responsible for. [131] Thus, they would be most happy to see all the citizens living in poverty, which allows themselves to hold power. Here is the best evidence of this: they do not look to how they might provide livelihoods for those in need but to how they can make as poor as the indigent those who think they have some wealth.

[132]⁶⁸ What escape might there be, then, from these present troubles? I have gone through most of my views on these things, not in a clear order but as each opportunity (*kairos*) offered itself. It might be better for you to remember if I try to gather together the most important points and summarize them again. [133] There are several ways we can restore the state of our city and make it better. First, we should make our advisors on public issues the same sort as we would want for our private affairs. We must stop thinking that the sykophants support democracy and that the best men⁶⁹ support oligarchy, since we know that no one is by nature either of these, but they wish to uphold the kind of government in which they find honor. [134] Second, we should be willing to treat our allies as our friends, not telling them we are giving them independence and in fact giving them over to generals to do whatever the generals wish; we must not stand over them as despots but as allies, knowing that while we are greater than any one of the cities alone, we are inferior to them all together. [135] Third, we should value nothing, after piety towards the gods, of course, more than our repute among the Greeks, for they willingly grant authority and leadership to those in this condition.

[136] If you follow what I have said and in addition show yourselves to be warlike in your training and preparation, but peaceable in your care to do nothing unjustly, you will make not only this city prosperous but all the rest of the Greeks as well. [137] For no other city will dare to do them wrong but will hold back and will keep very quiet

---

⁶⁸ Isocrates quotes the passage from here to the end of the speech (132–145), as well as sections 25–56, in his speech *Antidosis* (15.66) as an example of encouraging Athens to behave justly.

⁶⁹ The Greek phrase used here, *kalos kai agathos*, "noble and good," is a traditional phrase that often refers to the elite as the best sort of citizen.

when they see our force watching and prepared to give aid to the oppressed. But whatever they do, our situation will be good and advantageous for us. [138] If any of the leading cities decides to refrain from
oppression, we will get the credit, but if they try to act unjustly, then
everyone who is afraid and suffers harm will take refuge with us with
much pleading and supplication and will give us not only the hegemony but their own selves. [139] Thus, we will not lack allies with
whom we can hinder the offenders, but we will have many allies ready
and eager to fight alongside us. For what city or what person will not
want to share in our friendship and alliance when they see that we are
at the same time both the most just and the most powerful and are
both willing and able to save others, even while we need no help ourselves? [140] How much progress can we expect the city's affairs to
make if the other cities have the same goodwill toward us? How much
wealth will come flooding into the city if all Greece has been preserved
by our efforts? Who will not praise the people who have been responsible for so many great benefits? [141] But because of my age[70] I cannot cover everything in this discourse that I see in my mind, except
that it is a noble thing for us, in the midst of the vices and the madness of others, to be the first to think intelligently about the situation
and to stand as the leaders of Greek freedom; to be called the saviors,
not the destroyers, of the Greeks; and to become famous for our excellence, thereby regaining the reputation of our ancestors.

[142] To sum this all up, I can offer this conclusion, to which everything I have said so far points and to which we must look as we eval-
uate the city's affairs. If we want to remove the slander we currently
face, stop the wars that are futile and acquire a permanent hegemony
for the city, then we should hate all the tyrannical empires and powers, keeping in mind the disasters that have resulted from them, and
emulate and imitate the kings in Sparta.[71] [143] For it is less possible
for them to commit injustice than for private Spartan citizens, but

---

[70] This speech is traditionally dated to 355, and so Isocrates would be about
81 years old. Nonetheless, this is also a common apologetic motif in Isocrates; e.g.,
5.18, *Ep.* 1.1, *Ep.* 2.23, *Ep.* 3.4, *Ep.* 5.1, *Ep.* 6.2, *Ep.* 7.10.

[71] It is very odd to close by setting up the Spartans as examples. Laistner (1927:
124) criticizes the quality of the ending of this speech when compared with the
ending of *To Philip* (5), *Archidamus* (6), or *Areopagiticus* (7).

they have more blessed lives than those who hold tyrannies by force, since those who kill them receive the greatest gifts from their fellow citizens, whereas those who are not willing to die in battle for the kings are held in greater dishonor than those who abandon their battle lines or throw away their shields.[72] [144] This then, is the sort of hegemony we should strive for. And it is possible for us by our actions to obtain from the Greeks this position of honor that the Spartan kings had from their citizens, if they see that our power will not be a cause of slavery for them but of security.

[145] Although many other fine arguments could be made on this subject, two things advise me to stop my address: the length of this discourse and the number of my years. I advise and recommend those younger and more vigorous than I to say and write the sorts of words that will enable them to turn the greatest cities and those accustomed to cause trouble for others toward the path of virtue and justice, since it happens that when Greece prospers, the life of the mind (*ta tōn philosophōn*) also becomes much better.[73]

---

[72] These were especially serious offenses in Sparta, where soldiers were told by their mothers when they went off to war to come home "with their shield or upon it" (cf. *Ep.* 2.6n).

[73] Norlin (1929: 97) and Laistner (1927: 124) argue that this is an awkward closing, though Norlin tries to explain it by the connection between the state and philosophy in the mind of Isocrates. Benseler (cited in Laistner 1927: *ad loc.*) and Mathieu (in Mathieu and Brémond III 1942: 51) point to the close of *Panegyricus* as a parallel. The parallel is loose, however, and the abrupt change in this speech remains awkward. This sounds more like the end of a pedagogical exercise than a deliberative pamphlet.

12. PANATHENAICUS

INTRODUCTION

Isocrates says that he began *Panathenaicus* when he was 94 (3), just before the celebration of the Great Panathenaea (17), and completed it at age 98 (270); this was just before his death in 338. Like *Panegyricus* of 380, to which the discourse is often compared, *Panathenaicus* purports to be an address to a festival gathering, in this case, the Panathenaic festival at Athens.[1] The speech represents display oratory common at such festivals; it celebrates a special occasion of a group with narrative of its history and comment on its interests and values. In this case, the speech celebrates the greatness of Athens by discussing its notable history, its culture, and its leadership role among the Greeks.

The Panathenaea was held each year at Athens in late July or August, with a particularly elaborate version called the "Great Panathenaea" celebrated every fourth year. The festival lasted for several days and climaxed in a procession from the Ceramicus cemetery outside Athens, through the marketplace (Agora) along the Panathenaic Way, and up to the Acropolis. Tradition says that this procession is represented in the sculpted frieze of the Parthenon, the first time average humans were depicted in monumental sculpture.[2] Before this time, only gods and heroes were presented on buildings; but the Parthenon, built under the influence of Pericles in the high Classical Age of Athens, represents in many ways Pericles' perception of the greatness of

---

[1] On panhellenic gatherings in general, see the Introduction to *Panegyricus*. On the Panathenaea, see Neils 1992.

[2] Though Connelly (1996) has recently suggested that the frieze represents a myth. See Neils 1992, 2001 for other possibilities.

Greek culture generally and Athenian culture specifically. The spirit of
the Parthenon, which demonstrates the greatness of Athens, is also the
spirit of the Panathenaea.[3]

The ceremony included the presentation of a new robe to the goddess, carried in a procession from the harbor up to the city and presented to the cult statue of the goddess in the Erectheium, a second
temple on the Acropolis to the north of the Parthenon.[4] Like other
panhellenic gatherings such as the Olympic or Pythian games, the festival included athletic and musical contests.[5] Oratory was also certainly a part of the festival and would celebrate the greatness of Athenian culture, as Isocrates' discourse does.

Ceremonial oratory tends to be formulaic, offering common themes
in traditional ways. Standard topics of such discourse appear in this
speech: praise of the people, their ancestors, their city, and their important accomplishments. In addition to themes characteristic of the
genre, there are also themes particularly characteristic of Isocrates,
which can also be seen in *Panegyricus* of 380 and *To Philip* of 346. Jebb
(1962: 2.125–127) has outlined the arguments shared by *Panegyricus*
and this speech: early service to Greece by Athens, early wars of Athens, Athens' leadership in the Persian Wars, the naval empire, and the
crimes of Athens and Sparta against Greece. Isocrates also repeats his
lifelong desire that the Greeks make a unified campaign against the
Persians under strong leadership. Notions of who the leader should be
changed over the years for Isocrates because of changing political circumstances, but the basic idea lasted throughout his life.

In other ways, *Panathenaicus* is unique. Isocrates emphasizes the
greatness of Athens, as he had done in *Panegyricus,* but here he combines this with a stunning comparison with the Spartans, where the
Spartans do not come off very well.[6] Most notably, however, toward
the end of the discourse there is an unusual presentation of a discus-

---

[3] The festival was organized in 566 and was modified by the tyrant Peisistratus
to bring attention to Athens and elevate its status among the city-states of Greece.
In myth, its origins were attributed to Theseus or Erichthonius (Neils 1992: 13–27).

[4] This procession may be found on the east end of the Parthenon frieze.

[5] On the nature of the contests, see Neils 1992: 13–27, 52–75.

[6] This comparison strongly contrasts with the one Isocrates makes at the end
of *On the Peace* (8.142–144), where the Spartans look much more favorable.

sion between Isocrates and a former student (12.199–265). Isocrates relates how he called together some of his students to read the speech as he had composed it to that point. Since the speech included criticism of Sparta, he then summoned a former student who favored Sparta to see if the speech pleased him. After polite praise, as is normal from a student about the work of his former teacher, the man criticized the treatment of Sparta as too harsh and inaccurate. Isocrates points out the difficulties in the student's claims, but he also describes how he was led to adjust his presentation because of the comments.[7]

The speech also shows the adaptability of Isocrates, probably as a lesson to his students, in his revision of the text. He is open to criticism, and even if the criticism is not exactly accurate, as Isocrates points out, it can still help him think through the composition process and is therefore welcome and helpful.

The analysis of the student's claims echoes the dialectic/elenchic method of Socrates as seen in the dialogues of Plato. After the initial narrative of the student's objection (199–203), Isocrates sets out the discussion between teacher and student in direct discourse: Isocrates, 204–214; student, 215–217; Isocrates, 219–228; student, 235–263. Isocrates works here in the dialogue genre that was popular in the fourth century, but he does so in the form of alternating extended speeches. The Platonic dialogue that presents the Socratic method of question and answer is familiar to all, but it tends to include discussion that is much more pointed and brief. The parallel for Isocrates' method may be the so-called Aristotelian dialogue, less well known but more apposite. In that form, the dialogue is carried on in longer speeches, as here. Norlin (1929: 371) has criticized this section of the speech, perhaps with some validity, but the dialogue may serve to show Isocrates working in yet another genre and presenting an example to his school.[8]

The speech is difficult to outline in any detail. On a superficial level, it can be broken into four sections: introduction (1–41), praise of Athens (42–198), digression about a discussion with a student

---

[7] On the interpretation of Isocrates' reaction to the student, see Kennedy 1989 and Gray 1994.

[8] On Isocrates' awareness of genres and his mixture of them, see Papillon 1998b.

(199–265), conclusion (266–272). Yet there is even controversy about where the introduction leaves off and how the introduction is to be understood. The regular body of the speech is made up of traditional topics of praise, many similar to those found in *Panegyricus,* as mentioned above, but they are not set out in a clearly defined organization.

The discourse presents many of Isocrates' ideas on his teaching, since it began as a defense against some sophists who not only criticized his work but were successfully making people—who remain unidentified—hostile to Isocrates (17–20). There is much self-defense here, parallel to what Isocrates says in *Antidosis* (15) or the discourse *Against the Sophists* (13). This self-defense becomes something of a characteristic of Isocratean discourse, where he says that his enemies admire his work but then abuse him, hoping to draw people away from him. Isocrates uses self-defense often as a preface to his topic— his discourse *Helen* (10) is a good example—and is artistic in the way that he unifies his introductory self-defense with the overarching themes of the discourse, such as the seriousness of purpose found in the call to a united expedition, the desire for elegant presentation, and the framing of the discourse by the introductory comments (1–41) and the closing scene with his pupil (199–265).[9]

Panathenaicus is the last major composition of Isocrates. The only later document is a brief letter to Philip of Macedon (*Ep.* 3), which was written perhaps shortly after Philip's victory over the Greek forces at Chaeronea in 338.

12. PANATHENAICUS

[1] When I was younger, I chose not to write discourses (*logoi*) that were mythic (*mythōdes*) [10] or full of wonders and fictions, the sort that

---

[9] On the connection between a self-conscious introduction and the body of a work, see Papillon 1996a.

[10] Isocrates echoes Thucydides (1.22) here with his view of the mythic. Both authors want to avoid the mythic, which might be perceived as aiming at entertainment and pleasure and to aim instead at discourse that will be useful for the reader. On Thucydides and myth, see Flory 1990. On myth in Isocrates, see Papillon 1996b.

the multitude enjoy more than those that concern their own security; I also avoided those that related the great deeds of the past and the wars fought by Greeks (although I knew that these were justly praised) and also those that when spoken seem simple and unadorned, such as people who are skillful in courts teach the young to practice if they want to have the advantage in litigation.[11] [2] I rejected all these and devoted myself to discourses that gave advice about what would be advantageous (*sympheron*) to Athens and the rest of the Greeks, and that were full of many ideas (*enthymēmata*), with frequent antithesis and parisosis and other figures (*ideai*) that make oratory shine and compel the audience to applaud and cause a stir.[12] But now, no more of this at all.[13] [3] For I do not think that it is appropriate for me to continue speaking in that manner, now that I am 94 years old,[14] nor generally for those who have gray hair, but instead to speak as all would hope they could, if they wished, though no one could do so easily except those who are willing to work hard and pay careful attention. [4] The purpose of these preliminary remarks is that if it becomes evident to some that the discourse to come is weak, they would not compare it to the ornamentation of those earlier ones but would judge it according to the thesis that I have chosen for the present occasion.[15]

[5] I will discuss the great deeds of our city and the valor of our ancestors; I will not begin with them, however, but with my own situation, for I think this is more urgent. Although I have tried to live a life free from error without hurting anyone else, I have been continually slandered by obscure and evil sophists, and then others assumed me to be what they heard from others, although they do not know me as I

---

[11] On the types of prose, see Wilcox 1943.

[12] Usher (1999: 318–319) discusses the stylistic individuality of this speech. It is less ornate in its use of some figures, but sentence length is considerably longer than the norm for Isocrates, and antithesis is about the same as in the earlier work *Panegyricus*. Cf. Usher 1973. On *idea*, see Lidov 1983 and Sullivan 2001.

[13] Isocrates makes a similar claim in his discourse *To Philip* (5.27–28).

[14] Isocrates was 94 years old in 342. He says at the end of the discourse (266–270) that he then fell ill and did not complete the work until he was 98, in 338.

[15] Norlin (1929: 369–370), Jebb (1962: 2.125), and Usher (1999: 318–319) are among those who judge it inferior to his earlier work, *Panegyricus*.

really am.[16] **[6]** I want to speak, then, first about myself and about those who feel this way about me so that, if possible, I can stop some of them from slandering me and make others know how I really spend my time. For if I can manage this properly in my discourse, I hope that I will be able to live the rest of my life without trouble and that those who are present will pay closer attention to the speech I am about to deliver.

[7] I will not hesitate to speak out about the present turmoil in my mind, the oddness of what I am thinking at present, or whether I am doing what I should. I have enjoyed the greatest benefits that anyone would wish to have: first, I have had health, both in body and soul, and not just to an average degree but as much as those who are particularly fortunate in each of these respects. Second, I have had a prosperous life, so that I never lacked the ordinary necessities of life or anything that reasonable men desire. **[8]** Next, I am not one of those who are slandered or ignored but one whom the best men would remember and speak of as excellent.[17] Though all these things are mine, some in abundance, others in sufficient amount, I do not enjoy living in this way, but my old age is so unpleasant, trivial, and full of complaints that I have often blamed my own nature (which no one ever despised) **[9]** and lamented my fate, though I have nothing to fault this for—except for some difficulties and malicious accusations (*sykophantiae*) that attach to the life of philosophy (*philosophia*)[18] that I have chosen—and I know that my nature is weaker and softer than it should be for practical matters, and not perfect or entirely useful for speeches either. It is more able to make reasoned judgments (*doxasai*) about the truth of any matter than are those who say that they have certain knowledge (*eidenai*),[19] but it is inferior to almost all others in speak-

---

[16] For more extensive remarks about the slander from others and a defense of his life, see Isocrates' *Antidosis* (15) and *Against the Sophists* (13) in *Isocrates I* of this series.

[17] An odd claim, given his complaint in section 5 that he is, in fact, slandered. Here, however, Isocrates refers to the success of his school and talks about a different group, those who admire him, rather than those who have attacked him.

[18] Isocrates calls his manner of life *philosophia* and sees himself in the tradition of Socrates when he calls himself and those around him to be responsible citizens.

[19] On judgment vs. knowledge, see 8.8n.

ing on this very subject in a public gathering of many men. [10] For as much as any other citizen I know, I lacked both things that possess the greatest power among you, a strong voice and confidence before the public.[20] Those who lack these are more dishonored (*atimoteroi*) in their public reputation than those who are in debt to the state.[21] For the latter can still hope to pay off their fine, but the former have no hope of changing their nature. [11] Nonetheless, I was not discouraged about these things and did not allow myself to lose my reputation or my visibility entirely, but because I lost the chance to take part in politics, I retreated to the life of philosophy and hard work and writing down my thoughts, choosing not to treat trivial things like private contracts or things that others babble on about, but the affairs of Greeks and kings and our city. In this way I thought it would be more appropriate if I received more honor than those who spoke in public[22] just as the subjects of my discourse were more serious and more noble than theirs.[23] [12] But none of this happened. Yet everyone knows that most public speakers (*rhētores*) have the daring to give people not advice that will benefit the city but what they expect will be profitable for themselves; I and the people around me, however, not only keep away from public funds more than others but we spend our own funds beyond our means for the needs of the city.[24] [13] Furthermore, while they are insulting each other in the Assembly about security deposits or abusing the allies or bringing suit against anyone they can find, I have become the leading proponent of discourses that urge the Greeks to unity (*homonoia*) with one another and to a campaign against the barbarians. [14] I also advocate discourses advising that we all together

---

[20] Most scholars have taken Isocrates' comments about his physical limitations at face value, but Too (1995: 74–112) has suggested that this may be a rhetorical pose.

[21] Those in debt to the state also incurred *atimia* or disenfranchisement, which entailed loss of certain citizen rights, e.g., admittance to temples, the Agora, and the lawcourts (cf. MacDowell 1978: 74–75).

[22] Isocrates refers here to the *bēma* or platform where a speaker addressed a gathering in the Assembly or a jury in a court case.

[23] Isocrates also prioritizes his work at the beginning of *Panegyricus,* when he says his effort is more valuable than that of athletes in the panhellenic games (4.1–4).

[24] For a vivid picture of evil speakers and their desire for personal financial gain, see *On the Peace* (8.124–131).

should send out a common colony to a land so large and fertile that whenever someone hears of it they agree that if we are wise and stop our foolishness against each other, we would quickly settle it without work or danger, and it would easily take in all of us who are in need of daily necessities. If we all came together in this plan, we would never find any achievement more noble or greater or more beneficial to us all.

[15] But nonetheless, even though we differ so much in our attitude and I have made a career choice much more serious than they have, most people have formed their opinion about us unjustly, in confusion, and quite illogically. For although they criticize the behavior of the orators, they set them up as leaders of the city and put them in charge of everything; by contrast, they praise my discourses, yet they envy me for no other reason than these very discourses, which they actually welcome. Such is the unfortunate treatment I get from them.

[16] Why should you be amazed at those who naturally feel this way about all who excel, when even some of those who think they are superior and who vie with me and strive to imitate me are even more hostile than private citizens are?[25] Would someone find anyone more wicked—for I will say it, even if I seem to some to speak more rashly and severely than befits my age—than those who cannot even present to their students a small part of my teachings and yet use my discourses as their examples and, even though they are making their living from my work, show so little gratitude for it that, not even content with simply ignoring me, they always spread some insult about me? [17] Therefore, while they abused my discourses, comparing them with their own in the worst manner possible, analyzing them wrongly, and tearing them apart and mistreating them in every conceivable way, I took no account of the reports brought to me and was indifferent. A little before the Great Panathenaea,[26] however, I grew angry at them. [18] Some of my associates came up to me and said that three or four of the common sophists who say they know (*eidenai*) everything and quickly appear everywhere were sitting in the Lyceum and were dis-

---

[25] For a fuller treatment of Isocrates' rivals in education, see his speech *Against the Sophists* (13).

[26] On the Great Panathenaea, see the Introduction to this speech.

cussing the poets, especially the poetry of Hesiod and Homer. They were saying nothing of their own but were reciting the poets' words and repeating the best of what others had said before. [19] As their audience was enjoying their presentation (*diatribē*), one of the more daring tried to slander me, saying that I look down upon all those topics and that I would destroy the philosophies of others and every educational system and that I claim that everyone else talks nonsense except those who attend my presentations (*diatribē*). When they said this, some of those present expressed their dislike of me. [20] I could not tell you how pained I was and upset that some had accepted these slanders. For I thought it was quite clear that I fought against those who thought too highly of themselves and that I always spoke modestly, even rather humbly, about myself, so that no one would ever believe those who said that I behaved so pretentiously. [21] So it was not without reason that in the beginning of this discourse [27] I lamented the misfortune that followed me all the time in this way. For this is the cause of the falsehoods going around about me and of the slanders and the envy; this is why I cannot gain the reputation I deserve, either the reputation that all agree I should have or one that some have attained by studying with me and watching me on many occasions. [22] It seems these things cannot be otherwise, but I must be content with what has already happened.

Although I have many ideas about this, I am uncertain whether to counterattack against those who always lie and speak maliciously about me. But if I should invest energy and make a lot of speeches about people whom no one thinks worth talking about, I would quite rightly seem a fool. [23] So should I ignore these men and defend myself against those individuals who unjustly bear a grudge against me and try to show them that they have this opinion about me unjustly and inappropriately? Who would not judge me stupid indeed if I thought that those who are hostile to me precisely because I seem to have spoken gracefully on some topic will stop being displeased at my words if I argue in the same way as before, and will not rather be even more upset, especially if it seems to them that even at my present age, I have not stopped speaking nonsense? [24] I am sure, however, that no one

---

[27] In section 5.

would advise me to ignore this issue, stop here in the middle, and complete the speech that I selected when I wanted to show that our city has been responsible for more benefits for the Greeks than Sparta. For if I did that now, not finishing up what I have been writing and not joining the beginning of the planned discourse to the conclusion of what I have now been saying, I would look like those who say whatever occurs to them, randomly, coarsely, and without a sense of order. I must avoid this. [25] Therefore, the best thing is for me to make clear my views on their most recent slanders and then to speak about those things I had originally planned; I think that if I bring these out in my writing and clarify my view of education (*paideia*) and the poets, then I will stop them from creating false accusations and saying whatever occurs to them.

[26] To begin, then: far from disparaging the education handed down by our ancestors, I even approve the education we have established today—I mean geometry, astronomy, and the so-called eristic dialogues, though the young enjoy the latter more than is proper, even while none of the older students would say that they are even tolerable.[28] [27] Nevertheless, I advise those who are setting out on these studies to work hard and pay close attention to all of them, for I would say that even if these studies are able to accomplish nothing else, they will at least turn the young away from many other harmful activities. Thus I think young students will never find subjects more useful or appropriate for them than these. [28] For older students, however, and those who have achieved adulthood, I do not think that these studies are appropriate any longer. For I see that some of those who are so devoted to precision in these exercises that they even teach others do not use the knowledge they have in the right way (*eukairōs*) and, in fact, in other subjects they have less good sense (*phronēsis*) than their students (dare I say even than their slaves).[29] [29] I have the same opinion about those who can speak in public assemblies and those who are famous for writing speeches and generally about all those who excel in arts

---

[28] Isocrates also talks of such subjects as preliminary in *Antidosis* (15.261–269) and in *To Alexander* (*Ep.* 5.3–4).

[29] On *phronēsis*, cf. *Ep.* 7.1n.

(*technai*), in sciences (*epistēmai*), and in specialized abilities (*dynameis*). For I know that most of these do not manage their own affairs well, are intolerable in private gatherings, have contempt for the opinions of their fellow citizens, and are filled with many other serious faults. As a result, I do not think even these men have the qualities I am talking about. [30] Whom then do I call educated, since I exclude those in the arts (*technai*) and sciences (*epistēmai*) and abilities (*dynameis*)? First, those who manage well the daily affairs of their lives and can form an accurate judgment (*doxa*) about a situation (*kairos*) and in most cases can figure out (*stochazesthai*) what is the best course of action (*to sympheron*). [31] Next, those who behave appropriately and fairly toward people who are always with them, endure the rudeness and unpleasantness of others calmly and easily, and conduct themselves as gently and modestly as possible toward those they come in contact with. Next, those who are always in control of their pleasures and are not excessively overwhelmed by their troubles but endure them with a stout heart and a nature worthy of our common humanity. [32] Fourth, and most important, those who are not corrupted by their good fortune, do not abandon their true selves, or become arrogant, but on the contrary, remain in the ranks of those with good sense and do not rejoice more in the successes that come to them by chance than in those that come through their own nature and good sense (*phronēsis*). So then, I say that the ones who are wise and complete and possess all the virtues are those whose minds are well fitted not only for one of these areas of life but for all them. [33] This then is what I know about those who are educated (*pepaideumenon*).

Now although I want to speak about the poetry of Homer and Hesiod and the others—for I think I could stop those who recite their works and talk nonsense about them in the Lyceum—I sense that I am going beyond the limits that are set out for an introduction.[30] [34] A

---

[30] Isocrates did not reject the poets, as some claimed, but took ideas from the poetic tradition that could raise the moral and political level of rhetorical discourse because of the moral advisory role poetry played in Greek society. Oratory had come under attack in the fourth century because of the questionable morality of the sophists, and Isocrates sought to counter this by taking the serious ad-

wise man should not be too fond of his ability to say more than others on the same topics but should keep a proper sense of proportion (*eukairia*) about any subject he happens to address. This is what I must do. Therefore, I will speak another time on the poets,[31] unless old age takes me first, since I have topics more serious to speak about than this.[32]

[35] I will now begin my discourse about our city's good deeds toward the other Greeks. It is not that I have not already expressed more praise about it than all the other poets and prose writers together, but the present speech will be different. For in the past I recalled the city in discourses concerned with other issues, but now I am making the city my main subject. [36] I am not unaware how great a task I undertake at my age, but I understand clearly and have often said that it is easy to magnify small deeds with words but difficult to make praise even equal to achievements that are superior in both size and nobility.[33] [37] Nevertheless, I must not shy away from this but must complete the task while I still have breath, especially since many things spur me on to write it: first, those who wantonly accuse our city; next, those who praise it pleasantly but rather amateurishly and weakly; [38] further, others who dare to praise it too much, not in human terms but in such a grandiose way that they turn many against them; finally and most of all, my present age, which would naturally frighten others away. For I hope that if I succeed, I will gain greater reputation

---

visory role of poetry into his own discourse. To do this, he borrowed from the poets' organizational principals, topics, and sense of needing an appropriate style for a given situation. See further Papillon 1998a.

[31] With this dismissal, Isocrates ignores one of the two topics he introduced in section 25, education and the poets.

[32] There is a textual difficulty in this last sentence. The Loeb edition of Norlin, following the most important manuscript (G) reads "or unless I have topics more serious to speak about." I prefer the reading of the vulgate tradition, followed in the Budé edition of Brémond, which reads "since I have topics more serious." This reading makes the clause an explanation for why he does not treat the poets.

[33] It is a commonplace of epideictic oratory, especially funeral orations, to point out that words cannot match deeds. Cf. 4.74, 6.100; Thuc. 2.35; Lys. 2.1; and, later, Hyp. 6.2 and Dem. 60.1. On funeral orations, see 4.74n.

than I have now, while if my discourse turns out to be insufficient, I hope my listeners will be very understanding because of my age. [39] This then is what I wanted to set out about myself and other things as an introduction, like a chorus before a drama contest.[34]

Now, I think that those who wish to praise a city accurately and fairly must devote their discourse not only to the city they have selected but just as when we view purple or gold and examine them by setting other things that have similar appearance and are of the same value alongside them for comparison, [40] we should do the same thing with cities: we should not compare small cities with great ones, or those that have always been under someone's control with those that are accustomed to rule, or those that need to be rescued with those that are able to rescue, but rather we should compare cities that have similar power, are involved in the same affairs, and have similar resources. For thus we would best get to the truth. [41] If someone looks at us in this way and does not compare us with just any city but with Sparta, which most people praise moderately but some recall it as though its government had been run by demigods, then it will be evident that we Athenians, in power, achievements, and benefits provided to the Greeks, are as superior to Sparta as Sparta is to everyone else. [42] I will speak later about the ancient struggles on behalf of the Greeks,[35] but now I will begin by speaking about when the Spartans took possession of the Achaean cities and divided the land with Argos and Messene, for it is appropriate to narrate from that point.[36]

You will see that our ancestors preserved their unity of spirit toward the Greeks and their hatred toward the barbarians (which they had from the Trojan War) and have kept it in the same way since then.[37] [43] First there were the Cycladic islands, about which there were many disputes during the rule of King Minos of Crete until finally the

---

[34] Aristotle mentions a flute prelude to contests in the *Rhetoric* (3.14), where he specifically mentions the introductory section of Isocrates' *Helen* (10). For discussions of Isocratean notions of unity, see Papillon 1996a, 1997a.

[35] He treats the Persian Wars in section 49, the Ionian colonization in 164, and the early mythic history of Athens (Eumolpus, Amazons) in 191.

[36] Tradition says that the Dorians came into the Peloponnese in the tenth century and took control of the area, subjugating the native populations. Cf. 6.7n.

[37] Cf. sections 42–48 on the early history with *Panegyricus* (4.34–37).

Carians occupied them. Throwing them out, our ancestors did not
venture to appropriate the land for themselves, but they settled there
those who were most in need of a livelihood.³⁸ [44] After this, they
founded many great cities on both sides of the Aegean, and they drove
the barbarians from the sea and taught the Greeks how to govern
their own homelands and against whom they should fight so that they
might make Greece great. [45] About this same time, the Spartans refrained from doing any of the same things we were doing, and, far
from fighting the barbarians or helping the Greeks, they were not even
willing to live in peace. Although they held a city that was not originally theirs, and land that was not only sufficient but larger than
that of any other Greek city, they were not content with this [46] but
learned from experience that according to the law, cities and regions
are thought to belong to those who acquired them rightly and legally,
but in truth they belong to those who are best prepared and can defeat their enemies in battle. With this in mind, they ignored farming
and the arts and other such things and never stopped attacking and
violating every single city in the Peloponnese until they had subdued
them all, except Argos. [47] The result of our actions, then, was that
Greece grew greater and Europe became stronger than Asia; in addition, impoverished Greek cities, in fact, gained territory, and the barbarians, who were usually insulting, lost their own land and were less
arrogant than before. The result of the Spartans' actions, however, was
that their city alone grew great, they ruled over all the cities in the
Peloponnese, and they were a cause of fear to other cities and thus well
served by them. [48] It is right, then, to praise the city that is responsible for many benefits for other cities but to consider dangerous the
city that acts only in its own interests; we should make friends with
those who treat themselves and others alike but dread and fear those
who consider their own interests as much as possible, while the government of their city is most inhospitable and violent toward others.
Thus was the beginning for each of these cities.

[49] Later, however, during the Persian Wars when Xerxes was

---

³⁸Isocrates refers to the Ionian Migration during the years after the Trojan
War; he does so again in section 164 and in *Panegyricus* (4.34–42).

king,[39] he gathered 1,300 triremes and a land force of five million soldiers in all, including 700,000 fit soldiers, and with this great force led a campaign against the Greeks. [50] The Spartans, though they controlled the Peloponnesians, provided only ten triremes for the naval battle that would decide the entire war, whereas our ancestors, though they were overpowered and had to abandon their city because it was not walled in at that time, provided more ships, and more powerful ones, than all their allies put together. [51] The Spartans sent the general Eurybiades, who, if he had accomplished the objective he had in mind, would have done nothing to keep all the Greeks from being destroyed; we, on the other hand, sent Themistocles, the one universally recognized to be responsible for the naval battle being fought as it was and for all the other successes at that time. [52] The greatest sign of this is that those who fought with us took the hegemony away from the Spartans and gave it to our ancestors. And indeed, whom would anyone select as more qualified and reliable judges of those events than those who were at our side in those very same battles? And what greater service could anyone name than this, one that was able to preserve all Greece?

[53] After this, it happened that each city gained control of a naval empire, and whichever has this command has most of the cities under its control. In general I praise neither of the cities, for someone could fault them for many things.[40] Nonetheless, we were better than the Spartans in our oversight,[41] just as we were in the events already mentioned. [54] For our ancestors persuaded the allies to make their government the one they consistently preferred. It is a sign of goodwill and friendship when people recommend that others use the same system that they take to have helped their own situation. The Spartans, on the other hand, did not set up governments that resembled their own or that were found anywhere else, but they put just ten men in

---

[39] The Persian Wars lasted from 490 to 479. They are treated here (49–52) and again in 189. Cf. this treatment with that of *Panegyricus* (4.71–74, 85–98).

[40] On the difficulties of the naval empires, see *On The Peace* (8.74–105).

[41] Isocrates changes from the word for empire (*archē*) to the much more general and less pejorative word oversight (*epimeleia*).

charge of each city.[42] If someone were to lay complaints against them for three or four days continuously, it would still seem that he had not covered even a small portion of their crimes. [55] Therefore, it would be foolish to catalogue each of their many serious crimes, but if I were younger, I might perhaps have found a way to describe the whole situation in a few words that would rouse anger in the audience appropriate to what they did. As it is, however, I have no such words but only what comes to everyone, namely, that those men went so far beyond their predecessors in lawlessness and greed that they not only destroyed themselves and their friends and their homelands, but by discrediting the Spartans in the eyes of their allies, they caused them such great troubles as no one ever imagined would happen to them.

[56] From these events one could most clearly see how much fairer and gentler we were in managing these affairs, but one will see it again in what I am about to say. For the Spartans had the rule for barely ten years, while we held our empire for sixty-five years continuously.[43] And yet, all know that cities that fall under the control of others remain for the longest time with those under whom they suffer as little harm as possible. [57] At the end of their rule, moreover, both cities were hated and ended up in war and turmoil; but one would find that in this period, when our city was attacked by all the Greeks and barbarians, it was able to hold out against them for ten years, whereas when the Spartans were still powerful on land, they fought against the Thebans alone and were defeated in just one battle, losing all they had and experiencing nearly the same misfortune and troubles that we did.[44] [58] In addition, our city took back its power in fewer years than

---

[42] At the conclusion of the Peloponnesian War in 404, the Spartans set up oligarchic panels of ten men (decarchies) in each city to oversee their government. These were accompanied by a garrison and commander and were often perceived as tyrannical by the cities occupied. See too *Panegyricus* (4.110).

[43] Athens' empire lasted from 479 to 404 (cf. 4.106n). Sparta by tradition was considered to be in power from 404 to 371, when it lost power at the battle of Leuctra. Isocrates has been talking about naval powers, however, so he may be thinking of Athens losing her fleet in Syracuse in 415 and Sparta's loss at Cnidus in 394.

[44] That is, after the disastrous defeat at Syracuse, the Athenians held out for another ten years before finally surrendering to Sparta in 404. The Spartans lost

it took to defeat it, whereas the Spartans after their loss were not able to regain the same position from which they fell even after a much longer time, yet even now are still the same.

[59] I must also show how each city behaved against the barbarians, for this still remains. During the period of our empire, the Persians were not allowed to lead a land army past the Halys river or sail past Phaselis with its warships. In the period of Spartan supremacy, by contrast, not only did the Persians take the liberty to march and sail wherever they wanted, but they also became despots of many Greek cities. [60] The city, then, that made the treaty with the King that was nobler and prouder, the city that was responsible for the most and greatest troubles for the barbarians and benefits for the Greeks, the one, furthermore, that took the coast of Asia and much other land away from our enemies and gave it to our allies, [61] that puts an end to the arrogant violence of one side and to the distress of the other, and in addition that fights for its own security better than the city with a reputation for doing this, that gets rid of troubles faster than these same people, how is it not right to praise and honor this city above the one that was inferior in all these areas? This, then, is what I had to say at the moment about the contrast between the deeds of each side and the dangers they faced at the same time and against the same enemies.

[62] Now, I think those who are not happy to hear these arguments will not object to what I have said on the grounds that it is not true, and they will not be able to mention any other actions by which the Spartans were responsible for many benefits for the Greeks, but I think that they will try to accuse our city[45] [63]—as they always do— and will relate the most unpleasant things that happened during the time of our naval empire, and will criticize the trials and verdicts imposed on the allies as well as the war taxes we collected. And they will spend most time on the sufferings of the Melians and the Scionians

---

their empire at the battle of Leuctra in 371 against the Boeotian League, which was led by Thebes (Hammond 1986: 493–494). For rhetorical effect, Isocrates exaggerates about Thebes being alone. In any event, it is a very odd argument that Athens should be praised because it was able to avoid collapse longer than Sparta was.

[45] Cf. the treatment of the misdeeds of both sides here (62–107) with the treatment in *Panegyricus* (4.100–132).

and the Toronians,[46] thinking that these accusations might taint the benefits I mentioned a little before. [64] I could not deny everything that might justly be said against our city, nor would I even try. For I would be ashamed—as I have already said before[47]—if I were to work hard to persuade you that our government has never done anything wrong when people think that even the gods make mistakes. [65] Nevertheless, I think I will do the following: I will show that the city of the Spartans was much more harsh and cruel in the matters I just spoke of, that those who criticize us to defend them are as foolish as anyone can be and are, in fact, responsible for the bad reputation their friends have among us. [66] For whenever they level accusations against us that are more appropriate for the Spartans, then I have no trouble describing crimes of theirs that are worse than what was said about us. For example, as I just noted, they may try to mention the trials we hold for the allies in Athens; but who is so foolish that he cannot find a response to this, that the Spartans killed more Greeks without a trial than stood trial in our city from the time we first settled it?[48]

[67] If they mention the collection of war taxes, I will have the same sort of response: we will show that we provided far more advantages than the Spartans to the cities that contributed these taxes. First,

---

[46] Isocrates lists these events of the Peloponnesian War in order of fame, not chronology. Scione was besieged in 423 (Thuc. 4.120–123, 129–133) and destroyed in 421 (5.32). The Plataeans colonized the area until they were thrown out again at the end of the war. Torone was a city at the tip of the second finger of the Chalcidice in northern Greece. It was sacked by the Athenians in 422 under Cleon (Thuc. 5.1–3). The men were sent to Athens as prisoners of war, the women and children enslaved. In 416 the people of Melos wanted to assert their independence when Athens wanted them to join their side. Thucydides describes this situation in an unusual and famous passage called the Melian Dialogue (5.84–116). The two cities talk as if characters in a play, the Melians asserting their rights based on justice, the Athenians asserting the interest of the stronger. The Athenians eventually took the island, killed all the men, and enslaved the women and children. Thucydides makes the act look tyrannical on the part of Athens, bullying a small independent island, but inscriptional evidence seems to show that Melos was contributing to the Spartan cause (Meiggs and Lewis 1969: 181–184). Cf. 4.100.

[47] *Ep.* 2.16 is very similar.

[48] Probably a reference to the carnage that occurred under the Thirty at Athens in 411. This is also mentioned in *Panegyricus* 4.113.

they did not do this at our command, but they decided it themselves right when they entrusted the naval hegemony to us. [68] Second, they did not make these payments for our security but to preserve democracy and their own freedom so they would not experience such huge misfortunes if an oligarchic government should take over, such as happened during the time of the decarchies and the Spartan regime.[49] Next, they did not make these payments from funds that they had saved by themselves but from funds that they received with our help.[50] [69] They would rightly have been grateful to us for these funds, if they had taken the time to do even a small calculation. For when we took control of their cities, some entirely destroyed by the barbarians and others plundered, we brought them to such prosperity that even giving us a small portion of their revenues, they still had estates that were no smaller than those of the Peloponnesians, who paid no war taxes. [70] Next, as for the cities that were destroyed by each of our cities—a charge some make against us alone—we will show that those whom they continually praise did much more terrible things. It fell to us to commit our crimes against little islands so unimportant and small that many of the Greeks do not even know of them.[51] The Spartans, by contrast, on their own destroyed the most important cities in the Peloponnese and ones that were superior in every way to other cities. And they now have their wealth, [71] although these cities, even if they had not otherwise distinguished themselves, deserved to receive the greatest possible gifts from the Greeks because of their expedition against Troy where they offered themselves as leaders and gave generals with such great virtues, not only virtues that all share, even many of the lowly, but also those virtues that no bad person could have. [72] For Messene offered Nestor, the wisest man of all

---

[49] See above, 54n.

[50] Isocrates' description is accurate for the Delian League at its founding in the 470s. The difficulties come when that association is transformed from the Delian League into what tradition has called the Athenian Empire as the fifth century progressed. It is not the Delian League that led to the Peloponnesian War but the way Athens reacted to its position of authority in that league as time passed. See further, Norlin 1929: *ad loc.*

[51] A morally questionable argument, but from the point of view of practical politics and military tactics, perhaps a bit more acceptable.

those alive at that time; Sparta gave Menelaus, who, because of his good sense (*phronēsis*) and justice, was alone thought worthy to be the son-in-law of Zeus;[52] the city of the Argives gave Agamemnon, who had not one or two virtues but all that one could mention, and these not just in an average way but in abundance. [73] For we will find no one anywhere who accomplished tasks more notable, more noble, more important, or more beneficial to the Greeks or worthy of more praise. Now, some might not believe these things when they are set out like this, but if the details were stated in each case, then they would admit that I am telling the truth.

[74] I cannot see clearly but am at a loss what sort of arguments to use after this to give the right advice. I would be ashamed if I said such high things about Agamemnon's virtue but then brought up none of the deeds that he did, making my audience think I am just like those who boast and say whatever occurs to them. But I see that accounts of deeds that lie outside of the subject (*hypothesis*) are not well received and seem confusing; there are many who behave like this, but even more who fault them for it. [75] Thus, I am afraid that such a thing might happen to me. Nonetheless, I choose to help out someone who has had the same experience as I and others have experienced, namely, of missing out on the reputation that he should have; although he was responsible for many benefits at that time, he is praised less than those who accomplished nothing of note.[53]

---

[52] Menelaus was married to Helen, the daughter of Zeus by Leda. Tradition says that Zeus came to her in the form of a swan. In Isocrates' discourse *Helen* (10.61–63), the treatment of Menelaus is different; there he is only important as the husband of Helen and, in fact, achieves heroic status only through his connection with her.

[53] Thus Isocrates joins himself to Agamemnon; he has suffered the same slight as Agamemnon. Isocrates follows two different poetic arguments here, seen most vividly elsewhere in the victory odes of Pindar. First, he connects himself with the object of praise, so that by raising up the object of praise, he raises himself. Second, he joins Pindar in asserting that some heroes of the period of the Trojan War receive less credit than they are due. Pindar says that Ajax gets less credit than he deserves, and Odysseus more, because of the influence of Homer (*Nemean* 7.20–34). Pindar hopes to give Ajax a larger reputation through his poetry, just as Odysseus has received a greater reputation through the poetry of Homer. Isocrates will

[76] [54] What did that man lack, who had a position so honorable that no one would find a better one if everyone came together and searched for it? He alone was judged worthy to be the commander of all Greece. I cannot say whether he was chosen by all or whether he obtained this position himself, but whichever way it happened, he left no opportunity for a higher reputation for those who might be honored in some other way. [77] Taking this authority, he did not injure a single Greek city but rather was so far from wronging any of them that, finding the Greeks in war and turmoil and many difficulties, he relieved them of these troubles and established harmony among them; he ignored tasks that would be amazing and wondrous but of no practical use to anyone and instead formed an army and led it against the barbarians. [78] You will find no one, either among the best of that time or those who followed, who has made a more noble campaign than this, or one more beneficial to the Greeks. But he did not gain the reputation that he should have for what he did and for the example he set for others, because of people who love wonders more than real benefits and false stories more than the truth; instead, although he was so great, he had a lower reputation than those who did not have the courage to emulate him. [55]

---

try to increase Agamemnon's reputation through his prose encomium here. On Isocrates' debt to the poetic tradition, see Papillon 1998a.

[54] Sections 76–88 are an extensive digression in praise of Agamemnon. Cf. Race 1978. Blass (1892: 2.331–334) thought it was meant to represent Philip of Macedon. Norlin (1929: 418–419) thought he represented an example of the leadership of Greece against the east. See Papillon 1996b on the use of such myths in Isocratean discourse.

[55] Isocrates here vies with Homer, because Homer paints an uncomplimentary picture of Agamemnon in the *Iliad,* a poem meant to praise Agamemnon's rival, Achilles, who was called "the best of the Achaians." Pindar had made a similar argument on behalf of Ajax (cf. above, 75n). From the point of view of rhetorical strategy, it is interesting to look at the motivations of Isocrates and Pindar. Pindar champions Ajax because he is the mythic ancestor of the athletic victor he seeks to praise in *Nemean* 7, Sogenes from the island of Aegina, which was connected in ancient times with Ajax. Isocrates defends Agamemnon because he provides the perfect example of Isocrates' political goal of leadership of a unified Greece against an eastern enemy (cf. Papillon 1996b).

[79] One might praise him not just for these reasons but also for the things he did at this same time, for he was so great-hearted that he was not satisfied to recruit as many soldiers as he wanted from the private citizens of each city he wanted, but he persuaded the kings, who do whatever they want in their own cities and give orders to others, to come under his command, to follow him no matter whom he led them against, to do what he ordered, and to give up the royal life and live as a soldier. [80] He also convinced them to put their lives at risk and fight not for their own homeland and kingship but in theory for Helen, the wife of Menelaus, though in reality so that Greece would not suffer at the hands of the barbarians the same sorts of indignities that they suffered before, during the time of the capture of the whole Peloponnese by Pelops or the capture of Argos by Danaus or Thebes by Cadmus.[56] Who else will you find who took such forethought for these things, or would have stood in the way of their happening again, if not someone of the nature and power of Agamemnon? [81] There is one thing left, less than what I have already said but more than what has been often praised and more worthy of mention. The army he gathered together from all the cities was of such a size as you would expect when it had so many soldiers, some from divine lineage, some born from the gods themselves. These were not similar to the common people and did not have the same character as the rest, but they were filled with anger, aggression, envy, and love of honor. [82] Nonetheless, he kept them together for ten years without resorting to large salaries or the lavish expenditures that all now use to maintain their control, but through superiority in practical wisdom, being able to provide supplies to the soldiers from the enemy, and especially because they recognized that he could plan better for their security than the others could do for themselves. [83] And his last accomplishment

---

[56] These are examples of foreign invasions. Pelops invaded from the north and took control of the whole of the Peloponnese. This is the mythic explanation of the historic occurrence of the Dorian invasion from the north. Cadmus came to Thebes from the east and Danaus to Argos from Egypt. The Near Eastern and North African influences on Greek culture and history are evident in their myths as well as their archaeology. Many Greek cities celebrated these influences; only the ethnocentric Athenians argued for their autochthonous "purity" and therefore superiority.

was even greater than all these and is no less worthy of admiration: although clearly he did nothing inappropriate or unworthy in all that I have already described, he also used the pretext of fighting against one city, when in reality he fought not only against all those who inhabit Asia but also against many other races of barbarians, and he did not cease or turn back until he had enslaved the city of that man who dared to wrong us and had put an end to the arrogance of the barbarian.

[84] I am aware that I have said many things about the excellence of Agamemnon and that if people were to examine each one of these to find which they would reject, no one would dare remove any. Still, when they are read out continuously, everyone would fault me for having said much more than is necessary. [85] For my part, if I were unaware that I went on too long, I would be ashamed that I was so imperceptive when I tried to write on a subject that no one else had dared undertake. But, in fact, I knew more clearly than those who would dare abuse me that many will fault this. Nonetheless, I thought that it would not be so terrible if I should seem to some to miss the mark in this section of my speech, rather than if I should leave out of my description of such a man some good thing that belongs to him and would be appropriate for me to mention. [86] I thought that I would gain a good reputation among the best members of the audience if I were seen to make my discourse about the excellence of this man and to be more concerned about how I might speak in a manner worthy of that excellence than about the symmetry of the discourse. I did this although I knew clearly that even if the absence of proportion in my discourse would make me less popular, my sound judgment in assessing their accomplishments would benefit those who receive my praise.[57] In spite of this, however, passing over any advantage to me, I

---

[57] He refers to his praise of Agamemnon here, even though he speaks in the plural. The plural reference allows this statement to be more programmatic and allows him latitude elsewhere too. Isocrates digresses on Theseus (10.18–37) and Paris (10.41–48) in *Helen* and on Heracles in *To Philip* (5.109–115). A similar approach can be seen with his treatment of the fourth-century general Timotheus in *Antidosis* (15.101–139). Isocrates uses a similar, and perhaps more expected, form of this argument in *On The Peace* (8.39), where he says that he would be ashamed if he were more worried about his reputation than the security of the state,

chose what was right to do.[58] [87] And I will not be found to adopt this attitude only in what I said now, but I do the same in all my writings, since it will be clear that I take more joy in my students who gain a good reputation for their life and deeds than those who have a reputation for cleverness in their discourse. And yet when one of them says things well, even if I add nothing to it, all would give the credit to me, whereas when someone achieves success in action, even if everyone knew that I was an advisor, still everyone would praise the person who actually performed the deeds.

[88] But I do not know where I am being taken, for since I always think that I need to add the next point to what I have already said, I am now very far from my subject. There is nothing left to do, then, but to ask pardon in my old age for my forgetfulness and long-windedness, common habits of people of my age, and then return to that place from which I veered into this digression. [89] I think that I already see where I went astray.[59] I was responding to those who abused our city for the sufferings of the Melians and other such villages not by arguing that these were not crimes but by pointing out that the people my attackers esteem have destroyed more and more important cities than we have. It was in this context that I talked about the excellence of Agamemnon and Menelaus and Nestor, saying nothing false, though perhaps a bit longer than appropriate. [90] I was doing this on the assumption that there is clearly no greater crime than that of daring to destroy cities that bore and raised such great men about whom one could even now deliver many fine speeches. But it is foolish to focus on one topic as if there were a lack of things one might say about the cruelty and harshness of the Spartans, when, in fact, there is a great abundance. [91] It was not enough for them to wrong these cities with their great men, but they also wronged those

---

whereas in the current speech, he is more concerned about his literary topic than his reputation.

[58] Isocrates remarkably alludes to political and deliberative motivations by inserting the ideas of advantage and justice into a statement about literary judgment. He chose to do what was right (*dikaion*) for his literary topic rather than to do what would be advantageous (*lusiteles*) for himself.

[59] Sections 70–73.

who set out from the same place, made a common expedition, and shared in the same dangers; I mean the Argives and Messenians. Wanting to heap the same troubles on these men as on those others, they besieged the Messenians and did not stop until they had driven them from their land, and even now they make war against the Argives for this same purpose. [92] Further, after saying all this, it would be strange not to recall what they did to the Plataeans, in whose land they once[60] joined forces with us and the other allies, took up their position against the enemy, and sacrificed to the gods worshiped by the Plataeans. Together, then, we freed not only the Greeks who were with us [93] but also those who had been forced to side with the Persians. We did this even though among the Boeotians we had only the Plataeans on our side.[61] Yet not long after this, the Spartans, to please the Thebans, besieged and put to death all the Plataeans except those who could escape.[62] Our city was completely different from the Spartans in its treatment of these people. [94] For they dared to commit such crimes against them when they were benefactors of Greece and related to them by birth;[63] but our ancestors by contrast resettled to Naupactus those Messenians who had been saved and made the Plataeans who survived Athenian citizens, sharing everything they had with them. Consequently, if we had nothing else to say about the two cities, from this it would be easy to learn what each city was like and which had destroyed more and greater cities.

[95] Now, I perceive my attitude becoming contrary to what I said a little earlier, for at that point I became uncertain and lost and forgetful, but now I know clearly that I am not preserving the gentleness in my discourse that I had when I began to write it, but I am now

---

[60] The battle of Plataea was the last and decisive battle of the Persian Wars in 479.

[61] The other major city in Boeotia, Thebes, had "Medized" (cf. 4.157n, 14.30n).

[62] Plataea was the location of one of the first battles of the Peloponnesian War. Thebes attacked it unsuccessfully in 431 (Thuc. 2.2–6) and then again with a siege begun in 429 (Thuc. 2.71–78). The Plataeans eventually surrendered in 427; the men were killed, the women enslaved, and the town razed (3.20–24, 52–68). A period of fifty-two years intervened between the battle of Plataea and the razing of Plataea in 427; Isocrates calls this "not long" here for rhetorical effect.

[63] The Spartans and the Plataeans were both of Dorian descent.

taking up matters I had not planned to address, and I am becoming bolder than I normally am, as well as losing control over some of the things I am saying because of the number of points rushing to me to mention. [96] Therefore, since the desire to speak frankly has come over me, and I have unleashed my tongue, and I have created such a large thesis that it is neither good nor possible for me to leave out those actions by which I can show that our city had become more worthy among the Greeks than that of the Spartans, I must not be silent about the other evils I have not yet related but that occurred among the Greeks. Rather, I must show that our ancestors were slow to learn such crimes, whereas the Spartans were either the first to commit them in some instances or the only ones to do so in others.

[97] Most people accuse both cities because they pretended to be fighting against the barbarians for the sake of Greece, but then they did not allow other cities to be independent and to manage their own affairs as they saw fit. Instead, as if they had captured prisoners of war, they divided the cities up and enslaved them all; they acted like those who take slaves away from others as if to give them their freedom but then compel them to be their own slaves. [98] Yet for these crimes or many others more bitter than these, we are not the ones responsible but those who are opposed to us, both in what they say now and more generally in everything they do. For no one could show that our ancestors, in all the countless years before, ever tried to rule over any city, either great or small, but all know that the Spartans, from the time they first arrived in the Peloponnese, have done and planned for nothing other than how they might rule over all Greece, or if not all, at least the Peloponnese. [99] And as for the accusations of factions, murders, and overthrow of governments that some people bring against both our cities, the Spartans clearly filled all the cities except a few with such troubles and afflictions, but no one would ever dare say that about our city, before the disaster in the Hellespont,[64] that it had done such things to its allies. [100] But when the Spartans, who had been masters of Greece, lost power over our affairs, and the other cities were

---

[64] The naval defeat at Aegospotami in 405 is regularly mentioned only euphemistically by the orators.

mixed in factionalism, during this time two or three of our generals[65]—for I will not hide the truth—committed crimes regarding some of the cities, hoping that if they copied Spartan actions, they would be able to control them better. [101] Thus, all would rightly accuse the Spartans of being the leaders and teachers of such actions, but it would be only reasonable to forgive our ancestors, as you would forgive pupils who are deceived by their teachers' promises and have been disappointed in their hopes.

[102] Finally then, consider what they did alone and on their own: who does not know that during the time when we both together felt hostility toward the barbarians and their kings, and found ourselves in many battles and at times overcome by troubles, when our land was often ravaged and destroyed, we never looked to friendship or alliance with our enemy but continued to hate them because of their designs on Greece even more than we hate those who now treat us badly? [103] The Spartans, on the other hand, although they suffered no harm and had no expectation or fear that they would suffer, became so greedy that they were not satisfied with having an empire on land but were so eager to take control of the sea as well that they induced our allies to revolt with the promise to free them, and also negotiated with the King for a treaty of friendship and alliance, offering to hand over all those who lived in Asia. [104] But after they gave pledges to both these parties and then defeated us, those whom they had pledged to free they enslaved more than helots, and to the King they showed such gratitude that they persuaded his brother Cyrus, although younger, to contest the kingship. They gathered an army to support him, put Clearchus in command of it, and sent it against the King. [105] When fortune failed them in these plans,[66] since their intentions were known and they were hated by all, they were thrown into war and confusion such as might be expected when someone wrongs both the Greeks and the barbarians.

---

[65] Chares and others of the Second Athenian League (cf. Hammond 1986: 516; Ghirga and Romussi 1999: 467).

[66] Cyrus was killed at the battle of Cunaxa in 403. The whole expedition is described by Xenophon, a participant, in the *Anabasis*.

I do not know that I need to spend more time talking about this, except to say that after they were defeated at sea by the King's forces under Conon's command,[67] they then concluded a peace treaty.[68] [106] You could not ever find any peace treaty that was more shameful or more open to reproach or more demeaning to the Greeks or more contrary to what some call the virtue of the Spartans.[69] When the King made them despots over the Greeks, they tried to take away his kingship and all his success, but when he defeated them at sea, they handed over to him not just a small part of Greece but all Asia. [107] They wrote explicitly in the treaty that he should treat them as he wished, and they were not ashamed of making such agreements about men they had as allies when they defeated us and became masters of Greece and hoped to take control of all Asia. They inscribed treaties like this on stones,[70] placed them in their temples, and forced the allies to do this too.

[108] I do not think that others will want to hear about any more deeds, but they will assume that they have learned enough from what I have said about how each city has behaved toward the Greeks. I have a different view, however. I think the subject I proposed needs many other additional arguments, especially those that will demonstrate the foolishness of those who will try to oppose what I have said. I think that it will be easy to find such arguments, [109] for of those who approve all the achievements of the Spartans, those whom I consider the best and wisest will praise the Spartan constitution and will have the same opinion about it as before but will agree with what I have said about their treatment of the Greeks. [110] Those critics who are worse than this first group and, in fact, worse than most people, and who

---

[67] At the battle of Cnidus in 394.

[68] The Peace of Antalcidas, also known as the King's Peace, of 387/6. Notice how quickly Isocrates moved through Spartan history in this section. Events that occurred over seventeen years (from the end of the Peloponnesian War in 404 to the Peace in 387/6) are narrated as if they came in rapid succession. Such rapidity increases the energy of the passage and also the sense of Spartan wrongdoing.

[69] Cf. Isocrates' comments in *Panegyricus* (4.120–125) written forty years earlier. For a similar view of Spartan skepticism about peace, see *Archidamus* (6).

[70] On inscribed treaties, see 4.176n.

cannot say anything tolerable on any subject but cannot stay quiet about the Spartans, these imagine that if they make their praise of them excessive, they will gain the same reputation as those who are more eloquent and seem much better than they are. [111] Such men, when they sense that all their points have been anticipated, and they have nothing to say against my arguments, will turn, I think, to an argument about governments, comparing the one there with the one here in Athens, and particularly setting their prudence and obedience against our slackness, and they will praise Sparta on these grounds. [112] If they try to do this, sensible people should realize that they are talking nonsense, for I set this out not to have a discussion about constitutions but to show that our city is much more praiseworthy than Sparta in its relations with the Greeks.[71] Therefore, if they were to refute any of these points or mention other joint actions in which the Spartans were better, they would deserve credit. But if they try to speak about things I have not mentioned, all would rightly consider them senseless. [113] Not only that, but since I think that they will bring their discussion of constitutions into this discussion, I shall not hesitate to talk about that topic. For I think that in this too I will show that our city is even more superior than in what I have already said.

[114] And let no one assume that I am speaking about our present constitution that we were forced to accept but about the government of our ancestors. Our fathers did not find fault with this older one when they adopted the present government. Indeed, they judged the older one much more serious in many regards but thought that the present one would be more suited for a naval empire; they adopted the new one, and, caring for it well, they were able to ward off the plots of the Spartans and the whole Peloponnesian force, for it was important for our city to prevail over them in battle, especially at that time. [115] Thus, no one could justly fault those who chose this government, and indeed they did not err in their hopes and were not wrong about the advantage and disadvantage stemming from each; they knew clearly that hegemony by land is maintained by order, pru-

---

[71] It is true that when Isocrates sets out his thesis in sections 39–42, he makes it a comparison of the two cities and their "power, achievements, and benefits provided to the Greeks" (41).

dence, obedience, and other such qualities yet power by sea is not increased by these [116] but by the skills pertaining to ships and by men who can row them, namely, those who have lost their own livelihood and are used to making a living by receiving pay from others. With the arrival of these factors in the city, it was clear that the order established in the former constitution would be destroyed and the goodwill of the allies would quickly be reversed when they forced those states to whom they had formerly granted land and cities to hand over contributions and war taxes so that they might have money to pay the men I just mentioned. [117] But nevertheless, although they were aware of these considerations, they thought that for a city of such size and reputation, it was both advantageous and proper to endure all these problems rather than be ruled by the Spartans. For when two actions that are unappealing are presented, the better choice is to do something terrible to someone else rather than suffer it yourself and to rule unjustly over others rather than avoid this reproach but end up unjustly as slaves to the Spartans.[72] [118] This is what all who are wise would choose and prefer, but there are a few who claim to be wise who would disagree if asked. These then are the reasons, though perhaps I have spent too much time discussing why they changed their form of government from one praised by all to one faulted by some.

[119] So I will now turn to the topic I proposed, the constitution and our ancestors, starting from the time when the names oligarchy and democracy were not even known but when monarchies governed the tribes of barbarians and all the Greek cities. [120] I have chosen to begin in the distant past, first because I thought that those who lay claim to excellence should be better than others right from the beginning, and next because I would be embarrassed if, having talked at length about good men—though men quite different from me—I did not make even a small mention of our ancestors who governed our city very well and [121] who were just as superior to those who hold monarchies, as the wisest and gentlest men are superior to the wildest and most savage beasts. For what example of extreme impiety or terrible behavior would we not find in those other cities and especially in

---

[72] Quite in contrast to Socrates, who, in Plato's *Gorgias* (469) says that doing injustice is worse than suffering injustice.

those that we considered the greatest then and are reckoned so now? Has there not been an abundance of crimes: murders of brothers and fathers and guests? [122] Also the slaughters of mothers and incest and bearing of offspring from their own parents? And the eating of children that was planned by family members? Were there not exposures of children, drownings, blindings, and a multitude of other evils? With so many, there will never be any shortage for those who present stories of such calamities in the theater every year.[73]

[123] I went through this not because I wanted to abuse them but to point out that no such crimes ever occurred with our ancestors. This is not a sign of their excellence but only that they did not have the same nature as those who are most impious. Those who try to praise anyone extravagantly must demonstrate not only that they are not base but that they are superior to others past and present, in all the virtues. And one can say this about our ancestors. [124] They managed both the affairs of the city and their own affairs piously and well, as was only fitting for those who were born from gods, who were the first to inhabit their city and establish laws, and who always cultivated piety toward the gods and justice toward humans. They were not of mixed race nor invaders but the only autochthonous Greeks,[74] [125] for this land was their nurse from the time they were born, and they loved it as the best children do their fathers and mothers. In addition, they

---

[73] These are general references to famous myths of the Greeks. The list is organized by activity, not by myth, though the references highlight the Theban house and the Argive house. Oedipus killed his father; Orestes murdered his mother; Oedipus committed incest with his mother and produced offspring; Thyestes unknowingly ate his own children because of a plot of his brother Atreus; Oedipus was exposed; Orestes was exiled; Danae and her son were sent into the sea to drown by her father; Oedipus blinded himself. There is no mention of one of the more objectionable stories from myth—at least it was so to Lucretius—the sacrifice of Iphigenia by Agamemnon. There are two reasons for this. Isocrates cannot criticize this act, since he has just finished praising Agamemnon, and if he made a general reference to the sacrifice of daughters, it could also recall the sacrifice by Erechtheus, the early king of Athens. Isocrates avoids the stories of Athens that might be objectionable to make his point (cf. Papillon 1996b).

[74] The notion of autochthony, being born from the land and therefore native, is common in praise of Athens (cf. 4.24–25).

were so loved by the gods that they alone had what seems to be a most difficult and unusual achievement, the stability of a royal or tyrannical family lasting four or five generations.[75] [126] For Erechthonius, who was born from Hephaestus and Ge (Earth),[76] took the household and kingship of Athens from Cecrops, because he had no male children. Beginning with him, all those born afterwards, and there were many, handed down their possessions and their power to their children, down to the time of Theseus. I would much prefer not to have spoken about Theseus' excellence and his accomplishments already,[77] for it would have been much more fitting to discuss them here in a discourse about the city.[78] [127] For it would be difficult, even impossible, to move the thoughts I had at that time to this occasion, which I did not then foresee would come. Therefore, I will pass over these matters, since for now I have used them up. I will mention only one thing, which turns out not to have been addressed before, nor to have been accomplished before by anyone else but Theseus, which is the greatest sign of that man's excellence and prudence. [128] For although he had the safest and greatest kingdom, where he had accomplished many noble things, both in war and in governing the city, he looked past all these things and chose the glory that will be remembered for all time because it comes from labor and struggle instead of the leisure and prosperity that was available at that time because of his kingship. [129] And he did this not when he was older and had already experienced all the good things available to him but when he was in the prime of life. It is said that he handed over the city to the people to

---

[75] It is true that the house of Athens lasted many generations according to their own myth, but this longevity is also true of other cities, such as Thebes or Argos.

[76] The story of the birth of Erichthonius is variously told. Hephaestus is usually the father, but the mother is sometimes Earth (here and in the *Iliad*) and sometimes Athena (Apollodorus 3.14.6; Hyginus, *Fabula* 166). In the latter story, Hephaestus tries to rape Athena, but she escapes, and his semen falls on the ground, from which Erechthonius springs. Thus, Athena can stay a maiden, a virgin goddess, while still narratively the "mother" of Erechthonius and Athens.

[77] Isocrates treated Theseus at length in his discourse *Helen* (10.18–37).

[78] For the idea that the discourse on Helen was, in fact, really about the city and Greece at large, see Kennedy 1958. For an alternate view that she did not function as an analogy for Greece, see Papillon 1996a.

govern and himself turned to warfare on behalf of the city and the other Greeks.

[130] Thus I have recalled the excellence of Theseus now as best I could, even though I related all his deeds with some care earlier. As for those who took over management of the city that he passed on, I do not know what kind of praise I could give that would adequately express their wisdom. Although they were not experienced in government, they did not fail to choose a constitution that was acknowledged by all as not only the most inclusive and just but also the most advantageous to all and the most pleasant for those affected by it. [131] For they established a democracy (*dēmokratia*), not one that was administered arbitrarily, where lack of restraint was considered freedom or happiness was being able to do whatever you wished, but one that found fault with such attitudes and relied on the guidance of the best citizens (*aristokratia*).[79] Now, most people wrongly count this sort of government, which is, along with rule by the wealthy, the most useful, to be one of the distinct types of government, making this mistake not through ignorance but because they have never been concerned with what they ought to have cared for. [132] I assert, however, that there are only three forms of government: oligarchy, democracy, and monarchy. Those who live in such governments and who generally put in charge of the government and other matters the most capable citizens who will oversee affairs in the best and most just manner, these men will have the best life in each type of government, both for themselves and in their relations with others. [133] The ones, however, who enlist the worst and most daring men for these positions, the kind who do not consider the interests of the city but are ready to

---

[79] This passage (130–134) is a good example of Isocrates' thinking on government, where he espouses democracy but considers an aristocratic form of it best. He presents a traditional division, as seen in Pindar (*Pythian* 2.87) or Herodotus (3.80–83), that will be treated with more specificity by Plato (*Republic* 8–9) and Aristotle (*Politics* 3.7). Norlin (1929: *ad loc.*) points out that Isocrates argues that the best form of any of his three categories is the aristocratic version, where the best man is king, or the best people make decisions, or the best people lead the group. Statements like these have led some scholars to question Isocrates' dedication to democratic Athens, but he advocates only what most democracies advocate, that the best people should hold the leadership positions (cf. *Areopagiticus* [7.22]).

endure whatever they must for their own advantage, the cities of these people will be managed in a way similar to the baseness of those in charge of it. A third group, different from the two groups I have mentioned, who, when they are confident, honor those who say what they want to hear but when fearful, run to those who are the best and wisest, will do well or ill alternately. [134] This, then, is the nature and power of each form of government. I think, however, that these topics will provide much more material for others than what I have said just now, though I must not say any more about them;[80] I will speak only about that of our ancestors, for I propose to show that this was more serious and brought more benefits than the constitution in Sparta.

[135] For those who gladly listen to me discussing the useful kinds of government, this discourse will not be troublesome or inappropriate but fitting and in accord with what I said before. To those, however, who do not take pleasure in things said with great earnestness but prefer abusive discourses at gatherings, or if they do not go in for this foolishness, those who celebrate either things that are very trivial or the most lawless people who ever existed, to these sorts of people I think my discourse will seem longer than necessary. [136] But I have never cared about this sort of audience, and neither do most wise people. I am concerned, rather, with those who will remember what I have said before in the preface to the discourse and who will not fault the length of my discourse, not even if it extends to tens of thousands of words,[81] but who will understand that it is up to them to read and consider as large a part of it as they wish; and I am especially interested in those who especially enjoy hearing a discourse that presents the virtues of men and the structure of a well-governed city. [137] If someone wishes and is able to imitate these examples, they will them-

---

[80] This could be an instance of Isocrates laying out an example of how to treat a topic (130–134) and then leaving room for his pupils to do exercises on it. It is important to note here that this topic is not trivial but a serious one of types of government and what makes each attractive. Exercises (or topics for them) were not trivial, as some detractors of rhetorical education have said.

[81] This translation of *Panathenaicus* is something over twenty-five thousand words.

selves lead a life of great reputation and will make their own cities prosperous.

This, then, is the sort of audience I want to have, but I fear that if I had them, my discourse would fall far short of the topic I intended to treat in it. Nonetheless, I will try to speak about it as best I am able. [138] It would be fair, then, to give credit for our city being governed better than others at that time to its kings about whom I spoke a little earlier. For they were the ones who instructed the people in excellence (*aretē*) and justice (*dikaiosynē*) and great prudence (*sōphrosynē*) and who taught by their example the lesson that I will describe long after they actually practiced it, that every government is the soul of its city and has as much power as practical wisdom (*phronēsis*) has in the body. For it is this that plans everything and preserves the good things we have and avoids troubles and is responsible for all that happens in cities.

[139] The people learned this and did not forget it when they changed to democracy,[82] but more than anything else, they paid attention to how they might get leaders who favored democracy, but had the same character as their earlier leaders had, and would not intentionally choose leaders for the government to whom no one would entrust their private affairs. [140] They did not want to let anyone handle the affairs of the city who was recognized to be evil, or listen to people who have reprehensible personal lives and yet think that they should advise others about how they might govern their city prudently and thus fare better, or who use up what they received from their fathers in shameful pleasures while trying to aid their own private needs from public funds, who are always eager to say what people want to hear and then bring great discomfort and pain on those who are persuaded by them. [141] Everyone will agree that one should keep all such men away from advising them and also those who say that the property of others belongs to the city while daring to steal and plunder the city's own property and who pretend to be friends of the people but make the people hated by everyone else. [142] They say

<hr>

[82] Traditionally assigned to the reforms of Solon and Cleisthenes in the sixth century, but Isocrates makes Theseus responsible. Isocrates discusses the Athenian polity also in *Areopagiticus* (7.19–28).

that they fear for the Greeks' welfare, but in their actions they mistreat them, maliciously accuse them, and make them so hostile toward us that some cities going to war would more gladly and quickly take in their besiegers than accept help from us. But anyone would soon tire of writing if he tried to enumerate every crime and depravity.

[143] Our ancestors hated these faults and the people who had them. They appointed as their advisors and leaders not any random people but the best and the wisest, those who had lived the finest lives, and they chose these same men as their generals and sent them as ambassadors too, whenever they had need. They bestowed all leadership positions in the city on them, because they considered those who wish to and can give counsel from the speaker's platform would also have the same views on their own in any place and facing any task. This is what happened. [144] Because of these decisions, they saw their laws written down in just a few days, not like those we have now, full of such confusion and contradictions that no one is able to understand which are useful and which are not. First of all, there were just a few of them, but enough for those who would use them and easy to understand; second, they were just, useful, and consistent, as well as more serious about public conduct than private contracts, as must be the case where cities are well governed.

[145] About this same time they appointed as magistrates those who had already been selected by their tribes (*phylae*) and demes (*dēmoi*).[83] They made the offices not so much something to fight for or desire but much more like liturgies,[84] which are a burden for those assigned them but also bring some honor. For those chosen to lead had to set aside concern for their own possessions and refrain from taking the profits that often are given to people in office as well as the temple proceeds. What current leader would endure such restrictions? [146] Those who were careful about these things were praised appropriately and assigned another similar duty, but those who transgressed

---

[83] Tribes (*phylae*) were local units, originally by family, then geographic, used to organize the Athenian population. The ten tribes of Athens were created to assist in the choice of leaders by Cleisthenes during his political reforms of the late sixth century. These were broken into geographical demes (*dēmoi*) to ease the process. Cf. 8.88n.

[84] On liturgies, see the Series Introduction.

even a little met with the greatest shame and punishment. Thus, none of the citizens had the same attitude toward the magistracies as people do now, but they avoided them in those days even more than citizens pursue them now. [147] And everyone thought that there never was a democracy more honest, stronger, or more advantageous for most of the people than one that removed such concerns from the people but gave them authority over filling offices and punishing those who misused them. This is what happens to the best of tyrants too. [148] The greatest proof that they valued this government even more highly than I say is that elsewhere the people fought against governments they did not like, overthrew them, and killed their leaders, but people kept this form of government no less than a thousand years[85] and remained with it from the time they got it to the time of Solon and the tyranny of Peisistratus; Peisistratus became a demagogue, did much harm to the city, exiled the best citizens by claiming they were oligarchs, and finally overthrew the people's power and set himself up as a tyrant.

[149] Now, perhaps some might say it is strange—for nothing keeps me from interrupting this discourse—that I dare to speak as though I know precisely about events at which I was not present. But I think that I am doing nothing unreasonable in this. If I were the only one who trusted what was said about ancient times and what was written at that time and handed down to us, I might reasonably be faulted. But, in fact, many sensible people clearly feel the same way as I do. [150] And apart from this, if I had to prove this logically, I could show that everyone gets more knowledge (*epistēmē*) from what they hear than from what they see, and the actions they hear from others are more numerous and better than those at which they were actually present. Nonetheless, it is not right to ignore such responses—for perhaps they might injure the truth if no one refutes them—nor is it right to waste a lot of time refuting them but only as much as shows other material with which they could prove that they are speaking nonsense; then you should go back and finish up, beginning where you left off. This is what I will do.

[151] Thus, I have sufficiently shown the organization of their government and how long they had it. There remains only to relate the

---

[85] A very general number. Isocrates is thinking from the time that Theseus passed the government to the people (cf. 130) until Peisistratus.

actions that resulted from their good government. For from these you will understand even better that the government of our ancestors was better and wiser than others and that they had leaders and advisors who were the kind of men the wise should have. [152] Still, I must not address these points before I say a few preliminary words about them. For if I overlook the criticisms of those who can do nothing except complain, and describe in order all their achievements, especially the military practices they used to overcome the barbarians and become famous among the Greeks, there is no way that someone would not say that I am actually describing the laws established by Lycurgus that the Spartans use.

[153] I agree that I should talk about many of the customs at Sparta not because Lycurgus found or invented them, however, but because he was imitating the government of our ancestors as best he could: he established a democracy for them that was mixed with aristocracy, just as it was with us, prescribed that offices not be assigned by lot but by election, [154] passed a law prescribing the selection of a council of elders to oversee all matters with the same seriousness as they say our ancestors had concerning matters that came before the Areopagus, and gave them the same power that he knew the Council of the Areopagus had among us. [155] Anyone who wants to know the truth can learn from many sources that Lycurgus established the same kind of government there as existed in our city in ancient times among us. That the Spartans did not cultivate military skills before us or use them better than our ancestors, I think I can show clearly from the wars that people agree took place at that time. Thus, even the foolish adherents of Sparta will not be able to disagree, nor will those who admire our deeds and at the same time abuse them but then strive to imitate them.

[156] I will begin what I am going to say with something that may be unpleasant for some to hear but not unhelpful to say. For if someone should say that these two cities were responsible for the most benefits for the Greeks and also for the most harm after the time of Xerxes' campaign, to those who know something about the past he would certainly seem to speak the truth. [157] For they struggled in the best way possible against his forces, and having done this, when they ought to have planned well about the things to follow, they became not just so stupid but so crazy that though they could easily have defeated him both on land and at sea, they concluded a permanent peace treaty with

the man who marched against them and who wanted to completely destroy our two cities and enslave the rest of the Greeks, [158] as if they were making a treaty with someone who had been a benefactor.[86] On the other hand, jealous of each others' strengths, they entered into war and rivalry against each other and did not stop destroying each other and the rest of the Greeks until they had put their common enemy, the King, in control so that he could put our city in the greatest danger because of the force of the Spartans and similarly could put their city at risk because of our city. [159] And although they fell so far short of the cleverness of the barbarian, at that time they did not feel the pain they deserved for what they suffered or that was fitting for them, and even now, the greatest cities of Greece do not feel ashamed to fawn on his wealth, but the cities of Argos and Thebes fight together with him against Egypt, so that he might have the greatest force possible when he plots against the Greeks. But we and the Spartans, although we had an alliance, were more hostile to each other than to those against whom either of us happened to be fighting in battle. [160] No small sign of this is that although we do not plan together about a single issue, separately each of us sends ambassadors to him, hoping that he will put whomever he more prefers in charge of the surplus funds of the Greeks. We do not understand very well that he usually mistreats those who curry his favor but tries in every way possible to make amends with those who oppose him and show contempt for his power.

[161] I have gone through this, not ignorant that some will have the daring to say that I have gone beyond the subject of my discourse with these arguments. I, however, think that never have words been spoken that were more directly connected to the preceding argument than these, nor could any words show someone more clearly that our ancestors were wiser about our most important affairs than those who managed our city or Sparta after the war against Xerxes. [162] For it is clear that these cities during those times were making peace with the barbarians and were destroying themselves and the other Greeks. Now they think they deserve to rule over the Greeks while sending ambassadors to the King to negotiate friendship and an alliance. But those

---

[86] The Peace of Antalcidas, also known as the King's Peace, in 387/6.

who lived in our city in the past did none of these things, and in fact quite the opposite. [163] For they had made a firm commitment to stay away from other Greek cities just as the pious keep their hands off the offerings in the temples, and they assumed that the most necessary and most just war, after the war all humans wage against the savage beasts, was the one between the Greeks and the barbarians, who are by nature hostile toward us and are always plotting against us. [164] The principle I have stated is not my own invention but was drawn from their actions. For when they saw that the other cities were caught in great troubles, and wars, and conflicts, and that only their own city was well governed, our ancestors did not believe that those who were wiser and better off than others should ignore this and allow cities of the same lineage to perish,[87] but should, rather, investigate and take action to free all cities from their present evils. [165] With this in mind, they tried by means of embassies and negotiation to alleviate discord from those who were less troubled, but to those cities that were more divided by factionalism, they sent their citizens who had the best reputations to advise those cities about their current situation. Finally, they met with those who could not live in their own cities and who were in worse condition than the law allows, who for the most part do harm to a city, and persuaded them to join their campaign and seek a better life than the one they had. [166] As there were many who wanted this and were persuaded by them, they gathered an army from these men, overthrew the barbarians who occupied the islands and the coast of either continent, expelled them all, and then settled those lands with those Greeks who were especially destitute. They continued to do this, providing an example for others, until they heard that the Spartans, as I had said, had put all the cities in the Peloponnese under their control. After this, they were compelled to pay attention to their own situation.

[167] What good, then, came from this war and other colonizing

---

[87] Isocrates refers in these sections to historical migrations of different clans of Greeks, who shared local dialects. The Athenians spoke a version of the Ionian dialect, and the people connected with this dialect spread to the east in the ninth and eighth centuries. In section 166, he will make this period of colonization coincide with the Dorian invasion. This will help his persuasive presentation, even though historically the Dorian invasion occurred earlier.

activity (for I think that many people especially want to hear this)? The Greeks became more prosperous with respect to life's necessities and were more unified once they got free of the large number of people like this; the barbarians fell from power and had less confidence than before; and those who were responsible for these results had a great reputation and appeared to have made Greece twice as powerful as it was in the beginning. [168] I could not find a greater benefit from our ancestors, or one more advantageous to all Greece, than this. But perhaps I can mention one that is more relevant to preparing for war, no less deserving of fame and better known to all. For who does not know or has not heard from the tragedians at the Greater Dionysia[88] of the troubles that befell Adrastus in Thebes?[89] [169] Wanting to restore the son of Oedipus to power, who was his own son-in-law, he lost many Argive soldiers and saw all his captains killed. He himself escaped, though with reproach, and when he could not arrange a truce or take back his dead for burial, he came as a suppliant to Athens while Theseus was king and asked him not to allow such men to go unburied or allow an ancient practice and ancestral law to be broken that all people continue to use, not because it was established by human nature but because it was decreed by divine authority. [170] Hearing this, the people lost no time sending ambassadors to Thebes; they advised the Thebans to have a more pious attitude on the issue of collecting the bodies and to give a more lawful response to the request than they had made earlier; in this way, they also used this as an example to show that their city would not allow others to violate a law that was common to all Greeks. [171] When they heard this, those who were in charge at Thebes made a decision at odds with the reputation they have among some people, as well as

---

[88] The Dionysia was the major dramatic festival at Athens, where three poets would present plays as part of the worship of the god and as part of the dramatic competition.

[89] Eteocles and Polynices, sons of Oedipus, contested for control of Thebes, and Polynices brought an army from Argos to assist his attack on his brother, including the Argive king Adrastus. When the two brothers died at each other's hands, Adrastus enlisted Theseus to rescue the fallen Argives for proper burial. This was a common story for tragedy, as seen in Aeschylus' *Seven against Thebes,* Sophocles' *Antigone,* and Euripides' *Phoenissae.*

with their previous thinking, but after fairly presenting their own case and the case against those who had attacked them, they granted our city the right to recover the bodies.

[172] And let no one think that I am unaware that I am saying the opposite of what you will find I said in my *Panegyricus,* when I wrote about the same topic.[90] For I surely do not think that anyone who can understand these things is so foolish or envious that he would not praise me and consider me prudent for speaking about them in that way then and this way now. [173] I know that I have written about them nobly and appropriately, but I think this event will make it clear to all our city's superiority in war at that time, which is what I wanted to show when I related the events at Thebes, for it forced the king of Argos to become a suppliant at our city [174] and influenced the Theban authorities to choose to abide by the advice given by our city more than the laws set down by divine authority. Our city would not have been able to manage any of this if it had not been far superior to others in reputation and power.

[175] With so many noble actions of our ancestors to mention, I wonder how I should talk about them, for this is a bigger concern for me than anything else. I am now at the topic I have saved for the end, in which I said I would show that our ancestors are superior to the Spartans in wars and battles far more than in other areas.[91] [176] My argument will contradict the opinion of most people, but in this way it will seem true to the rest. Just now I was at a loss about whether I should relate the dangers and the battles of the Spartans or of our ancestors first, but I have now decided to speak about theirs first so that I might finish my discussion of this subject with the more noble and just events.

[177] When the Dorians who marched into the Peloponnese had divided into three parts the cities and lands that they had taken from their rightful owners, those who were allotted Argos and Messene managed their affairs just like the rest of the Greeks; according to those

---

[90] Cf. 4.54–60. The story of Adrastus and the Argives is also told in *Plataicus* (14.53–54). Usher (1990: 162) points out parallels with other authors. The version told here gives Athens more active involvement, but the tellings are quite similar.

[91] Cf. this section on the early history (175–198) with that in *Panegyricus* (4.51–70).

who know these things best, however, the third part that we now call Lacedaemon[92] was factionalized as no other Greek city ever was, and when those who scorn the masses got control, they devised policies about what happened that were not at all the same as those of others who had already been through similar events. [178] For the rest of the Greeks allowed those who had opposed them to live with them in the city and to share in everything except public offices and honors; the Spartans who were sensible thought these people were mistaken if they thought they could run a state securely while living with those men against whom they had committed the greatest crimes. So the Spartans did not do this but rather established for themselves the kind of equality before the law and democracy that those who are always going to agree ought to have, and they made the people into serfs (*perioikoi*), enslaving their souls no less than the souls of actual slaves.[93] [179] After this, they divided the land: although there were just a few of them, they took for themselves not only the best part (which all should have shared equally) but also more of it than any Greeks ever possessed before; to the common people they granted only a small portion of the worst land, just enough that with hard work, they could scarcely obtain their daily needs. After this, they divided up the people as best they could into very small groups, settled them into many small areas, and gave them names as if they lived in cities, but they actually had less power than our demes have.[94] [180] And after robbing them of all the things that free people should have, they subjected them to the greatest dangers, for in military campaigns that the king led, they were arranged in order, man to man, next to each other; some were put in the front ranks, and if the Spartans ever needed to

---

[92] Cf. 6.16n.

[93] Spartan society consisted of three parts: Spartan citizens; helots, the people who were conquered by the Spartans when they entered the region and were then subjected by them (cf. 5.49n); and *perioikoi* (lit. "dwellers around"), free persons who owned land and businesses outside Sparta proper but were under the control of the Spartan government. *Perioikoi* had civic rights and responsibilities but no say in the Spartan government. On *perioikoi*, see Demand 1996: 121–123 and Hammond 1986: 99–100.

[94] That is, they pretended that they were separate communities, though they were smaller than the demes (precincts) of Attica.

send help somewhere and feared the work, the danger, or the length of time involved, they would send the *perioikoi* to face the risk instead of the others. [181] Yet why should we go on at great length, listing all the outrages they committed against the people and not just mention the greatest of their crimes and leave the rest be? The Ephors had the right to put to death without trial as many as they wanted of these people, who had from the beginning suffered terribly but were now useful to them, whereas for the rest of the Greeks, it is impious to stain their hands with the murder of even the worst of slaves.

[182] I have described their internal relations and their crimes against the *perioikoi* at greater length so that I might ask those who approve all the actions of the Spartans if they approve these too and if they think that their battles against the *perioikoi* are pious and noble. [183] For I think that these are the most terrible acts, which have caused many evils for the losers and many gains for the winners, though the Spartans continue to fight for these all the time, but they are not pious or noble or appropriate for those who claim to be virtuous, at least if virtue is defined not as a matter of technical or artistic skill or any other such thing but as a quality found in the souls of good men together with piety and justice. This virtue (*aretē*) is the topic of this whole discourse. [184] Some people dismiss this virtue and praise those who commit more crimes than others, not realizing that they are showing their own character when they praise those who have more than they need but would dare to kill their own brothers and friends and associates so as to get the possessions of these people too. These sorts of deeds are similar to those of the Spartans, and those who approve these must have the same opinion about those I just described. [185] But I am amazed if some do not think that battles and victories that are contrary to justice are more shameful and more full of reproach than defeats that one suffers without doing wrong, especially when they know that great but evil powers are often stronger than men who are worthy and choose to face dangers for their country. [186] It would be much more just to praise these men than those who are willing to die to gain the prosperity of others and who are similar to mercenaries in foreign armies. For these are the deeds of evil men, and even though sometimes noble men fare worse in these contests than those who willingly do evil, this might be said to be due to the inattention of the gods. [187] I could make this argument about the

Spartan misfortune at Thermopylae,[95] and all who have heard about it praise and admire it more than victorious battles over enemies who should not have been attacked. Some dare to praise the latter, not understanding that there is nothing pious or noble in words or deeds that are without justice. [188] The Spartans never cared about such things, for they look to nothing other than how they might get possession of as much of other peoples' property as possible; our ancestors, on the other hand, strove for nothing so much as having a good reputation among the Greeks. For they realized that no judgment would ever be more true or more just than the one made by an entire people. [189] It was clear that they had this view both in the regular governing of the city and in the greatest of their actions. For in all three wars, not counting the Trojan War, that the Greeks waged against the barbarians, they put Athens at the front: one was against Xerxes where the Athenians' superiority to the Spartans in every battle was greater than the Spartans' superiority over the others; [190] second was the fighting over the founding of colonies, where none of the Dorians came to fight along with us, while our city became the leader of those who could not provide for themselves and of others who willingly went, and we caused such a change that although the barbarians were used to capturing the greatest of the Greek cities before, we made the Greeks able to inflict on the barbarians the same fate that they themselves had suffered before.

[191] I think I have said enough about the two earlier wars,[96] and so will move on to address the third war that occurred after the Greek cities had just been founded and our city was still ruled by kings. At that time, we faced many wars, and great dangers fell upon us, all of which I could not find out about or describe, [192] and so will leave aside the bulk of the things that happened at that time and that do not need to be discussed now. I will try, as briefly as I can, to describe the men who marched against us, the battles we faced that are worth re-

---

[95] On the battle at Thermopylae, see 4.90. The battle became an emblem of sacrifice for the good of the cause and was commemorated in ancient times by the poetry attributed to Simonides, still seen today on an inscription on the top of the burial mound where the Spartans lay.

[96] He spoke of the Persian Wars in sections 49–52 and the colonization of Asia in sections 164–168.

membering and discussing, and their leaders; in addition, I will try to show the excuses they gave and the power of the different peoples that accompanied them. This will be enough to say in addition to what we said about our opponents.

[193] First, the Thracians invaded our land led by Eumolpus, son of Poseidon, who contended with Erechtheus for control of the city, claiming that Poseidon had acquired it before Athena did. The Scythians invaded too, with the Amazons, born from Ares, who made the campaign to recover Hippolyta because she had transgressed their existing laws by falling in love with Theseus, returned with him from there, and lived with him in Athens. [194] The Peloponnesians also invaded, with Eurystheus, who refused to compensate Heracles for all the wrong he had done him and even made a campaign against our ancestors in an attempt to seize by force the children of Heracles who had fled to us for protection. He suffered what he deserved; far from gaining control over the suppliants, after being defeated in battle and taken prisoner by our ancestors, he ended his life as a suppliant himself of those people he had come to demand from us. [195] After this, those sent by Darius to sack Greece landed at Marathon and, meeting with more troubles and greater disasters than they had hoped to inflict on our city, left in flight from all Greece.

[196] All these groups I have mentioned did not invade all together or at the same time but as the opportunity and the self-interest and desire occurred to each.[97] Our ancestors conquered all of them in battle, put an end to their arrogance, and in spite of the magnitude of their accomplishments, did not betray themselves in the process,[98] avoiding the experience of those who by planning well and wisely, obtain great wealth and a fine reputation but then because of an excess of these benefits become arrogant, lose their good sense, and are brought

---

[97] Isocrates points out here that he is gathering a broad array of evidence. In fact, he combines what traditionally would be called both historical occurrences (Darius) and mythic accounts (Theseus and Hippolyta, the children of Heracles). Elsewhere, he refers to both the Persian Wars and the Trojan Wars as *mythoi*, thus making fewer distinctions between these than modern scholars and even many ancients such as Thucydides would. See further Papillon 1996b.

[98] Isocrates says in section 32 that keeping true to oneself is one of the signs of an educated person. For the full description of an educated person, cf. 30–32.

down to lower and poorer circumstances than they experienced before. [197] Instead, our ancestors escaped such dangers and kept to the character they always had by governing their city well and paying more attention to the conditions of their souls and the quality of their minds than to the battles they had fought; they were admired by others for their strength of character and prudent wisdom more than for the valor they displayed in battle. [198] For all saw that many people have spirits adept at war, even when they are experts in vice, but base men have no share in a spirit that is adept at everything and can help everyone, for this belongs only to those who are nobly born and raised and educated well, as were those who governed our city then and were responsible for all the goods I have mentioned.

[199] Now, I see others ending their discourses with the greatest and most memorable deeds, but although I think they are wise to think this way and do this, it turns out that I cannot do the same as they, but I am compelled to keep speaking. I will explain the reason for this a bit later, after a very few preliminary remarks.

[200] I was revising this discourse up to the point just read with three or four young people who regularly spend time with me. Although it seemed fine to us when we had gone through it, lacking only a conclusion, I decided to send for one of my former students, who was now part of an oligarchic government and liked to praise the Spartans, thinking that he would notice and point out if we had inadvertently said something wrong. [201] When I sent for him, he came and read through the discourse. I will not waste time reporting the intervening events, but nothing I had written troubled him, and he praised it as much as he could and discussed each of the parts just as we were doing. Nonetheless, it was clear that he was not pleased with what I had said about the Spartans. [202] He pointed this out quickly, for he ventured to say that even if the Spartans had done nothing else good for the Greeks, still, all should rightly be grateful to them because when they discovered the finest way of life, they adopted it themselves and revealed it to others.

[203] This brief and insignificant statement was responsible for my not completing the discourse as I had wished. It caused me to realize that I would be acting shamefully and shockingly if I would allow one of my former students to use inferior arguments in my presence. With this intention, I asked him if he thought nothing of those who were

present and was not ashamed to have made an assertion that was impious, false, and full of many inconsistencies. [204] "You will see that it is such, if you ask some of the wise what way of life they consider to be the best, and then how long the Spartans have lived in the Peloponnese. For there is no one who would not prefer a life of piety towards the gods, justice towards other people, and good sense (*phronē-sis*) in all other actions, but they would also say that the Spartans had inhabited their land no more than seven hundred years. [205] If these things are true, and if you turn out to be speaking the truth when you claim that they are the discoverers of the best way of life, then it is necessary that those who were born many generations before the Spartans settled there did not live such a life, not those who campaigned against Troy or who lived at the time of Heracles or Theseus, or Minos the son of Zeus, or Radamanthus or Aeacus or any other of those we praise in song for their virtues; they must all have a false reputation. [206] But if you turn out to be speaking nonsense, and, in fact, it is fitting that those born from the gods had this way of life more than others and showed it to their descendants, then there is no way that the whole audience will not think you are crazy, since you praise anyone you happen to think of so randomly and unjustly.

"Next, if you praise them when you have not heard my arguments, then you might be talking nonsense, but you at least would not seem to contradict yourself. [207] But as it is, when you have praised my discourse, which shows that the Spartans have done many terrible things both to their own people and to the rest of the Greeks, how could you still say that they have been leaders for the best way of life when they are responsible for such things? [208] In addition, you have failed to see that it is not just random persons who discover the customs, the skills, and everything else that was previously unnoticed but those who excel by nature and who are able to learn the most about earlier discoveries and more than anyone else want to focus their attention on finding others. The Spartans are further from this than even the barbarians. [209] For the barbarians can be considered to have learned and taught others many discoveries, but the Spartans are so far behind in general culture (*paideia*) and study (*philosophia*) that they do not even learn their letters, which have such great power that those who know and use them gain experience not only of events in their own time but of all the events of the past too. [210] Nevertheless, you have the audacity to say that those who are ignorant of such things are the discoverers of the finest way of life, even though you know that they teach their own children to develop ways of behaving that, they hope, will not make them benefactors of others but will make them most able to mistreat the Greeks.

[211] "If I were to go through all their crimes, it would be burdensome for me and my listeners, so I will mention only one, which they love and are particularly enthusiastic about, and by this I think I will show their whole character. The Spartans send out their sons every day, as soon as they get up, with any friends they want, allegedly to hunt but actually to steal from those who live in the country. [212] Those who are caught doing this pay a fine and are beaten, but those who do the most evil and are able to escape detection have a higher reputation among the children than the rest, and when they reach adulthood, if they maintain the way they practiced as children, they will be ready for the highest offices. [213] If someone can show any lesson they love more or consider more important than this one, I will admit that I have never said anything true on any topic at all. Yet is there anything noble or righteous in this practice? Is it not shameful? Must we not think that they are idiots when they praise those people who are so far outside common decency and share none of the attitudes that are common to Greeks and barbarians? [214] Others think that criminals and thieves are the most wicked slaves, but the Spartans assume that those who are the best at such acts are the finest of their children, and they honor them particularly. And yet what sane man would not prefer to die three times rather than be known as one who trains himself in excellence by means of such practices?"

[215] Hearing this, he did not respond to anything I said rashly, but he was not entirely silent either.[99] He said, "You (he meant me) have presented your argument as if I approved of everything there and

---

[99] The rhetorical device of presenting an absent person as though he were present and speaking directly is called *prosōpopoieia*. It is rare in Isocrates. When Isocrates presents the former student, though, he seems to give the student his own style. The student uses guarded phrases like "seems" and "appears to be" frequently, as would be appropriate for a student who wishes to criticize but still feels subordinate. The student also uses extended infinitive constructions more than Isocrates normally does.

thought everything was just fine in Sparta. In my opinion, however, it is reasonable to fault them for the freedom they give their children and on many other grounds, but you accuse me unfairly. [216] For when I read your discourse, I was pained by what you said about the Spartans, but even more because I could not reply to what you had written about them, since I usually praise them. But I was so perplexed that I gave the only answer left to me, that if for no other reason, at least we should all justly be grateful to them since they have the best way of life. [217] But I said this not with an eye to their piety or justice or good sense (*phronēsis*)—topics that you treated—but to the gymnastic training they have there and to the cultivation of bravery and their sense of unity and in general their preparation for war; all would praise these practices and would say that the Spartans are particularly good at them."

[218] When he said this, I accepted it not because he had refuted any of my criticisms, but because he had covered over the most bitter part of what he had said, not crudely, but quite thoughtfully, and had defended himself on the other points, more prudently than when he spoke frankly before. In any case, I let that go and replied that I had a much stronger attack on these very points of his than on their children's habit of stealing. [219] "For they harmed their own children with this practice, but with the ones you mentioned a little earlier, they destroyed the Greeks. And it is easy to see that this is the case. For I think all would agree that those who are the worst men and deserve the greatest punishment are those who take acts invented to help others and use them instead to do harm, [220] not against the barbarians or against those who wrong them or those who invade their land but against their closest friends and kinsmen. This is what the Spartans do. So how can you righteously say that they make good use of the practice of war when they spend their whole time destroying those they ought to be protecting? [221] Nonetheless, you are not alone in your ignorance of who makes good use of these practices, for nearly all Greece is ignorant too. For when they see or hear from someone that some people are devoting their time to practices that are thought to be good, they praise them and make great speeches about them, though they do not know the results. [222] But those who want to reach a correct judgment (*orthōs dokimazein*) about such people must hold their peace in the beginning and not form an opinion about them; but

when they come to that time when they see them speaking and acting, in private matters and in public affairs, then they should examine each of them carefully. [223] They should praise and honor those who make lawful and good use of their preparation, but they should criticize and hate and avoid the lifestyle of those who do wrong, whether deliberately or not, keeping in mind that things in themselves are neither helpful nor harmful, but the use people make of them and their actual conduct are responsible for all that happens to us. [224] You can understand this from the following: things that are entirely the same and not at all different turn out to be useful for some people and harmful for others. And yet it is not logical that each thing should have a nature that is not the same but the opposite of itself. On the other hand, what right-thinking person would not think it quite reasonable that nothing turns out the same for those who act rightly and justly as for those who act wantonly and wrongly?

[225] "This same argument would apply to their sense of unity too, for this is not different in nature to what I have already mentioned, but we would find that some of them are responsible for the greatest goods, while others are responsible for the greatest evils and misfortunes. And I would say that the Spartans' sense of unity is like this. For I will tell the truth, even if some of my claims appear to be completely contrary to general belief. [226] For the Spartans, by their unanimity among themselves about outside issues, were like professionals at making the Greeks fall into factions, and they thought that if the other Greek cities suffered the harshest misfortunes, this would be the most advantageous thing of all for them, for they could do what they wished with these cities if they were in such circumstances. Thus, no one could justly praise them for their sense of unity, no more than pirates and robbers and other criminals. For these too agree among themselves but then destroy others. [227] Now, if I seem to some to make a comparison that is inappropriate for their reputation, I will let this one go and bring up the Triballoi.[100] All agree that they have a sense of unity unmatched among men, but they destroy not only their neighbors and those who live near them but everyone else they can reach. [228] Those who lay claim to virtue (*aretē*) must not imitate these

---

[100] On the Triballoi, see 8.50n.

people but should much rather imitate the force of wisdom and justice and the other virtues. For these do not benefit others by their own natures but make those people happy and blessed with whom they permanently reside. The Spartans, however, are quite the opposite; they destroy those they are near, and they appropriate for themselves all the goods of others."

[229] With these words, I put the man to whom I made these arguments in his place, even though he was clever, very experienced, and trained in discourse no less than any of my former students. But the young men who were present for all this did not have the same opinion as I; although they praised me for having argued more vigorously than they expected and for making a fine argument, and they showed contempt for him, they were wrong to do so and misjudged both of us. [230] For he went away wiser and more humble in his mind, as sensible men should, and he experienced what it says at Delphi, so that he "knew himself" as well as the nature of the Spartans better than before. I, on the other hand, was left thinking that I may have argued successfully, but I felt that I was more foolish because of it and that I thought more of myself than is fitting for someone my age, so I was filled with youthful agitation. [231] This state of mind was clear to me, for when I calmed down, I did not stop before I had dictated to my slave the discourse that shortly before I had recited with such pleasure, but a little later would cause me pain. When three or four days had passed and I reread it and examined it, I was not bothered by what I had said about Athens, for everything I had written about the city was right and fair, [232] but I was pained and troubled by the things I said about Sparta. The passages about them seemed to me too immoderate and not like the other parts; they were demeaning, excessively harsh, and entirely thoughtless. Often I started to erase them or burn the work, but I changed my mind, taking pity on my own old age and the hard work I had put into the discourse.

[233] While I was so upset and kept making many changes, I decided it would be best to summon my former pupils who were in the city and consult with them whether the discourse should be entirely destroyed or distributed to those who wished to have it so they could do with it whatever they wished. Once I had decided this, I did not delay but immediately summoned those I had mentioned, and after I told them why they had been gathered, the discourse was read out

loud to them; it was praised and applauded, getting a reception like the ones that win in oratorical contests (*epideixeis*). [234] When all this was finished, the others began talking with one another; clearly, they were discussing what had been read. But the man whom I had summoned at the beginning to give advice, the one who always praised Sparta, to whom I had said more than I should, after a period of silence looked at me and said that he was uncertain what to make of the present situation, for he said he did not want to doubt my words, but he was unable to trust them entirely either.

[235] "I am wondering if you were so pained and troubled, as you say, by your remarks about the Spartans—for I see no such problem in what you have written—or if you gathered us together because you wanted to get our advice about the discourse, when you know clearly that we praise everything that you say or do. But intelligent people generally seek advice on matters that are important to them, especially from those who are wiser than themselves or else with those who will give their honest opinion. But you have done the opposite. [236] Therefore, I accept neither of these reasons; rather, you seem to me to have summoned us together and made your eulogy of Athens not simple-mindedly nor for the reasons you explained to us but because you wanted to test us to see if we were still lovers of wisdom, if we remember what you said during our studies, and if we could understand how you happened to write this discourse—[237] that you were wise to choose to praise your own city so that you might please the bulk of the citizens and have a good reputation among those favorably disposed toward you. Having decided this, you assumed that if you devoted your discourse to Athens alone and told the mythic stories about it that everyone keeps telling, your words would appear just like what others had written, and this would be most disgraceful and painful for you. [238] But if you put aside those myths and described those achievements that are acknowledged by all and have brought so many benefits for the Greeks, and if you contrasted them with the achievements of the Spartans and praised the actions of your ancestors but criticized those of the Spartans, then the discourse would appear more splendid to the audience, and you would remain true to your purpose, which some would admire more than those discourses written by others. [239] At the beginning, you seemed to me to organize and plan your discourse in this way, but since you knew that you had

praised the Spartan government as no one else has,[101] you feared that
the audience would view you like those who say whatever comes to
them because now you criticize those whom you earlier praised more
than others.[102] Reflecting on this, I think you studied how you could
describe each group and still appear to speak the truth about both—
how you could praise your ancestors as you wish but also make it appear to those who are hostile to the Spartans that you are accusing
them while they do not notice that, in fact, you are not doing this but
praising them. [240] Seeking such approaches, you seemed to find arguments easily that had subtext (*amphiboloi*),[103] and were equally supportive of those who praise and those who criticize, but could be used
on both sides and would provide many points for debate. If someone
uses such arguments in disputes over private contracts or for his own
gain, it is shameful and a sure sign of wickedness, but when used in
discussions of the nature of human beings or their behavior, it is noble
and philosophical (*philosophon*). [241] Such, in fact, was the discourse
that was just read, in which you made your own ancestors peace-
loving, devoted to the Greeks, and the leading supporters of equality
among cities but made the Spartans haughty (*hyperoptikous*), warlike
(*polemikous*), and interested in gain (*pleonektas*), just like all people assume them to be.

"But although each city has this sort of a nature, the Athenians be-

---

[101] Isocrates speaks highly of the Spartans throughout *Archidamus* (6) and in a
section of *On the Peace* (8.142–144).

[102] The issue here is whether Isocrates will be considered hypocritical, praising
Sparta in one place and criticizing it in another. Isocrates does not want to be put
in a category with groups such as the sophists. The sophists of the fifth and fourth
centuries were reputed to display their talent by speaking on any topic suggested by the audience, by giving speeches defending controversial topics, by arguing both sides of an issue, by praising trivial or evil subjects, and by making
"the lesser seem the greater cause." Plato's *Gorgias,* Aristophanes' *Clouds,* and Isocrates' own discourse *Against the Sophists* (13) discuss orators who present any idea
given to them, without thought for whether the issue was just or not. On the last
phrase, which might better be translated "make the weaker argument stronger,"
see Schiappa 1999: chap. 6 and Gagarin 2002: 24–26.

[103] On Isocrates' use of arguments with subtext or double meaning (*amphiboloi*), see Bons 1993.

ing praised by all and appearing to be well disposed toward the people, while most envy the Spartans and are hostile toward them, there are nonetheless those who praise and admire them [242] and have the courage to say that they, in fact, have more good qualities than your ancestors possessed. For haughtiness (*hyperopsia*) shares in dignity, a respected quality, and people with this quality seem to everyone to be more high-minded than the proponents of equality. Those who are warlike (*polemikos*) are far superior to peace-loving people, for the peace-loving are not grabbers of other people's possessions nor intimidating protectors of their own, but the warlike can do both: they can take what they want and protect anything they have, once they have it, and those who do this seem to be men in the most complete sense.[104] [243] They also think they have better arguments regarding the idea of being 'interested in gain' (*pleonexia*) than those you presented, for they do not think that those who break private contracts and deceive and cheat should rightly be called interested in gain, since in any situation they end up losing because of their bad reputation. In fact, this desire for gain by the Spartans and by kings and tyrants is something people pray for and that all people want. [244] Moreover, those who have such power are abused and cursed, but there is no one whose nature is such that he would not pray to the gods to have this power above all for himself or, if he cannot have it, then that his closest family members have it. From this it is clear that we all think the greatest benefit is to have more than others.[105]

---

[104] The pupil's point here—is it Isocrates' point too?—is that Isocrates is using terms that people hostile towards Sparta will take in a negative way but that those friendly to Sparta can take positively. There is an interesting parallel notion in the *History* of Thucydides, where the historian talks of how words changed their meaning to rationalize behavior that would otherwise be thought blameworthy. In his commentary on the revolution at Corcyra (3.82.4), Thucydides points out that audacity became known as courage, hesitation as cowardice, or moderation as unmanliness. Isocrates' former pupil is arguing for a positive outlook for Spartan characteristics, but one can see how easily it could be taken as rationalizing negative traits; this is precisely Isocrates' intent, according to the student. This is what makes the passage *amphibolos,* having double meaning.

[105] Sections 243–244 sound very much like the sort of argumentation attributed to the sophists and faulted by the Greeks, as described in the preceding note.

"It seems to me, then, that this was your intention when you designed the overall plan of the work. [245] If I thought you would leave what you said alone and let the work be unedited, I would not have tried to say anything more. But now, I do not think you will be worried that I ignored the matter I was summoned to advise on, for even when you summoned us, you did not seem to me to be serious about it. [246] Rather, you chose to compose a discourse unlike any other, one that seemed simple and easy to understand for those who read it cursorily, but for those who went through it carefully (*akribōs*) and tried to detect what others had failed to see, it was evidently difficult and hard to learn, full of much history and philosophy, and all sorts of decoration and fiction [106]—not the usual fiction that with evil intent harms fellow citizens but the kind that can help or please its hearers through education.[107] [247] But you will say [108] that I do not allow the discourse to have the quality you planned for it, but by showing the force of your words and explaining your plan, I do not notice that to the extent that I made the discourse clearer and more understandable for the readers, I also made it less distinguished. By clarifying its insight to those who did not understand it, I made the discourse empty and robbed it of the honor it would have been accorded by those who study hard and did the work themselves.

[248] "Now, I admit that my intelligence is as inferior to yours as it can be; not only that, but just as I know that truth, I also am aware that when your city deliberates about the most important issues, those who are reputed to be the most intelligent are wrong about what is best for the city, and there are times when someone who is considered foolish and is viewed with scorn turns out to succeed and give the best advice. [249] So it is not surprising if something like this happened in

---

But "wanting more" (*pleonexia*) is not always a bad trait, in Isocrates or elsewhere in Greek thought, and so the pupil has a valid point. Isocrates makes a similar defense of true and honorable *pleonexia* in *Antidosis* (15.275–284).

[106] Cf. the opening section of this speech.

[107] The best manuscript, G, gives *paideias,* education; other manuscripts give *paidias,* sport or game.

[108] In a discourse that is a fictive presentation of a real situation, we have the fictive orator presenting a fictive student presenting a fictitious response of the orator.

the present situation, where you think that you will be especially famous if you conceal as long as possible the intention you had when
you composed this discourse. I, on the other hand, think that you will
best achieve your goal if you can as quickly as possible make clear to
everyone your intentions in composing the discourse, especially to the
Spartans, who are the objects of many of your arguments, some just
and reverent, others reckless and excessively contentious. [250] If someone were to show the discourse to the Spartans before I discussed it
with them, there is no way they would not hate you and be very hostile to you for having written an accusation against them. But now I
think that although most Spartans will continue to live in the same
way they always have, and will pay no more attention to discourses
written here than to those written outside the pillars of Heracles,
[251] nevertheless the wisest of them, who have a few of your works
and admire them, if they find someone to read it and have the time to
spend on it, will not miss anything in it but will recognize the praise
of their city and the arguments supporting it and will scorn the random abuse of their actions and the harsh words. They will conclude
that envy provoked the slander found in the book (*biblion*) [252] and
that you have written for all to remember the achievements and
battles, on which they pride themselves and their reputation with others is based, gathering them all together and setting them next to each
other, and that you are responsible for many people wanting to read
them and examine them in detail not just because they want to hear
their acts but because they want to learn what you said about them.
[253] Keeping this in mind and working it over, they will not forget
the ancient deeds for which you have praised their ancestors, but they
will often relate them to each other: first, that when they were still Dorians, they despised the condition in which they saw their own cities—without reputation, small, and extremely poor—and so they led
their army against the leading cities in the Peloponnese: Argos, Lacedaimon, and Messene. [254] Victorious in battle, they drove the defeated people out of their cities and their land, and they themselves
took all their property, which they still hold even now. No one will
point to a greater or more admirable deed at that time than this, nor
one more fortunate or blessed by the gods, for it freed those who accomplished it from their own need and made them masters of other
peoples' happiness. [255] They achieved these successes together with

all who had marched with them. But when they had divided the land with the Argives and the Messenians and settled in Sparta themselves, you say that at that moment (*kairos*) they had so much confidence that though they were no more than two thousand, they thought they would not deserve to live unless they could become lords over all the cities in the Peloponnese. [256] With this in mind, they engaged in war and did not stop, although they encountered many dangers and hardships, until they had gained control of all of them except the city of the Argives. In control of the most land and with the greatest power and a reputation befitting those who have accomplished such great deeds, they were no less proud because they alone among the Greeks had a uniquely fine reputation. [257] For they could say that although they were so few in number, they never were the followers or obeyed the orders of any of the well-populated cities but had always been independent and, in fact, were themselves the leaders of all the Greeks in the war against the barbarians. They achieved this position not illogically but because, although they had fought the most battles of any people at that time, they did not lose a single one of them when one of their kings was in command but won them all. [258] No one could give a greater sign of courage, strength, and unity of purpose than this, except for the following: of the large number of Greek cities then in existence, among the others you could not mention or find a single one that has not encountered the troubles that usually plague cities, [259] whereas in Sparta, no one could point to any faction, or slaughter, or illegal exile, or seizure of property, or abuse of wives and children, or change of government, or cancellation of debts, or redistribution of land, or any other sort of incurable trouble.[109] When they list all these things, there is no way that they will not remember that you gathered these deeds all together and spoke so nobly about them, and they will be very grateful for this.

[260] "I do not have the same opinion of you as I had before, for in the past, I admired your nature, the organization of your life, your industriousness, and especially the truth of your philosophy, but now

---

[109] Isocrates uses a very similar paragraph to describe Athens under the general Timotheus in *Antidosis* (15.127). Many of these troubles can be found in Athenian history.

I envy you and congratulate you on your good fortune. For it seems to me in your life that you will not have gotten a reputation greater than you deserve—that would be hard—but one that will be recognized by more people and more unanimously approved than it is now. When you die, you will have a share of immortality, not that of the gods but the kind that creates memories of those who have excelled in some noble deed for those who come afterward.[110] [261] And you have come upon this justly, for you have praised both cities well and appropriately. The one, Athens, is praised according to the judgment of the multitude, a judgment that no famous person would despise; all long for it and would endure anything in order to get it. The other, Sparta, is praised according to the reasoning of those who try to get at the truth, among whom some would prefer to have a better reputation than among other people, even if the latter were twice as many as they are now.

[262] "Though I have a great desire to keep speaking at present, and still have many things to say about you and the two cities and your discourse, I will put these aside and will only reveal my thoughts on those matters you say you summoned me to address. I advise you not to burn the discourse or conceal it but if it needs anything, edit it and then add an account of all the discussion of it that has occurred and give it to those who want it, [263] if you want to bring pleasure to the best of the Greeks and to those who are truly devoted to philosophy and do not just make a pretense of it. Do it also if you want to bring pain to those who admire your works more than others but criticize them to the crowds at the panegyric festivals, where those who sleep are more numerous than those who actually listen. They expect that if they mislead this kind of audience, their own works will rival yours, for they fail to understand that their work is further behind yours than that of those who write the same kind of poetry as Homer are behind his reputation."

[264] When he had said all this, he urged those present to reveal their opinions on the matter for which they had been summoned, and they did not just applaud, as they usually do when they are pleased with

---

[110] A statue of Isocrates was set up in Athens by his son Aphareus, as well as one at Eleusis by Timotheus. Cf. Richter 1965: 151–152.

what has been said, but they cried out that he had spoken superbly. Gathering around him, they praised him, admired him, congratulated him; they had nothing to add to or remove from what he had said, but they expressed the same opinion and advised me to do what he suggested. [265] I too did not stand there in silence but praised his nature and his concern, but I did not comment at all on what he said, either how his suppositions had hit on or missed my own thoughts, but I let him continue to hold the opinions he had expressed.[111]

[266] I think, then, that I have now said enough about the subject I set myself, for a detailed review of my argument is not appropriate for discourses such as this one.[112] But I want to discuss my own personal experience while I was composing this discourse. I started it at the age that I said at the beginning.[113] [267] When it was already half written, I contracted a disease that is not appropriate to discuss[114] but that can in three or four days kill older men, and even many who are in the prime of life. I fought this disease continually for three years, each day working so hard that those who knew the situation or who learned of it from them admired me more for my perseverance in this than for my achievements that had been praised before. [268] Thus I had already given up the project, both because of the disease and because of my old age, when some of those who used to visit me and who had often read the part of the discourse that I had written, begged and urged me not to leave it behind half finished and unrevised but to work a bit longer and attend to what remained to be done. [269] They did not say this as if they were just fulfilling their duty, but instead they accorded the written text such extreme praise that if someone heard them who was neither my friend nor favorably disposed toward me, there would be no way that he would not assume these people

---

[111] Isocrates allowed his former pupil to exercise his training and then did not tell him if his thoughts were correct or not. He apparently wanted the process to be a creative one for the pupil.

[112] Isocrates means an epideictic work like a panegyric address, since for a judicial and deliberative oration, one of the chief functions of a peroration is to summarize the arguments given earlier. Cf. Eden 1987: 60–63.

[113] Isocrates had said in section 3 that he was 94 years old.

[114] Isocrates does, however, discuss it for a whole section. To discuss something after you say that you will not discuss it came to be called *praeteritio.*

were mocking me and that I was deranged and a complete fool if I believed what they said. [270] Although I felt this way about what they said, I was persuaded—for why should I dwell on this point?—to return to work on the rest, although I was now just three years shy of one hundred,[115] and my condition was such that no one else in the same condition would have tried to write and would not even have wanted to be in the audience when another person was presenting the work he had done.

[271] Why then have I reported all this? Not because I thought I deserved sympathy for what I have written—for I do not think that my discourse is the sort that needs this[116]—but because I want to show what happened to me and to praise those of my audience who approve of this discourse and who think that discourses that are written to instruct (*didaskalikous*) and are carefully written (*technikous*) are more serious and philosophic than those that are written for public display (*epideixis*) or for litigation (*agōnes*), those that aim at the truth (*tēs alētheias stochazomenous*) rather than those that seek to deceive the opinions (*doxas*) of the audience, and those that rebuke and admonish wrongdoers more than those delivered to please or delight. [272] I also have this advice for those who think the opposite of this: first, they should not trust their own views or think that decisions made by those who are lazy are true. Next, they should not make rash pronouncements about subjects they know nothing about but should wait until they can agree with those who have much experience in these types of discourses. If they form their opinions this way, there is no one who would think such people are fools.

---

[115] Isocrates was now 98 years old (in the Greek inclusive way of counting, 98 is three less than 100); the year is 338.

[116] See above, section 4, where he entertains the possibility.

14. PLATAICUS

INTRODUCTION

This discourse takes the form of a speech delivered by a Plataean official before the Assembly at Athens. Plataea is a city about 40 miles northwest of Athens in Boeotia. It has a storied history, most famously as the location of the battle against the Persians in 479 that insured Greek victory at the end of the Persian Wars. The present speech concerns the relationship between Plataea and Thebes. The two cities shared a long-standing hostility going as far back as 519, when Thebes tried unsuccessfully to control Plataea (Herod. 6.108). In 431, at the opening of the Peloponnesian War, Plataea was besieged and then sacked by Thebes (Thuc. 2.2–6). Plataea continued to be an important city in the early years of that war (Thuc. 2.71–78, 3.20–24, 3.52–68). In 373 Thebes destroyed the city once again, exiled the inhabitants, and redistributed the land to Theban citizens. This speech is cast as a plea for aid after this calamity, presented by a Plataean representative to Athens, where Plataean exiles had fled.

There is no evidence that the speech was actually presented to the Athenian Assembly, even if Isocrates wrote it for actual delivery by a Plataean representative. Other possibilities exist: it may have been an exercise for Isocrates' pupils to use as a model, an advertisement for his school, or a political pamphlet in favor of Athens or against Thebes. If Isocrates wrote this for a Plataean official, the speech would represent a rare example of logography for use in the Assembly rather than the courts.[1] We cannot know which function it served, or whether

---

[1] See the Introduction to this volume. Antiphon wrote speeches on behalf of two cities (Lindus and Samothrace), protesting the tribute they were required to

it perhaps served multiple functions.² We do know that Athens offered little help in 373 (Xen., *Hellenica* 6.3; Seager 1994: 178–179), and Plataea was restored only with the help of Philip II of Macedon after the battle of Chaeronea in 338. Thus, the speech may be dated to 373, if it represents a real plea, or sometime after that date, if it is an exercise or advertisement. In any event, the dramatic date of the discourse is 373.

The speech shows the normal rhetorical organization: introduction (1–6), narration (7), proof (8–55), and peroration (56–63). The narrative is truncated, as it often is in deliberative orations. The proof combines logical argumentation (8–44) with emotional appeal (45–55). The peroration (56–63) summarizes and rouses the emotions a final time.

14. PLATAICUS

[1] Athenians, since we know that you usually give enthusiastic help to those who have been wronged and that you are most grateful to those who treat you well, we have come to ask that you not ignore us when we have been driven from our homes by the Thebans during a period of peace. Although many people in the past have taken refuge with you and have obtained everything they requested, we think that it is especially proper for you to show concern for our city. [2] You would find that no one has been more unjustly beset by great calamities than we have and that no one has been more loyal toward your city for a longer period of time. Further, we are here to request the kind of help for which there is no risk for you; in fact, all people will consider you the most pious and just of all the Greeks, if you agree.

[3] Now, if we did not see that the Thebans are getting ready to persuade you in any way they can that they have done nothing wrong to us, we would have kept our speech short. But since we have reached

bring to Athens (Blass 1892: 120–121, 123–124). We have only a few fragments of these, but it is likely that they were delivered in the Assembly.

²Grote (1846), Jebb (1962), and Seager (1994: 178) think that a Plataean actually presented the speech. Mathieu (in Mathieu and Brémond II 1938) and Blass (1892) believe it was not intended for actual delivery. Van Hook (1945) does not express an opinion.

such a height of misfortune that we have this contest[3] not only against the Thebans but also against the most powerful orators, whom the Thebans have bribed with our own money to speak on their behalf, we must make a longer speech to clarify the situation.

[4] It is difficult, then, not to have our speech fall short of what we have suffered, for what sort of speech would be equal to our troubles?[4] What orator could be skilled enough to denounce the crimes committed by the Thebans? Nonetheless, we must try to the best of our ability to make their violation of the law clear. [5] What particularly upsets us is that we are so far from being treated on an equal footing with the rest of the Greeks that even though there is peace and a treaty has been made,[5] we not only have no share in the common freedom but we are not even thought fit for mild slavery. [6] We ask you, therefore, Athenians, to listen to what we say with a favorable mind, remembering that it would be the most absurd thing of all if you should be responsible for the liberty of those who have always been most hostile toward your city,[6] while we, who come before you as suppliants, should not even obtain what your worst enemies get.

[7] I do not think I need speak at length about what has happened.[7] Who does not know that they have occupied and redistributed our

---

[3] The Greek word used here, *agōn*, represents a struggle or contest. It is used in a number of ways. It can represent any kind of physical or mental struggle (6.104). It can also be used as a technical term: in drama, to show the confrontation between two characters; in courts, to represent a competition between two orators (12.271); or in education, as a rhetorical exercise. If this speech is a fiction, Isocrates may be tipping his hand here about it being a rhetorical exercise.

[4] It is a commonplace of epideictic oratory, especially funeral orations, to point out that words cannot match deeds. Cf. 4.74, 6.100; Thuc. 2.35; Lys. 2.1; and, later, Hyp. 6.2 and Dem. 60.1. On funeral orations, see 4.74n.

[5] In 375 the so-called King's Peace of 387/6 (the Peace of Antalcidas) was renewed, calling a halt to hostilities between the factions of Athens, Thebes, and Sparta. Plataea had been under Spartan control.

[6] That is, the Thebans.

[7] Deliberative speeches often delete the narrative portion of a speech, since there is the assumption that the background information is clear to all gathered in the Assembly. This would be the case here because many Plataeans took refuge in Athens and most Athenians would thus be aware of the situation. Alternately, if the speech was not actually delivered, then this is more of a rhetorical strategy.

land and razed our city? But I will try to show you what they will say in their hopes of deceiving you.

[8] First, sometimes they try to assert that they were driven to treat us this way because we were unwilling to pay tribute as a member in their alliance. But you must consider first whether it is just to inflict such terrible and illegal punishments for such charges, and then whether it seems right to you that the city of the Plataeans, when it could not be persuaded, be compelled by the Thebans to pay. Indeed, I think there is no one more audacious than those who obliterate each of our cities and then compel us to take part in their type of government when we have no need for it. [9] In addition, their treatment of us does not seem consistent with their treatment of others. When they were unable to persuade our city, they should have compelled us to pay tribute only to Thebes, as they did with Thespiae and Tanagra,[8] for then we would have suffered none of the incurable troubles we have. But now it is clear that they did not want to do this, but rather they coveted our territory. [10] I wonder what precedent they will cite and how they will define justice when they say that they are giving us these orders. For if they examine ancestral customs, they will see that they should not be ruling others but rather should be paying taxes to Orchomenus, for that is how it was in ancient times.[9] But if they reckon that the treaty is valid[10]—which is right—how can they not admit that they are acting unjustly and violating its terms, for this treaty requires that both large and small cities be autonomous?

[11] I do not think that they will dare to be so shameless about these issues; they will turn to the argument that they were at war with the Spartans and that by destroying us, they were doing things that helped their whole alliance. [12] I believe, however, that no grievance or accusation should be more powerful than oaths and treaties. Not only that, but if some city had to suffer on account of its alliance with the Spartans, it is not just that the Plataeans, of all Greeks, should be

---

[8] The Boeotian town of Thespiae had been recently (373) subdued by Thebes; Tanagra, also in Boeotia, was under Theban control as well.

[9] Orchomenus was the most ancient of Boeotian cities, having an important Bronze Age history. Isocrates mixes current notions of taxes with the ancient notion of the prominence of the city for rhetorical effect.

[10] Above, 5n.

chosen, for we did not serve Sparta willingly but under compulsion. [13] Who would believe that we had come to such a pitch of insanity that we would more highly value those who had enslaved our city than those who had allowed us to share in theirs?[11] But I think it was difficult to revolt when we ourselves had a small city, and they had become so powerful, and in addition, there was a Spartan harmost[12] in charge, and a guard troop and a large army were present at Thespiae. [14] We would have been destroyed by them not only more quickly than by the Thebans but more justly as well, for it was not proper for the Thebans to hold a grudge about past events during peacetime, but it would have been reasonable for the Spartans to punish us most severely if we had betrayed them during the war. [15] I think you are aware that many other Greeks too were compelled to follow the Spartans with their bodies, but in their minds they felt loyalty to your side. What opinion do you expect these people will have if they hear that the Thebans have persuaded the Athenian people that none of those who submitted to the Spartans should be spared? [16] The Thebans' argument will clearly have no other effect than this, for they have destroyed our city without making any charge specific to it, but only a charge they could equally make against any other city. You must plan with these cities in mind to make sure that the arrogance of the Thebans does not change those who formerly hated Spartan rule and make them think that their safety lies in an alliance with Sparta.

[17] Consider, then, that you took up the most recent war[13] not for your own security or for the freedom of your allies—for these already existed for all of you—but on behalf of those deprived of their autonomy in violation of the oaths and the treaty. This, then, would be the most disturbing thing of all, if you allow these cities, which you thought should not be enslaved to Sparta, to be destroyed now by Thebes. The

---

[11] The Athenians had offered the Plataeans citizenship rights in Athens in 427, at the outbreak of the Peloponnesian War.

[12] The Spartan Sphodrias was *harmostēs*, harmost or governor (cf. 4.117n), in Thespiae and Plataea after Sparta took control in 378. See Xen., *Hellenica* 5.4.15.

[13] Athens, with Theban aid, opposed Sparta with what has been called the Second Athenian League during the Corinthian War, beginning in 378. The goal was to curb the imperialistic tendencies of Sparta (Seager 1994: 166–168). They put an end to Spartan control at the battle of Leuctra in 371.

Thebans are so far from matching your gentleness [18] that it would be better for us to be prisoners of war, which is thought to be the worst fate of all, than to turn out to be their neighbors. This is because the cities that you captured by force were immediately freed of their Spartan harmost and their condition of slavery and now share in your council and in freedom.[14] But some of those who live near the Thebans are slaves no less than those bought with money, while for others, the Thebans will not stop until they have brought them to the same condition as us. [19] The Thebans were faulting the Spartans because they captured the Cadmea[15] and placed garrisons in the cities, but they themselves, while not sending in garrisons, do not think it at all terrible to destroy the walls of some cities and kill the men of other cities. They have thus become so shameless that they think that all their allies should look out for the security of Thebes, but they keep for themselves the power to enslave others. [20] And yet who would not despise the greed of those who seek to rule over any who are weaker than they, but think it necessary that they be on equal terms with those who are stronger, and who begrudge you the land that was given to you by the Oropians,[16] while they themselves use force to claim and redistribute land belonging to others.

[21] In addition to the rest of their evil pretexts, they say that they did these things for the common good of the allies. And yet, since there is a common council, and your city can give better advice than Thebes, they should not have come now to defend what they have already done, but they should have come to consult with you before doing anything. [22] Instead, they have unilaterally plundered our possessions and have come to make all the allies share in their ill repute. If you are sensible, you will guard against this, for it is much better to compel Thebes to emulate your righteous behavior than to let yourselves be persuaded to share in the lawlessness of these people, whose values have nothing in common with the rest of the world. [23] I think it is clear to everyone that during war, it is fitting for the wise to try in

---

[14] Above, 13n.

[15] The Cadmea, named after Cadmus, the legendary founder of the city, was the citadel of Thebes.

[16] Oropus was a city in northeastern Boeotia. Control of it went back and forth between Athens and Thebes throughout the fifth and fourth centuries.

every way to be superior to their enemy; but when there is peace, they should value nothing more highly than oaths and treaties. [24] In contrast, every delegation these men sent used to make speeches about freedom and autonomy,[17] but now that they think they are immune from harm, they give no thought to anything else but speak boldly only in support of their own gain and their own use of violence. [25] They also say that Thebes' possession of our land is an advantage for the allies, not understanding that it was never an advantage for them to seek their own gain unjustly. Many people, in fact, who desire others' land unjustly, quite justly put their own land in the greatest danger.

[26] Further, the Thebans will not, at any rate, be able to say that they will stay loyal to their allies while there is reason to fear that we Plataeans will go over to the Spartans after we get our land back. For you will find that we were twice besieged because of our friendship with you, whereas they have often wronged this city. [27] It would take a lot of work to describe their past betrayals, but during the Corinthian War—which resulted from their arrogance[18]—when the Spartans were marching against them, and they were rescued through your help, far from showing any gratitude for this, when you put an end to the war, they abandoned you and went over to the Spartan League. [28] The Chians and Mytileneans and Byzantines remained with you,[19] but the Thebans, although they inhabit such a great city, did not even dare to remain neutral but were so cowardly and base that they solemnly swore to follow the Spartans against you, even though you were the ones who saved their city. They were punished by the gods for this, and when the Cadmea was captured,[20] they were forced to flee here to Athens. And then they gave the best demonstration of their untrustworthiness. [29] When they were saved yet again through your power and came back to their own city, they did not remain loyal

---

[17] Thebes had asked Athens for help against Sparta in 379/8, when they were trying to retake the Cadmea from Spartan control. Cf. Seager (1994: 164–165).

[18] The Corinthian War lasted from 395 to 386 with Thebes and Athens against Sparta. It was ended by the King's Peace (Peace of Antalcidas) in 387/6. Isocrates overstates here the culpability of the Thebans and their arrogance.

[19] Seager (1994: 163) is more cautious about the allegiance of these cities.

[20] In 382, with the help of some Thebans who sympathized with Sparta.

for a moment, but they immediately sent ambassadors to Sparta and were ready to act as slaves and leave the former agreements they had made with Sparta completely unchanged. But what need is there to go on about this? For if the Spartans had not ordered them to receive back their exiles and to drive out the murderers, nothing would have kept them from joining in a campaign with those who had injured them against you who had treated them well.[21]

[30] Now, even though they behaved in this way toward your city recently, and in the past betrayed the whole of Greece,[22] the Thebans thought they deserved forgiveness for such terrible crimes—so willingly committed and so serious—but thought that we deserved no forgiveness for what we did under compulsion. Yet being the Thebans that they are, they dare to criticize others for siding with the Spartans when we all know that they have for the longest time behaved like slaves to Sparta and have fought more eagerly on behalf of the Spartans' command than for their own security. [31] What invasion of your territory did they ever fail to take part in? Who has been more continuously hateful or hostile to you than they were? In the Decelean War,[23] were they not responsible for more troubles than all other invaders? When you were in grave trouble, were they not alone among the allies to cast their vote that your city must be enslaved and the region must be put to pasture just like the Crisian Plain?[24] [32] Thus, if the Spartans had held the same opinion as the Thebans, nothing

---

[21] In 379, Thebans who had been in exile in Athens reclaimed the Cadmea with Athens' help, hoping to institute a democracy in Thebes. They exiled the Spartan leaders from the Cadmea and killed some of the Thebans who had helped the Spartans gain control. The Thebans then tried to appeal to Sparta, perhaps to hedge their bets; the Spartans demanded the return of the pro-Sparta, antidemocratic leaders and the exile of those who had killed pro-Spartan Thebans. Thebes would not do this. Seager (1994: 164–166) thinks that this account by Isocrates may be correct in its core, though other historians doubt it.

[22] Thebes had to deal constantly with its reputation for "medizing" (cf. 4.157n).

[23] The last part of the Peloponnesian War (413–404) was called the Decelean War from the time when the Spartans captured Decelea, a city in Attic territory (cf. 8.37n).

[24] A plain declared holy and therefore inviolable. The Theban proposal would have made Attica a holy place and would have forbidden any habitation after Athens' defeat in 404.

would have kept those who were responsible for the security of all Greece from themselves being enslaved by Greeks and falling into the greatest misfortune. What good deed of theirs could they mention that would suffice to undo the hatred that you justly feel toward them because of these things?

[33] They have no line of defense left, given the magnitude of the crimes they have committed, and those who wish to speak for them have only one argument: Boeotia now fights to protect your land, and if you should dissolve the alliance you have with them, you will act against the interests of your allies, for the balance of power will change substantially if Thebes should side with Sparta.[25] [34] But I do not believe that it is to the allies' advantage that the weaker be slaves to the stronger—indeed we fought the past war to protect the weaker[26]— or that the Thebans are so crazy that they will revolt from the alliance and give their city to the Spartans. It is not that I trust they will have the strength of character to do the right thing, but rather I know that the Thebans are aware that one of two fates necessarily awaits them if they do revolt: either they will die while resisting and suffer the same treatment they themselves inflicted on others, or they will go into exile and suffer destitution and loss of all hopes. [35] Do the Thebans have good relations even with their own citizens? They kill some; they exile others from the city and appropriate their property. Are they on good terms with the other Boeotian cities? They not only try to rule them unjustly, but they have destroyed the walls of some and banished others from their own land. [36] Surely they cannot possibly return to your city, which (you will see clearly) they have repeatedly betrayed. Thus, there is no way that they will want to dispute with you about some other city and thus very likely lose their own city for no good reason; more likely, they will act more properly in all their dealings with you, and the more they fear you, the more they will cultivate good relations with you. [37] Their treatment of the Oropians made it clear to you how you must deal with people of that sort. For when they hoped that they would have the chance to do whatever they wished, they did not treat you as allies but dared to commit the sort

---

[25] Thebes was a part of the Boeotian alliance.

[26] Above, 17n.

of crimes they would have committed against their worst enemies. But when you voted to remove them from the peace treaty because of this behavior, they dropped their arrogant attitude and approached you more meekly than even we now come.[27] [38] Thus, if some of their speakers frighten you by mentioning the risk that they might cross over and side with the enemy, you must not believe them. The forces holding Thebes back from this are so great that they would much sooner endure your rule than an alliance with the Spartans.

[39] Therefore, even if they were about to change everything and do just the opposite, not even then, I think, would it be right for you to give more credit to Thebes' appeal than to the previous oaths and the alliance. Consider first that it is your custom to fear not dangers but rather a bad reputation and shameful behavior, and second that those who win in war are not those who violently overthrow other cities but those who manage Greece with more justice and tact. [40] Someone could show this with many examples, but who does not know what has happened during our own lifetime? The Spartans destroyed your power when you appeared invincible; at first they had only a small naval force, but later on they drew the Greeks to their side through their high reputation in this area.[28] Then in turn you took away their supremacy;[29] with justice on your side, you rebuilt a city that had lost its walls and was in dismal condition.[30] [41] That the Persian King was

---

[27] The Second Athenian League, formed in 377, to which Thebes belonged, served as an antidote to the rising authority of Sparta at the time. This alliance was much more clearly and carefully delineated than the Athenian empire of the fifth century. Athens' power was still dominant, however, and the threat to Thebes of expulsion from that alliance, as Isocrates describes it here, as well as Thebes' own tense relations with members of its own Boeotian League, made any chance of Theban revolt from the alliance unlikely.

[28] Athens was defeated by Sparta and its allies at the end of the Peloponnesian War in 404. In the Peloponnesian War, Sparta did not have a strong fleet until the defeat of the Athenians at Syracuse in 413. After this, the balance of naval power shifted significantly, and in 405 the Spartan naval victory at Aegospotami made the defeat of Athens in 404 inevitable.

[29] At the battle of Leuctra in 371; see above, 17n.

[30] At the end of the Peloponnesian War in 404, one of the terms of the Athenian surrender was that they pull down the defensive walls that stood around the

not responsible for these events, recent years have made perfectly clear. For when he had no involvement in our affairs, and you were in a hopeless condition, and nearly all the other cities were enslaved to Sparta, nevertheless you gained such an advantage over it in battle that the Spartans were glad to see a peace treaty concluded.

[42] Therefore, let none of you shrink from taking on dangers when you do it with justice. And let none of you think that you will lack for allies, should you wish to give aid to all those who are unjustly treated and not just to the Thebans. If you vote against them now, you will make many others desire your friendship; if you show that you are prepared to make war equally against all on behalf of the treaty, [43] who will be so foolish as to want to remain with those who are enslaving them rather than side with you, who fight for their freedom? Otherwise, if war breaks out again, what will you say to justify leading the Greeks, should you offer them autonomy but then allow the Thebans to sack whatever city they wish? [44] How will you avoid acting inconsistently if you do not prevent the Thebans from violating their oaths and breaking the treaty, but you then claim you are making war against the Spartans for the same reasons? Further, when you give up your own possessions, hoping to make the alliance as strong as possible, are you going to allow the Thebans to possess the land of others and to do things that will make everyone think less of you?

[45] But most shocking of all would be if you had decided to give aid to those who have always been allied with the Spartans—should the Spartans tell them to do something in violation of the treaty—but allowed us to become the most wretched of all just because, although we have been on your side most of the time, in this last war we were compelled to be on the Spartan side. [46] Could anyone find someone more unfortunate than we are, who lost everything—our city, our land, our possessions—in one day and now, lacking every possible necessity, are reduced to vagrants and beggars, unsure where to turn, unhappy wherever we stop? If we find other people faring badly, we

---

city and led to the port of Piraeus; this was done to the accompaniment of flutes, according to Xenophon (*Hellenica* 2.2.20–23). In the first decade of the fourth century, under Conon's leadership, the walls were rebuilt (cf. Wycherley 1978: 19). This would be important for Athens' later attempts to reassert itself in the Second Athenian League; see above, 37n.

are pained because we are compelled to share the troubles of others in addition to our own. [47] But if we come to people who are doing well, we are even more unhappy, not because we envy their good fortune but because we see our own troubles more clearly in contrast to the blessings of our neighbors. Because of these troubles, we pass no day without tears but spend all our time longing for our home and lamenting the change that has come upon us. [48] So what do you think is our reaction when we see our own parents cared for inappropriately, our children raised without the hopes we had for them when we bore them, many of them reduced to slaves for the sake of paltry debts, others hiring themselves out as day-laborers, still others getting their daily needs by whatever means they can, lives inconsistent with our ancestors' behavior, their own youthfulness, or our own ideals? [49] And the most painful of all is when someone sees us separated one from another, not just citizen from citizen but even wives from their husbands, daughters from their mothers, and every family connection torn apart. This has happened to many of our fellow citizens because of their poverty. And the demise of our common life together has made each of us think only of our own private hopes. [50] I think you are aware of all the other shameful effects of poverty and exile. Although we feel these more painfully in our hearts than the rest, we do not speak of them, ashamed to set out our own sufferings too accurately.

[51] With this in mind, we think that you should feel some consideration for us, for we are not strangers to you, but all of us are related to you by our goodwill and most of us are related by blood. Through the right of intermarriage you gave us, we have been born of Athenian mothers,[31] and thus it is impossible for you not to be concerned with the request we have come before you to make. [52] Indeed, it would be most shocking of all if you, who once shared with us the right of your citizenship, should now vote not even to give us back our own citizenship. Further, it is unreasonable for you to take pity on each individual who suffers unjustly and yet not to show the slightest pity for a whole city that has been destroyed, especially since

---

[31] Plataeans were given the right of citizenship (and intermarriage) in 427, after Thebes had attacked them and destroyed their city at the opening of the Peloponnesian War.

it has come to you for refuge, and never before have you suffered shame or dishonor when you have taken pity on suppliants. [53] Take, for example, the time when the Argives came to your ancestors and asked them to rescue the bodies of those who had died at the foot of the Cadmea.[32] Your ancestors were persuaded by them and compelled the Thebans to act more suitably; as a result, not only did the Athenians gain glory on that occasion, but they also gave their city an undying reputation for the rest of time. You should not betray this reputation, for it is a disgrace to take pride in the actions of your ancestors but then openly to treat suppliants in just the opposite manner.[33] [54] And yet the requests we have come to make are much greater and more just, for the Argives appealed to you while campaigning against a foreign land, but we have lost our own land; they were asking for help in retrieving their dead, but we ask you to save those who are still alive. [55] Further, the evil is not equal, or even similar, that the dead should be deprived of their burial, and the living should be bereft of their own homeland and all the other goods that go with it. The former is a more serious matter for those who prevent burial than for those who go unburied; but to suffer hardship on a daily basis because you have no place of refuge and are homeless and to see the suffering of those close to you without being able to help, why must I say how much worse this situation is than all other troubles?

[56] For this reason, we beseech all of you to restore our land and our city to us.[34] We remind your elders how pitiable it is to see the elderly suffering, bereft of their daily needs, and we entreat your young men and ask them to help their age mates and not let them suffer even more evils than I have described. [57] You alone of all the Greeks owe

---

[32] In the story of the Seven against Thebes, Adrastus led Argives against Thebes but was defeated. He then turned to Athens for help in recovering the dead for proper burial. Isocrates also treats this story in *Panegyricus* (4.54–60) and *Panathenaicus* (12.168–171).

[33] Note the progression from logical argument (8–44) to emotional argument (45–55), highlighted by the use of myth (53). The myth is nicely appropriate, since it shows Athens helping a suppliant and since the enemy in both situations is Thebes.

[34] The peroration (56–63) has the dual purpose of summarizing the arguments and rousing the emotions of the audience to the speaker's aid.

us this gift—to give us aid when we have been dispossessed—for
they say that when your forefathers had left this land during the Persian Wars, our ancestors were the only ones outside the Peloponnese
to share in your ancestors' troubles and help preserve their city for
them.[35] So now we would justly receive the same aid from you that,
in fact, we initially gave you. [58] Therefore, even if you have decided
to take no thought for our persons, still it is not in your interest to
allow our land to be destroyed, since it contains the greatest sign of
your own courage and the excellence of the others who fought with
us. [59] While other trophies stand for one city's victory over another,
those in our land stand as a sign of victory for the whole of Greece
against the whole force from Asia.[36] The Thebans, however, would
likely destroy these markers, since these memorials are a source of
shame for them about what happened then. In contrast, you should
preserve them, for as a result of those deeds, you became the leaders of
the Greeks. [60] It is right, then, that you should be mindful of the
gods and heroes who protect the place and not look aside while the
honors due them are destroyed. When you received favorable signs
from sacrificing to them, you engaged in a battle so important that it
freed these and all other Greeks.

It is necessary as well to consider your ancestors and not to neglect the respect you owe them. [61] How would they feel about
you—if those there have some perception of what happens here—if
they should see that although you are in control, those who once decided to enslave themselves to the barbarians[37] are now established as
rulers of the other Greeks, while we, who fought together with them

---

[35] Isocrates tells the story of the Plataeans fighting with the Athenians against
Persia in *Panathenaicus* (12.93).

[36] Since Plataea was the site of a decisive Greek victory over the Persians in 479,
the Plataeans could make a legitimate claim to their land being a sort of national
memorial. Because the Thebans had joined the Persian side, they would not be included in this victory. Cf. above, 30n. Herodotus tells us (9.85) that each Greek
city buried its dead at Plataea. He also says that other national tombs were set up
for some time after the battle, even by cities that did not take part in the battle.
The Greeks also set up a panhellenic festival in honor of Zeus Eleutherius in Plataea, for which there is no remaining archaeological evidence.

[37] A reference to Thebes' medism in the Persian Wars (cf. 4.157n).

for freedom, should be the only Greeks to lose our land, and that the tombs of those who fought by their side lack the proper offerings for want of people to bring them, while the Thebans, who joined the army of the opposition now have control of this land? [62] Keep in mind that you used to make the strongest accusations against the Spartans because as a favor to the Thebans, the betrayers of Greece, they destroyed us, its benefactors. Do not, then, allow these criticisms to be made of your city, and do not choose the arrogance of these people ahead of your own reputation.

[63] Although there are many things to say that would lead you to be more concerned for our safety, I cannot include everything. Rather, you must think of everything I have left out and recall especially the oaths and the treaty, as well as our own goodwill and the Thebans' hostility. Then cast your vote about us justly.

LETTERS

GENERAL INTRODUCTION
TO THE LETTERS

~~~~~~

In this translation, the letters are set out in their traditional order, with those pertaining to Philip and his house first (1–5), then those addressed to other persons (6–9).[1] The dating of each letter is to varying degrees conjectural, but if they were to be set out in chronological order, a good approximation would be as follows (and this is the order that Mathieu presents them in the Budé edition):

1. To Dionysius	ca. 368
6. To the Children of Jason	359
9. To Archidamus	356
8. To the Rulers of the Mytileneans	ca. 350
7. To Timotheus	ca. 345
2. To Philip 1	342
5. To Alexander	342
4. To Antipater	340–339
3. To Philip 2	338

If these dates are close to correct—and that is far from certain[2]—then the letters all come from the second half of Isocrates' career. They include the common theme of Isocrates' old age and the resulting dim-

---

[1] *Epistle* 1 is addressed to Philip in some manuscripts. This explains its presence in the opening half of the collection.

[2] The dating for each is only conjectural, based on internal evidence. The whole notion of dating may be moot, however, if we follow Too's notions of the writings as conscious fictions (1995: 75–81).

inution of his ability to produce full artistic discourse, though shorter letters may still be possible.[3]

The authenticity of some letters has been questioned in the past, but current consensus attributes all of them to Isocrates. The most unusual one, letter 4 to Antipater, has been questioned because of oddities in form and style, including more use of colloquialism and the appearance of words not otherwise seen in Isocrates; this is, however, probably more a result of the change in genre than of a different author. It is a personal letter of reference for an otherwise unknown Diodotus.

Several of the letters (1, 6, 9) are truncated in a way similar to the discourse *Against the Sophists.* Traditionally, it is assumed that a portion of the original letter has been lost. Too, however, has argued that Isocrates intentionally breaks off the works to allow the readers/students their own creative chance (1995: 199).

Work on the letters (Sullivan 2004) has shown that they do not follow the rules that Isocrates sets out for letters. Rather, they work in the same way as his other discourses. In many ways, the letters serve the same function as the discourses and present the same themes: Greek unity, hostility to Persia, the need for strong leadership, and the proper way to lead. Isocrates' discourse *To Philip* for example, has themes similar to those of the two letters to Philip. Since the identification of these writings as letters is ancient, however, this edition will continue that tradition.[4]

---

[3] E.g., *Ep.* 5.1, where he defends his age against suspicion. He also says that he would travel to speak to the recipient if he were not so old. Cf. *Ep.* 1.1, 3.4, 6.1–2.

[4] On the difficulty of genre categories, especially for Isocrates, see Papillon 1995, 1998b: 4, 15.

EPISTLE 1. TO DIONYSIUS

INTRODUCTION

Epistle 1 is addressed to Dionysius, tyrant of Syracuse, in the best manuscripts. In other manuscripts, the addressee is Lycophron or Philip, but a reference in *To Philip* (5.81) confirms Dionysius as the recipient.

The passage in *To Philip* uses a verb that seems to refer to the time when Dionysius first took on the tyranny at Syracuse, in 405. Thus the epistle might be dated to 405 or shortly afterwards. It is very unlikely, however, that Isocrates was writing this kind of letter in 405, a period when he was still engaged as a logographer, writing private judicial speeches for others. The content of the epistle seems to place it in 368 or early 367, a period in which Dionysius was being courted by Athens, with whom he concluded a treaty at the beginning of 367, shortly before his death. Most scholars therefore accept this later date.

The epistle is incomplete, perhaps left unfinished at Dionysius' death (so Mathieu in Mathieu and Brémond IV 1962: 168), intentionally truncated (so Too 1995: 199), or simply defective from the transmission process. If it is the incomplete beginning of a larger whole (so van Hook 1945: 371), it may be more akin to the discourse *To Philip* (5) than to one of the other letters. Isocrates' goal may be the same as that found in many of his writings, an appeal to a leader to unify the Greeks and lead them against Persia. He never gets to his point in this introductory section, however. This "prelude," as he calls it (10), justifies his need for writing, the dangers of written vs. oral discourse, an appeal to Dionysius' prudence, and the importance of advice over display. Such a "prelude" also occurs in other Isocratean discourses, such as *To Philip* (5) and *Helen* (10).

EPISTLE I. TO DIONYSIUS

[1] If I were younger, I would not be sending you a letter, but I would sail myself and speak with you there.[1] But since the period of my youthful vigor and your actions do not coincide—I have already given out, while you have reached the peak of your activity—I will try to make my views as clear as I can in the present circumstances.

[2] I certainly know that it is much better for those who wish to give advice not to communicate through letters but rather to be present in person, not only because it is easier for someone to speak to someone else face to face than to make his views clear through a letter, and not only because all people trust the spoken word more than the written word, for they receive the spoken word as a proposal for action but receive the written word as if it were literature, [3] but in addition to these factors, when you are present, if someone does not understand something that is said or does not believe it, the person who presents the address is there and gives aid in both these situations. In written discourse, on the contrary, should such a situation arise, there is no one to correct matters, for when the writer is absent, the discourse has no supporter.[2] Nonetheless, since you will be the judge in this case, I have great hopes that I will be seen to say what is needed, for I think that you will dismiss all the difficulties I just mentioned and will pay close attention to the matters at hand.

[4] Still, some of those close to you have already tried to alarm me by saying that you respect flatterers and look down on those who give sound advice. Now, if I believed their reports, I would have held my tongue. But, in fact, no one could convince me that it is possible for someone to excel so much in both thought and action unless he has

---

[1] Cf. *Ep.* 3.4, 6.2.

[2] Isocrates says something very similar in 5.25–29. Greeks of the classical age often debated the values of spoken vs. written discourse. Socrates, according to Plato's *Phaedrus* (274B–278B), prefers oral discourse because of this same idea of the inability of writing to defend itself; he prefers it also because of its ability to create ideas, where writing can only remind one of what a person already knows. Demosthenes had a reputation for carefully worked out speeches and was often abused for this (Plut., *Life of Demosthenes* 5–10). Alcidamas argues for the importance of extemporaneous speech in his work *On the Sophists*. Cf. O'Sullivan 1992.

become a student and a listener and searcher, and further, has brought together and gathered from every quarter people through whom he could train his mind.

[5] Because of this, then, I was roused to write to you. Moreover, I will speak about important matters, things that no living person is more fit to hear. And do not think that I am exhorting you in this way so that you become the audience for a literary performance; I do not have any interest in display speeches (*epideixeis*), and I am well aware that you are already inundated by such types of flattery. [6] In addition, it is clear to all that panhellenic festivals are fitting for those who want to make display speeches (*epideixeis*)—for in those someone might demonstrate his talent to the most people—but those who wish actually to accomplish something must speak to the person who is most likely to complete the tasks proposed in the speech.[3] [7] If, therefore, I were counseling one city, I would make my address to the leading citizens of that city. But since I am preparing to offer advice about the security of all Greeks, to whom would I more justly speak than to the one who is the foremost of our race and who has the greatest power?

[8] And indeed, it will be clear that my mentioning these things is timely. For when the Spartans held power, it was not easy for you to be concerned about affairs in our region or oppose the Spartans while at the same time fighting against the Carthaginians. But since the Spartans are in such dire straits that they will be pleased if they can just keep their own territory, how could a better opportunity for you arise than the one before you now, when our city would gladly offer itself to you as an ally if you would act on Greece's behalf?

[9] And do not be amazed, even though I am not a public speaker, or a general, or otherwise in a position of authority, if I take up such a weighty issue and attempt two very important things, to speak on be-

---

[3] A display speech (epideictic oratory) is meant to show off the talent of the speaker. Advice oratory (deliberative oratory) seeks to rouse the audience to accomplish the speaker's goal. This is akin to the distinction Isocrates makes in 5.25–26; it also parallels the treatment of Aristotle in the *Rhetoric* (1.3). In this instance, the audience is a single person, but the division of display vs. action still holds. On the lack of distinction between discourse and epistle in Isocrates, see the Introduction to the letters.

half of Greece and to offer you advice. From the beginning, I abstained from engaging in public affairs—it would be too much work to explain why⁴—but it would be clear that I have participated in that kind of education (*paideusis*) that frowns upon trivial matters and seeks to accomplish important ones. [10] Thus it would not be strange if I were better able to see what is advantageous than those who make policy at random, although they may have gained a high reputation. Indeed, I will show, not by further prelude, but from what I am about to say, whether I am worth hearing . . .⁵

---

⁴ Isocrates says elsewhere that he had a weak voice and a natural fear of public speaking (12.10; 5.81; *Ep.* 8.7). Too argues that this claim is largely a rhetorical construct.

⁵ The letter breaks off here, apparently bringing introductory remarks to a close but not continuing to the body of the address. See the Introduction to this letter and Too (1995) for discussion of this break.

EPISTLE 2. TO PHILIP 1

INTRODUCTION

Isocrates writes to Philip to chide him for being careless in battle and not taking his leadership role seriously enough. Isocrates uses the opportunity to call on Philip to lead the Greeks against Persia, repeating a theme that is popular in his works. Isocrates was an advocate of Philip of Macedon and often addresses him and his court. In addition to this letter, he wrote a lengthy discourse asking Philip to take a leadership role with the Greeks (Isoc. 5), a letter to Antipater, Philip's regent (*Ep.* 4), and a second letter to Philip himself (*Ep.* 3). *Epistle* 5 has traditionally been taken as an addendum to the present letter, written to Philip's son Alexander ("the Great").

The letter has been dated to 342, when Philip had been wounded in a war with the Thracians (Blass 1892: 2.326–327). Others, however, date it to 344, when he was wounded in a war with the Illyrians (Mathieu in Mathieu and Brémond IV 1962; J. R. Ellis 1976; and Merlan 1954). If the latter is the case, then *Epistle* 5 to Alexander cannot accompany it (which is the traditional approach), for *Epistle* 5 is most likely dated between 343 and 340. The easiest, but by no means surest, approach is to date *Epistle* 2 to 342 and treat *Epistle* 5 as an addendum to it.

EPISTLE 2. TO PHILIP I

[1] I know that as a rule, all people are more grateful to those who praise them than to those who offer advice,[1] especially if someone sets

---

[1] Cf. *Ep.* 1.2–3, 5, and *Ep.* 9.6–7.

out to give advice when he was not asked. Now if I had not formerly advised you with much goodwill with the result that you seemed to me to have accomplished things especially fitting for you, perhaps I would not be trying right now to reveal my thoughts on what has happened to you. [2] But since I chose to concern myself with your affairs for the sake of both my city and the other Greeks, I would be ashamed if I should turn out to have advised you about trivial things but said nothing about more pressing matters, for I know that the former only affect your reputation but the latter pertain to your own security, which you seemed to disregard, according to everyone who heard the criticisms directed at you. [3] For there is no one who has not condemned you for risking yourself more rashly than is appropriate for a king and for being more concerned about winning praise for your courage than about the situation as a whole. It is just as disgraceful not to show your superiority to others when enemies surround you as it is, when there is no pressing need, to throw yourself into the sort of combats where, should you succeed, you would accomplish nothing great but, should you die, you would destroy all the good fortune you currently have. [4] Not all deaths occurring in war must be judged noble; indeed, dying on behalf of one's country or one's ancestors or children is praiseworthy, but a death that injures all these and soils the success of previous deeds should be considered shameful and should be avoided as the cause of great dishonor.

[5] But I think that it would benefit you to imitate the way our cities[2] deal with military affairs; all of them, whenever they send out an army, insure the security of the government that will make decisions about matters that come up. Therefore, when they endure one misfortune, their ability is not destroyed, but they can endure many calamities and recover from them. [6] You too must consider this and assume that there is no greater good than your safety. This will allow you to make appropriate use of the victories you win and to correct any troubles that befall you.[3] You might notice that the Spartans take

---

[2] Macedon was a large ethnic territory ruled by a monarch, quite unlike an ordinary Greek city or *polis*.

[3] The last clause is omitted in many manuscripts. The most reliable manuscript, G, has it, and so I include it here.

great care for the security of their kings and set the most respected citizens as guards over them. For these guards, it would be a greater shame to allow their kings to perish than to throw away their shields.[4] [7] And I am sure that you are aware of what happened to Xerxes when he wanted to enslave the Greeks and to Cyrus when he was trying to gain the kingship: Xerxes encountered greater defeats and misfortunes than anyone else ever has, but because he preserved his life, he also kept his kingdom, handed it down to his children, and managed Asia in such a way that it was no less formidable to the Greeks than it had been before.[5] [8] Cyrus, on the other hand, defeated the power of the King and would have taken control of his domain had it not been for his own folly.[6] By this act he not only deprived himself of a great kingdom but also placed his followers in extreme danger. I can mention many who led great armies but who, by their premature deaths, destroyed many thousands of men along with themselves.

[9] Considering these examples, you must not value courage that comes with foolish stupidity and untimely ambition for honor. Many dangers specific to the monarchy already exist; do not seek out others that bring no glory and are more fitting for a common soldier, and do

---

[4] The idea of throwing away a shield is emphatic because it would be the ultimate shame for a Spartan. A famous legend about the Spartans is that mothers, when they sent their sons off to war, would say to them that they should return "with their shield, or upon it," that is, if they do not return victoriously with their shield, they should die trying and be carried home upon it. This legend presented one of the greatest statements of Spartan honor: the value of a shameless life; there is no option for compromise. Cf. 8.143n.

[5] Xerxes led the Persian forces against the Greeks in the second phase of the Persian Wars (480–79); his forces were defeated at Salamis and Plataea (cf. 5.147n), but he was able to retreat and rebuild his forces. Although he died before he could march again on Greece (465), he passed the consolidated empire on to his son Artaxerxes I.

[6] In 401 Cyrus hired Clearchus to lead a troop of Greek mercenaries into Persian territory and challenge the rule of his brother Artaxerxes. In the battle of Cunaxa, Cyrus was killed when he foolishly ran ahead of his army to pursue his brother. Xenophon, author of the autobiographical treatment of this event titled the *Anabasis,* had to lead the Greek troops back to the coast. Isocrates also tells the story in 4.145–149 and 5.90; he mentions it in 8.98 and 12.104–105.

not contend with those who wish to escape from their wretched lives or those who without thinking choose dangers in the hope of greater mercenary pay. [10] Do not desire the kind of glory that many Greeks and barbarians[7] obtain but rather the kind of glory that you alone out of all living people in the world are able to win. And do not excessively love the sorts of virtues that even the common men share, but seek only those that no base man can attain. [11] Do not wage wars that are difficult and have no potential for glory when it is possible to fight easy wars that will bring honor, and do not wage wars that give painful anxiety to those close to you but great hopes to your enemies (such as you now offer them). As to the barbarians with whom you are now fighting, it will suffice if you succeed against them only so far as guarantees the security of your territory, but you will try to put down the one now called The Great King[8] to enhance your reputation and to show the Greeks who it is against whom they must fight.

[12] I would have preferred sending such advice to you before your campaign, so that you would not have fallen into such danger if you had listened, and if you had not listened, I would not seem to be giving advice that is obvious to all because of your wound; rather, your experience would have confirmed the validity of what I said about these things.

[13] Although I have many things to say because of the nature of the subject, I will stop speaking, for I think that both you and the best of your advisors will add easily whatever you wish to what I have said. But in addition, I fear a certain inappropriateness, since in going on now, I have mistakenly moved beyond the appropriate length for a letter and have drifted to the length of a full discourse.

[14] Even though this is the case, I must not omit some words about my city but must try to encourage you toward a friendship and connection with it. For I think that many people are not just reporting the worst things said about you here but are adding their own comments too. It is not reasonable (*eikos*) to pay attention to these people, [15] for you would be acting illogically if you should fault our people for readily believing slanderous men and then you your-

---

[7] On Isocrates use of the general term "barbarian," see 4.3n.

[8] That is, the Persian King.

self turn out to trust people who practice this very tactic (*technē*), and should not recognize that when they portray the city as easily persuaded by whoever appears, they are only showing that the city is much more beneficial to you. For if some who are able to do no good to the city achieve whatever they want through speech, then it is certainly fitting that you should lack nothing from us, since you are the most able to help the city.

[16] I think that I should oppose those who bitterly attack our city with those who say that everything is just fine[9] and that the city has done you no wrong, either large or small. But I would not say such a thing, for I would be ashamed, seeing that others believe that not even the gods are without fault, if I should dare to say that our city has never made a mistake. [17] Nonetheless, I can say this about it: you would not find a city more useful than Athens, either for the Greeks or for your own interests. You should pay special attention to this, for our city might bring you many benefits not only as an active ally but even if it simply seems to be on good terms with you; [18] you would more easily maintain control over those now in your power if they had nowhere else to turn, and you might more quickly overcome any barbarians you might wish. How then can you not eagerly desire this kind of goodwill, which will not only maintain your existing empire securely but also add much more without risk. [19] I am amazed at how many of those in powerful positions hire armies of mercenaries and spend a great amount of money on them, even though they know that armies like this have more often harmed those who relied on them, while they do not cultivate the city that has such great power and has many times in the past rescued each individual Greek city and even Greece as a whole. [20] Keep in mind that many people think you have planned well because you treated the Thessalians justly as well as to their advantage, even though they are not easy to deal with, being arrogant and often factious. Now you should try to treat us similarly, knowing that although the Thessalians' border is next to yours, our

---

[9] The text is corrupt here. The reading in the Budé edition makes no sense; the Loeb edition takes a scholar's conjecture (Corais), which could be translated more literally as "saying that everything is just the opposite." When this phrase is contrasted with the accusers' attack, it would mean that everything is "just fine."

power is equivalent to yours, and you should seek in every means to win us over; [21] for it is much better to capture the goodwill of cities than their walls. This physical conquest not only creates envy, but people give the credit to your army; but if you can attain a friendship and goodwill, everyone will praise your intelligence.

[22] You are fully justified in trusting what I said about our city, for you will see that I am not accustomed to flatter it in my discourses but have condemned it most of all.[10] In addition, I am not well regarded by the common people and especially by those who form opinions casually, but just like you, I am misunderstood and envied. We differ only in this: they relate to you the way they do because of your power and good fortune, whereas they relate to me because I claim a greater intelligence than theirs, and they see more people wishing to talk with me than with themselves. [23] Now, I wish that it would be equally easy for both of us to escape our reputations. Although you can change yours without difficulty if you wish, because of my age and many other factors, I must be content with my present situation.

[24] I do not know what else I should say, except this, that it is a fine thing for you to entrust your kingship and present good fortune to the goodwill of the Greeks.

---

[10] A strong statement, but it is true that Isocrates often faults Athens for its excessively democratic notions and its tyrannical empire of the fifth century. See especially his discourse *On the Peace* (8.41–60) and *Antidosis* (15.63–65).

EPISTLE 3. TO PHILIP 2

INTRODUCTION

This is the last work Isocrates wrote. After Philip had defeated the joint Greek forces in the battle of Chaeronea in 338, Isocrates wrote a final time to ask him to lead the now (forcibly) unified Greeks against Persia. Thus, he finishes his life with the same message he had maintained throughout it, the need for a unified Greece and an expedition against Persia. The positive nature of this letter would seem to conflict with the tradition (Jebb 1962: 2.31–32) that Isocrates took his own life out of frustration after the battle of Chaeronea.

EPISTLE 3. TO PHILIP 2

[1] I am confident that I discussed sufficiently with Antipater[1] what was advantageous both to Athens and to you, but I wanted to write to you as well about what I think should be done after the peace. My comments are similar to those I wrote in my discourse to you[2] but are expressed much more concisely than there.

---

[1] Antipater served as Philip's close attendant during the struggle with Greece and oversaw the delivery of Athenian dead back to their city after Chaeronea (J. R. Ellis 1976: 199). He would be a leading figure in Macedonian politics even past the death of Alexander. Isocrates' letter to Antipater (*Ep.* 4) does not contain the kind of discussion Isocrates describes here, and so he may refer to a lost letter or to personal conversation between himself and Antipater after the battle.

[2] *To Philip* (5), written in 346. His cross-reference here might support the idea (cf. Sullivan 2004) that Isocrates does not distinguish between discourse and epistle, as mentioned in the Introduction to the Letters.

[2] At the time of that discourse, I kept recommending that you should bring the Greeks into agreement by reconciling our city with those of the Spartans, the Thebans, and the Argives.[3] I thought that if you convinced the leading cities to think in these terms, the other cities would quickly follow. That, of course, was a different situation (*kairos*); now it turns out that you no longer need to convince them, since, because of the recent battle,[4] all are constrained to be reasonable and to desire what they suspect you want to do, and agree that they should put an end to the madness and greed that they always exhibited toward one another and instead should wage a war against Asia. [3] Many ask me whether I advised you to make the expedition against the foreigners or whether I only agreed after you had already conceived the idea. I respond that I do not know clearly, for I had not met you before. Nonetheless, I think you had already decided on this, and I merely spoke in line with your thoughts. When they heard this, they all asked me to advise and encourage you to maintain the same course since you would never accomplish anything better, more advantageous, or more timely for the Greeks.

[4] If I had the same ability I did before,[5] and was not entirely worn out, I would not now be addressing you in a letter but rather would have come myself and spurred you on and urged you to these actions. But now, as best I can, I encourage you not to neglect this opportunity before you can bring it to completion. It is not right to have an insatiable desire for anything else, for moderation is approved in most circumstances, but for those like you who are clearly superior to others, it is fitting to desire a great and noble reputation and never to be satisfied. [5] Consider that your glory will be unsurpassable and worthy of your other accomplishments when you compel the barbarians to serve as helots[6] to the Greeks (except for those who fight on your side) and make the King, who is now called "the Great," do whatever you order him to. There would be nothing left to do but become a god. Indeed, it is much easier for you to accomplish these goals, start-

---

[3] Cf. 5.30.

[4] The battle of Chaeronea in August 338 that gave Philip control over Greece.

[5] Isocrates was 98 when he wrote this short letter. Cf. *Ep.* 1.1, 6.4. On the composition of this letter, see Worthington 1993.

[6] On helots, see 5.49n.

ing from your present situation, than it was to acquire the power and glory that you now possess, starting from the kingship you had when you began.

[6] I am thankful to my old age only for this: it has brought my life to the point where I now see that some of what I was thinking and tried to write about as a youth in my discourse *Panegyricus* and the discourse to you⁷ has already happened through your actions. I am hopeful that the rest will follow.⁸

------

⁷ At the age of 98, Isocrates looks back to *Panegyricus* (4), composed in 380 when he was already 56 years old. He composed *To Philip* (5) in 346, when he was 90.

⁸ On the tension between this attitude and the tradition about his suicide, see the Introduction to this volume, p. 18.

EPISTLE 4. TO ANTIPATER

≈≈

INTRODUCTION

This letter is quite different from the first three. It serves as a professional letter of introduction from Isocrates to Antipater, a regent of Philip, on behalf of a student, Diodotus and his son (who are otherwise unknown). Its authenticity has been doubted because of its different tone, but this may only be due to the difference in type of letter; it is less advisory than other letters. Most modern editors accept it. There are similarities between this letter and the portion of *Epistle* 7 that also serves as a letter of introduction.

The date is probably just after Athens renewed hostility with Philip in 340.

EPISTLE 4. TO ANTIPATER

[1] Although it is dangerous for us to send letters to Macedon, not only now when we are at war with you but even when there is peace, nonetheless I have chosen to write you concerning Diodotus, thinking it right to value highly all my students who have excelled, not least of whom is this man, both because of his loyalty toward me and because of his general fairness. [2] I would have especially liked to introduce him to you, but since it turns out that he has met you through others, I need only to add my recommendation for him and to confirm the acquaintance that has already arisen between you. For I have had many students from all over, some with high reputations.[1] Among

---

[1] Isocrates pupils include Timotheus, the famous general; the historians Ephorus and Theopompus; and orators Isaeus and Hyperides. Demosthenes is said by

all these, some have been impressive in discourse, some were skilled in thought and action, and others were prudent and refined in their lifestyle but without talent when it comes to the other useful life skills. [3] But this man has such a well-rounded natural ability that in every area I have mentioned, he is the most accomplished.

I would not dare say this if I myself did not have the most precise knowledge of him and if I did not expect you to gain the same sense of him from your own experience with him and from what you learn from others who know him; [4] everyone of these would agree (unless he were quite envious) that no one is better able to speak and advise than Diodotus and that he is the most just and the most prudent and the most disciplined with money. Further, he is the most pleasant and agreeable person to pass the day with or live with. In addition, he is extremely frank not in an inappropriate way but in a way that most reasonably gives evidence of his goodwill toward his friends. [5] Some rulers, who have a noble dignity of soul, honor this frankness as a useful thing; other rulers, whose nature is weaker than their circumstances would require, are displeased by it since it forces them to do something that they do not choose to do. They are not aware that those who dare to disagree with them about what is advantageous can, in fact, give them the most power to do what they want. [6] For it is likely that because of men who always choose to say what is pleasing, not only are monarchies unable to survive when they inevitably encounter many dangers but citizen governments cannot endure either with such men around. Yet because of those who speak openly in the interest of what is best, many of these are preserved, even when their affairs seem headed for ruin. Therefore, it is fitting that those who state the truth should be more highly valued by all monarchs than those who say everything with a view to pleasing but, in fact, say nothing that should please. Still, it turns out that the former are valued less among some leaders.

[7] Diodotus had this very experience among some leaders in Asia. He was useful to them in many ways, not just in advising but even in dangerous actions. Still, because of his frankness with them about

---

Plutarch (*Life of Demosthenes* 5) to have obtained a copy of Isocrates' handbook, since Demosthenes could not afford to study at his school. On the handbook tradition and Isocrates, see Papillon 1995. On his students, see Sanneg 1867.

their own interests, he was deprived of honors at home and of many other hopes. The flatteries of inconsequential men counted for more with them than the good services of this man. [8] Thus he considered approaching you but hesitated not because he thought that his superiors were all alike but because of the troubles he had had with them. He was discouraged about his prospects with you, rather like the feeling sailors have, I think, when they have experienced a storm: at first they are no longer eager to go to sea, even though they know that one can often have a good voyage. Nonetheless, since he has been with you, he is doing well. [9] For I think this will help him, judging from the kindness that outsiders think you have. Moreover, I think you are aware that it is the most pleasant and advantageous thing of all to obtain through your good deeds friends who are both trustworthy and useful and then to treat those well so that many others will also be grateful to you because of them. For all men of refinement praise and honor those who have close association with noble men, just as if they themselves enjoyed the benefits.

[10] I think Diodotus himself will especially cause you to take note of him. But I have also been urging his son to support your interests and to try to advance by offering himself to you as a student. When I said this, he remarked that he wanted your friendship but that he nonetheless had the same feelings about it as about athletic contests: [11] he would like to win the victory there, but he would not dare to enter the contest since he did not have enough strength to win the crown. He would like to gain honors from you, but he does not think he could achieve them, for he is intimidated by his own inexperience and your luminance. Further, he thinks that his poor little body, marred by certain defects, would impede him in many endeavors.

[12] This man, then, will do whatever seems advantageous. Nonetheless, whether he spends his time with you or lives quietly in your country, watch out for whatever else he might need and especially for his safety and that of his father. Think of them as a sort of pledge from my old age, which should justifiably return much favor, from the reputation I have, if it is worthy of any regard, and from the goodwill that I have always had toward you. [13] And do not be amazed if I have written a rather long letter or if I have spoken in it rather excessively and like an elder statesman, for I have ignored everything else and considered only this one thing, to show my eagerness on behalf of men who have become my very dearest friends.

EPISTLE 5. TO ALEXANDER

INTRODUCTION

This letter is of great interest because it may represent Isocrates' thoughts on the education Alexander received after Philip had brought Aristotle to Macedon to be Alexander's tutor. If it accompanied *Epistle* 2, it can be dated to 342, when Alexander was about 14 and Aristotle had just taken up his teaching post. Isocrates was 94.[1] In any case, the letter must surely have been written while Aristotle was in Macedon as Alexander's tutor from 343/2 to 340. Isocrates explains his sense of what Aristotle was teaching and gives his own evaluation of it. His views are not terribly positive, but they are not completely dismissive either, as Merlan (1954) points out.

The letter assumes that Isocrates and Alexander have an established relationship and have already discussed the nature of education. The third section seems to describe Alexander's discriminating, analytic evaluation of Aristotle's teaching, while section 4 presents Alexander's more synthetic and sophisticated approach, which parallels Isocrates' own ideas. There is the sense that Isocrates has already given Alexander pedagogical advice. We cannot be sure of the extent of Isocrates' relationship with the Macedonian court, but his advocacy of Philip as early as *To Philip* (5) in 346 may support the notion of contact. It is unclear, nonetheless, whether Isocrates' claim here is historical, a convenient fiction for address, or a rhetorical pose.[2]

---

[1] For more on the date, see the Introduction to *Ep.* 2.

[2] On the compositional technique of this letter (and *Ep.* 3), see Worthington 1993.

EPISTLE 5. TO ALEXANDER

[1] When I was writing a letter to your father, I thought that it would be odd if I did not address you—since you are in the same region as he—or greet you, or write something to you that might make those who read it[3] think that I have not already passed my mental prime because of my old age, or that I ramble a lot, but rather that the part of my ability that remains is quite worthy of the power I had when I was young.

[2] I hear everyone saying that you are kind toward others (*philanthrōpos*), a friend to Athens (*philathēnaios*), and a man of learning (*philosophos*),[4] not thoughtlessly but reasonably. Moreover, you do not receive any of our citizens who neglect their affairs and pursue base goals, but only those with whom you would not regret spending time and who would not cause you any harm or do you wrong, should you join together with them and share in their activities—just the sort of people with whom those who are sensible should associate.

[3] As regards philosophies, you do not reject eristic[5] but think that it gives you an advantage in private discussions; nonetheless, you do not think it is appropriate for the leaders in a democracy or for those who hold a monarchy, since it is not advantageous or proper for people of superior intelligence to engage in eristic with fellow citizens, or to allow others to contradict them.

---

[3] This phrase may indicate that Isocrates distributed his works, even these "private" letters, to a wider reading audience. A similar approach might be seen in the letters of Cicero or Pliny, but it is less clear whether this is true in the case of the letters of Demosthenes or Plato.

[4] Isocrates' alliterative pun of the three Greek adjectives *philanthropos, philathēnaios, philosophos* is impossible to render in English. It would be convenient to simply translate them "philanthropic, phil-Athenian, and philosophical," but these would be misleading. Isocrates gives a similar description of Philip (15.29).

[5] Eristic is close verbal debate such as was taught most famously by Plato and later, under Plato's influence, by Aristotle, though eristic education was common in the fourth century. Isocrates makes claims about eristic (and other studies) as "preparatory" in *Antidosis* (15.261–269) and in *Panathenaicus* (12.26–29). Isocrates' treatment in these passages is quite moderate. The term eristic, however, can often be pejorative, and Isocrates himself can be much harsher. See *Helen* (10.6) and especially *Against the Sophists* (13.1).

[4] And so you do not embrace this activity (*diatribē*) but prefer an education (*paideia*) involved with discourses (*logoi*), which we use to conduct our daily affairs and deliberate about public matters.[6] Through this education you will know how to make reasonable judgments (*doxazein*) about the future and direct your subjects intelligently about what each should do. You will know how to make the right decision about what is noble and just and their opposites and in addition reward or punish each group as it is fitting.

[5] Therefore, you are wise to be practicing this, for you give your father and the others hope that should you continue this education as you become older, you will surpass others in practical wisdom (*phronēsis*)[7] in the future as much as your father has thus far surpassed all others.

---

[6] Isocrates refers to the Aristotelian approach as a *diatribē*, a pastime or, more insultingly, a waste of time. He then refers to Alexander's preference in terms he uses of his own educational ideas, an education concerned with discourses (*paideia peri tōn logōn*).

[7] On *phronēsis*, see *Ep.* 7.1n.

EPISTLE 6. TO THE CHILDREN OF JASON

~~~~~~

INTRODUCTION

Jason ruled Pherae in Thessaly with great skill and intrigue until his assassination in 370. After a long and difficult period of tyrannical rule by their relatives, the children of Jason found themselves in authority in 359. Isocrates writes to praise them for leaving behind the excesses of tyranny and choosing the better form of life to be found in a constitutional government.[1] The letter thus becomes a discourse on the advantages of democracy over tyranny, though its incompleteness keeps Isocrates' comments from being clear.

EPISTLE 6. TO THE CHILDREN OF JASON

[1] One of the envoys sent to you reported back to me that you called him aside privately and asked if I might be persuaded to leave Athens and spend time with you. Because of my friendship (*xenia*)[2] with Jason and Polyalces, I would gladly come to you, for I think that this association would be advantageous for us all. [2] However, many things stand in my way; in particular, I am not able to travel, and it is inappropriate for people of my age to travel to a foreign city.[3] Also, everyone who learned of my journey might rightly fault me, if, when I chose to spend the earlier part of my life quietly at home, I now try

---

[1] See below, 11n.

[2] Isocrates refers to *xenia,* a quasi official relationship between two persons, households, or states, which implies mutual respect and aid. See Herman 1987.

[3] Isocrates was 77 when he wrote this letter. Cf. *Ep.* 1.1, 3.4.

to leave home in my old age; indeed, it would be more reasonable that even if I used to travel before, I should now be hastening home when the end of my life is so very near.⁴ [3] In addition to these reasons, I also fear for Athens, truth be told. For I see that alliances that the city makes are dissolved quickly. So if something like this should happen with you, even if I were able to escape the blame and the risks (which would be difficult), nonetheless I would be ashamed if I should seem to some to neglect you on account of Athens, or to slight Athens on your account. If the interests of the cities were to differ, I do not know how I could please both sides. These, then, are the reasons why I have not been able to do what I want.

[4] Still, I do not think that I should neglect your interests and write to you only about my own. Rather, I will try as best I can to discuss the same things now that I would have said to you had I been there with you. And do not assume that I have written this letter because I wanted to compose an artistic literary demonstration (*epideixis*) rather than because of our friendship. I am not so mad as to be unaware that I cannot write anything better than what I made public before,⁵ since I am so far past my prime (*akmē*), and so if I produce something inferior now, my reputation would become much worse than it currently is. [5] Further, if I had intended to compose an artistic literary demonstration (*epideixis*) and were not looking seriously to your interests, I would not have chosen this subject out of all the possibilities, a subject that is difficult to address well. Rather, I would have chosen others that are more attractive and have more potential for clever argumentation (*logos*). In fact, I was never eager to gain honor in such demonstrations before; I preferred other types, which most people did not understand, and I did not have the intention of composing a display in this work. [6] Rather, seeing that you were facing many great dangers, I myself wished to make clear my opinion about

---

⁴ Isocrates would live for another 21 years!

⁵ It would be somewhat misleading to translate the verb *diadidomi* as "publish," though this is how it is often understood later. We are not sure whether the letters were treated differently in this regard than other discourses of Isocrates (see Sullivan 2004). Thus, even if this letter was sent to the children of Jason, Isocrates most likely had multiple copies circulate among associates as well.

them. Now I think that I am in my prime (*akmē*)[6] for giving advice, for experience teaches those of my age and makes them more able than others to see what is best. Speaking about the proposed subject in a pleasing, artful, and polished manner is no longer in my power because of my age, but I would be grateful if I could discuss them in not too careless a manner.

[7] Do not be amazed if you find me saying something you have heard before; in some cases, I might do this unwittingly, while in others, I do so intentionally if it is appropriate for the argument. Indeed, it would be foolish, when I see others using my arguments, if I alone should avoid what I have said before. I preface my remarks in this way because my first point is one of those things that are commonly repeated. [8] For I am accustomed to say to those who devote themselves to our philosophy[7] that this is the first issue to consider: what ought to be accomplished by a discourse and by its parts. When we discover this and examine it thoroughly, then I say that we should seek materials (*ideai*) through which our aims can be fully worked out and the goal that we set can be attained.[8] Now, I propose this procedure for discourses, but it is also fundamental in all other areas and especially in your own activities. [9] For nothing sensible can be done if you do not first think through and plan with much forethought how you should manage the rest of your time, what sort of life you should choose, what sort of reputation you should seek, and which honors you should value, those that citizens give willingly or those they are forced to give. Once you have decided these matters, then you should examine how your daily activities may contribute to the goals set out in the beginning. [10] Searching and studying (*philosophountes*) in this

---

[6] Isocrates puns on the notion of *akmē* or prime of life. Isocrates says in section 4 that he is past his prime (*akmē*) for writing elegant discourse, but here says that he is in his prime (*akmē*) for giving advice.

[7] Isocrates refers here to his philosophy, which informs the content of his school. He describes what happens in his school and some of its priorities in *Ep.* 5 and in *Antidosis* (15.180–192). His philosophy emphasizes practical approaches to educational theory, political science, epistemology, rhetorical theory, and the threefold requirement of natural ability, training, and practice.

[8] On the process of composition, see Gaines 1990. On *idea*, see Lidos 1983 and Sullivan 2001.

way, you will take aim at the target (*stochasesthe*), so to speak, that lies before your mind, and you will more likely accomplish what is advantageous for you; but if you do not make such a plan, and instead try to do whatever occurs to you, then necessarily you will err in your thoughts and make serious mistakes in many situations.

[11] Now perhaps someone who lives his life without a plan might try to disparage such reasoning and ask me to give advice about what I have just said. So I should not hesitate to make clear what I think about it. For in my opinion, the life of private citizens appears to be superior and more desirable than that of tyrants, and I think that honors given in constitutional governments are more pleasant than those in monarchies;⁹ I will try to speak on these issues. [12] And yet, I am aware that I will have many opponents, especially among those close to you, because I think that these persons not the least are spurring you on toward tyranny. This is because they do not consider the nature of the situation from all sides but rather deceive themselves in many ways. They see the power, the profit, and the enjoyment and expect they will enjoy these, but they do not consider the uncertainties, the fears, or the calamities that affect rulers and their friends. Their experience is the same as those who undertake the most shameful and lawless crimes: [13] they are not ignorant of the baseness of their acts, but they hope to obtain the benefits they offer nonetheless, while avoiding all the terrible evils inherent in such crimes. They also hope to organize their affairs in such a way that will keep them far from dangers but close to profit. [14] I envy the simplemindedness of those who think this way, but I myself would be ashamed if, while advising others, I neglected their good and sought my own advantage and if I did not place myself entirely outside of considerations of profit or all other advantages when recommending what was the best.

And so, since this is my opinion, you should give me your attention as follows . . .¹⁰

---

⁹Isocrates contrasts *politeia* with *monarchia* here. The former could include a democracy (*demokratia*) or an oligarchy (*oligarchia*); the latter includes states controlled by a king (*basileus*) or a tyrant (*tyrannos*).

¹⁰The letter seems to be incomplete, ending in the middle of a sentence. On the question of the fragmentary nature of this letter and other discourses of Isocrates, see Too 1995.

EPISTLE 7. TO TIMOTHEUS

pppppppppppppppppppppppppppppppppppppppppppppppppppppppppp

INTRODUCTION

This letter serves two purposes. It first commends Timotheus, the new tyrant at Heraclea, on the benevolent rule he displays. This is particularly important to Isocrates because Clearchus, Timotheus' father, had been a pupil of Isocrates (as well as of Plato) and showed great promise. The temptations of tyranny, however, corrupted him when he returned to Heraclea, and his reign was wicked. Timotheus now shows the same promise as his father, and Isocrates encourages him to maintain this promise and not succumb to the temptation of tyranny, as his father had done. The frankness with which Isocrates describes Clearchus to his son is striking.

The second goal, connected with the first, is to introduce and commend Autokrator to Timotheus on account of Autokrator's excellence at giving counsel. This may be Isocrates' attempt to wield some influence over Timotheus, so that the latter might avoid the collapse that Isocrates saw in Clearchus.

Timotheus held control from 346 to 338, and the letter is usually dated to the early years of his reign but after he had enough time to show his potential, perhaps about 345.

EPISTLE 7. TO TIMOTHEUS

[1] I think you have heard from many about the friendship that exists between our houses, and I congratulate you, first because I know that you are exercising your present authority better and more wisely than your father, and second because you prefer to gain a noble reputation rather than amass great wealth. That you hold this opinion is

no small sign of your excellence (*aretē*); indeed, it is the greatest possible sign. Thus, if you live up to this reputation you now have, you will not lack those who will praise your practical wisdom (*phronēsis*) and moral purpose (*proairēsis*).[1] [2] But I think that what has been said of your father will give great credibility to your reputation for wisdom and superiority. For most people are accustomed to praise those who are born from well-respected fathers less than those who come from unpleasant or difficult fathers, if they show themselves to differ from those who bore them. For, in every case, a good that comes unexpectedly is more pleasing than one that comes predictably and expectedly.

[3] Keeping this in mind, you must investigate and study how and with whom and on whose advice you will right the misfortunes of your city, inspire your citizens to work hard and behave well, and make them live more happily and confidently than in past times, for these are the tasks of those who would rule rightly and wisely. [4] Some rulers look down on these tasks and consider nothing except how they themselves can live in the greatest extravagance or how they can abuse and collect tribute from the best and richest and wisest citizens; they fail to understand that intelligent men who hold this position of power should not seek pleasure for themselves from the troubles of others but should by their own care make their citizens more fortunate. [5] While they should not treat everyone harshly and cruelly, they should not ignore their own safety either but should order their affairs so mildly and lawfully that no one would dare to plot against them, while providing for their personal protection in rigorous detail as if all wished to attack them. With this attitude, they would themselves be free of all dangers and would have a high reputation among the rest of the citizens. Goods greater than these it is difficult to find.

[6] I have been thinking as I write this how fortunately all these things

---

[1] Practical wisdom (*phronēsis*) is one of Aristotle's five intellectual virtues (*Nicomachean Ethics* 6.3, 5). Isocrates defines it in *Antidosis* (15.271) as the ability "to succeed in finding the best solution most of the time through educated experience (*doxa*)." For an example of the complicated nature of *phronēsis*, see Schwarze 1999. Moral purpose (*proairēsis*) is the capacity for choosing the appropriate means to an end based on prior deliberation; it is active in the realm of the moral virtues, according to Aristotle (*Nicomachean Ethics* 3.2).

have turned out for you. For your father left you a prosperity that could be acquired only with violence and tyrannical behavior and with much hostility, but your task is to use it in a noble and humanitarian way, and you must give great attention to this task.

[7] Since this is my opinion, the situation is as follows: if you desire money and greater power and the dangers that are required to obtain these things, you should summon other advisors. If, however, you have enough of these things and set your heart on excellence and a noble reputation and the goodwill of your people, you should pay attention to my words, and you should compete with those who manage their cities well and should try to surpass them. [8] Now I hear that Cleommis[2] in Methymnia has this kind of power, is noble and wise in all his affairs, refrains from killing or exiling any citizens or confiscating their property or doing any other evil to such an extent that he provides great security for his subjects, he recalls former exiles, he restores their former possessions to those who return, [9] and he reimburses the cost of each item to those who had bought them.[3] In addition, he arms all the citizens, on the assumption that no one will try to overthrow his power, and if anyone should try it, it would be more advantageous for him to die after displaying such excellence to his citizens than to live longer after being responsible for the greatest evils for the city.

[10] Now, I would have discussed these things even more with you, perhaps even more elegantly, if it were not absolutely necessary to write this letter quickly.[4] I will advise you again later if old age does not prevent me, but for now I will turn to personal matters. Autokrator, the bearer of this letter, is a friend of mine. [11] We have been in the same profession, I have used his expertise many times, and now finally I have been giving him advice about his trip to see you. On account of this, I would hope that you would treat him well, to the advantage of us both,[5] and that it will be clear that part of what he needs is realized through my efforts.

---

[2] Cleommis ruled in Methymnia, on the island of Lesbos. Nothing more is known about him.

[3] He encourages this kind of activity to the rulers at Mytilene (*Ep.* 8.3).

[4] Quickly, perhaps, because Autokrator is about to leave.

[5] Some manuscripts read "you both," and some read "us both."

[12] And do not be amazed if I write to you so urgently, though I never asked anything of your father Clearchus. For nearly all those who have sailed here from your city say that you are like the best of my students. On the other hand, all those who knew Clearchus agree that at the time when he was in our school, he was the most liberal and gentle and humane man of those who belonged to our group; but when he took power, he seemed to change so greatly that all who knew him beforehand were shocked. [13] For this reason, I broke off relations with him. But I admire you, and I would value it highly if you would be friends with me. You yourself will reveal quickly whether you have the same view as I do, for you will treat Autokrator well, and you will send a letter to me renewing the ties of friendship and hospitality that existed between our houses.[6] Good-bye; write if you should need anything else from me.

---

[6] On *xenia,* see *Ep.* 6.1n.

EPISTLE 8. TO THE RULERS OF THE MYTILENEANS

INTRODUCTION

Isocrates writes this letter to the new members of an oligarchic government in the city of Mytilene on the island of Lesbos. He writes at the urging of his grandchildren. The democracy in the Lesbian city of Mytilene had been overthrown and replaced by an oligarchy in 351 or 350. Since the oligarchs had treated the exiled democrats leniently early in their reign, Isocrates' grandsons impose upon him to write a letter, requesting the safe return of their exiled former teacher Agenor and his relatives. The letter allows Isocrates to express his views on the benefits of culture. In this way, the letter is quite similar to the Latin speech *On Behalf of Archias* by Cicero, who also uses the occasion of danger to his teacher Archias to talk about the value of education.

The date is determined by references in section 8 to Conon being dead (who died in 354) and Diophantes' absence in Asia (during 351–350); it was thus most likely written in 350.

EPISTLE 8. TO THE RULERS OF THE MYTILENEANS

[1] The children of Aphareus, my grandchildren, who were educated in culture (*mousikē*)[1] by Agenor, have asked me to send you a letter asking that you receive Agenor back from exile, together with his father and brothers, since you have recalled some other exiles. When I told them that I feared it might seem rather strange and intrusive if

---

[1] The Greek word *mousikē* is much broader than "music." *Mousikē* would include all the areas of interest to the muses: music (in our sense), poetry, history, dance, etc. It thus designates culture in a broader sense.

I sought such a great favor from men with whom I had never before talked or been associated, they persisted even more. [2] When nothing turned out as they hoped, it was clear to all that they were unhappy and upset. And when I saw that they were more distressed than they should be, I finally promised to write a letter and send it to you. I mention all this in order that I do not justifiably seem foolish or troublesome.

[3] I think that you have planned well in reconciling your citizens, in trying to reduce the number of exiles, in increasing the citizen population, and finally in modeling yourselves on our city with your treatment of partisanship. But someone would especially praise you for restoring the property of those who return from exile,[2] since this makes it clear that you exiled them not from greed for the possessions of others but from fear for your *polis*. [4] Moreover, even if none of this had seemed to you the right approach and you had taken back no exiles, I think it would be to your advantage to receive these men back,[3] for it would be disgraceful if, when your city is recognized by all to be the most cultured (*mousikōtatos*)[4] and those who are most notable in this regard have been born in your city, nonetheless, the one who is foremost now in the study of such education is an exile from your city. Further, while other Greeks grant citizenship to those who are outstanding in some noble discipline, even if they are in no way connected to the city, you allow those who are famous everywhere and are your own natural citizens to live elsewhere. [5] I am amazed at how many cities think that those who excel in athletic contests deserve honor above those who rely on intelligence and hard work to discover something useful; they do not see that by nature, the powers of strength and speed die with the body, whereas knowledge remains for all time benefiting those who use it.[5] [6] Considering this, then, wise men should value most highly those who govern their cities well and

---

[2] As Timotheus had done in Heraclea (*Ep.* 7.8–9).

[3] That is, Agenor and his relatives.

[4] Isocrates refers here to Lesbos' reputation for the arts, as seen with the poets Sappho and Alcaeus. Mytilene was also the home of Pittacus, one of Greece's seven sages. Diogenes Laertius (*Vita Sophistarum* 8.82) talks of a certain Archytas of Mytilene who was *mousikos*.

[5] This section recalls the opening of Isocrates' *Panegyricus* (4.1).

justly, and secondly, those who can add honor and good reputation to the city; for everyone takes such persons as examples and thinks that their fellow citizens are similar to these men.

[7] Now, perhaps someone might say that those who wish to obtain something ought not only to praise the thing itself but to show that the person himself rightly received what he had been discussing. But this is the situation. I have held back from being active in politics or speaking in public. This is because I did not have a sufficiently strong voice or sufficient courage.[6] Nonetheless, I have not been entirely useless or lacking in reputation, but you would find that I have been an advisor and a participant with those who have chosen to speak well of you and our other allies and that I myself have composed more discourses about the freedom and autonomy of the Greeks than all those who ever mounted the speaker's platform. [8] Therefore, you might justifiably be very grateful to me, for you especially desire to live in such conditions. I think that if Conon and Timotheus were alive now and Diophantus were to come here from Asia, they would be very eager for me to get what I ask. I do not know what more to say on this issue, for none of you is so young or forgetful that he does not know their good deeds.

[9] I think you would be best advised about these matters if you consider who is making the request and on whose behalf. You will discover that I have been on the closest terms with those who deserve credit for the greatest benefits for you and others, and that those for whom I make this request are such as will cause no trouble for the elders or those in power, but will offer to the young an education that is pleasant, useful, and appropriate for their age.

[10] Do not be amazed if I have written a letter that is more earnest and lengthy than others. For I desire two things: to please my children and to make it clear to them that even if they take no part in public affairs or hold power in the military but rather emulate my own life, they can live lives that are not inconspicuous among the Greeks. One more thing: if you should decide to grant what I ask, make it clear to Agenor and his brothers that they have obtained what they want in part through my efforts.

---

[6] On Isocrates' reticence to speak, see *To Philip* (5.81), the Introduction to this volume, and Too 1995.

EPISTLE 9. TO ARCHIDAMUS

INTRODUCTION

Isocrates wrote this letter in 356, when he was 80 years old, as he says in section 16. Archidamus had recently succeeded his father as one of the two kings of Sparta. Isocrates covers three of his favorite topics: the superiority of his own type of discourse over mere epideictic, how a monarch should rule, and finding a man to lead a unified Greece against Persia.

The letter appears incomplete. It would have gone on to set out Isocrates' familiar call to a prominent state leader to take a role at the head of a united Greek force. Some have doubted the authenticity of this letter, but Smith (1940) has argued convincingly in favor of Isocrates' authorship.

Isocrates had written the discourse *Archidamus* in the voice of Archidamus in 366, when his father Agesilaus was still king. That discourse treated the difficult political situation in Sparta at the time, when Corinth was putting pressure on Sparta to give up control of Messene.

EPISTLE 9. TO ARCHIDAMUS

[1] Archidamus, knowing that many people are starting to praise you and your father and your family,[1] I chose to leave this sort of dis-

---

[1] This may refer to the common practice of praising a newly crowned monarch. Archidamus no doubt received many tributes when he succeeded his father. Isocrates explicitly says that he is 80 years old when he writes the letter (16), which would date the letter to 356; this may be slightly late for such tributes to continue,

course to others, since it was too easy to do. Instead, I thought I would encourage you to take on the generalship and lead an army unlike any that now exists and from which you will become responsible for great benefits for your own city and for all Greeks. [2] I made this choice, fully aware which discourse was easier but knowing exactly how difficult and rare it is to discover deeds that are noble, great, and useful, while it would have been easy for me to praise your excellence (*aretē*).[2] For in that case, I would not need to furnish material from my own work but would have found so many excellent sources of inspiration in the things you had accomplished that eulogies about others would not have rivaled in the least one spoken about you. [3] For how might someone exaggerate the lineage of those born from Heracles and Zeus, which all know belongs to your family alone, or the courage (*aretē*) of those who founded the Doric cities in the Peloponnese and who occupy this territory? Or who could exaggerate the number of dangers undergone or victory trophies set up through your command and kingship? [4] Who, indeed, would have any difficulty if they wanted to show the valor of your whole city and its discipline and the government established by your ancestors? How many words could one use to describe your father's practical wisdom (*phronēsis*)[3] or his management of troubles or the battle that was fought in the city in which you stood as general and fought, just a few against many, and surpassed all others in saving your city?[4] And no one could point out a deed greater than this. [5] For neither capturing cities nor killing many of the enemy is as great or hallowed as rescuing your own city from such dangers, and not just any city, but one that is so outstanding in excellence. No one could fail to win fame by recounting these events, even if they do it simply, not elegantly, merely listing the feats indiscriminately, not with great style.[5]

---

however, since Archidamus succeeded to the throne in 360/59. The letter might be dated earlier, with Isocrates only approximating his age, or he may have delayed his comments until the tributes were over, as he hints at here.

[2] On *aretē*, see 4.71n.

[3] On *phronēsis*, see *Ep.* 7.1n.

[4] Agesilaus defeated a much larger Theban force under Epaminondas in 362 at Sparta (Xen., *Hellenica* 7.5.9–10).

[5] As, in fact, Isocrates has just done. The rhetorical/poetic figure of doing something even while you say that you are not going to do it came to be known

[6] Now, although I could have spoken sufficiently on these matters, since I know first that it is easier to run quickly through the past than to speak thoughtfully about the future, and second that all people are more grateful to those who praise them than those who advise them (for they welcome the former, while they think the latter are annoying, should they give their advice without being asked), [7] nevertheless, knowing all this, I refrained from saying only what would please you. Rather, I intend to speak about matters that no one else would dare address, for I believe that those who claim to have a sense of fairness and intelligence should choose not the easiest of discourses but the most difficult, not those most pleasing to the audience but those that will help them aid their own cities and the rest of the Greeks. It is to such matters that I now turn my attention.

[8] I am amazed that it never occurred to those who have the power to act or speak to think about panhellenic affairs or to feel pity for the wretched situation of Greece, which now suffers so shamefully and shockingly. No part of Greece remains that is not completely filled with war and factional strife and slaughters and innumerable other evils. The greatest part of these falls on those Greeks living on the Asiatic coast, all of whom we abandoned in the treaty[6] not only to the barbarians but even to Greeks who, while sharing our tongue, have adopted the ways of the barbarians. [9] If we had any sense, we would not allow them to gather together and make campaigns under the leadership of just anyone or marshal armies of mercenaries that are larger and stronger than our forces made up from citizens. These forces damage only a small part of the King's land, but they destroy any Greek cities they enter, killing some, putting others to flight, and pillaging the property of still others.[7] [10] Still further, they violate the

---

later as *praeteritio*. Sections 1–5 form an elaborate example of this. Sections 1–7 also serve as a sort of priamel (priamel is the rhetorical/poetic term for listing a group of items in a category to build up anticipation and grandeur, only to sweep them aside and move on to the true topic at hand, which the author usually claims is the best in that category). The opening lines of Pindar's first Olympian ode, or Sappho 16 on what one finds beautiful, are famous examples of this. On the priamel, see Race 1982.

[6] The Peace of Antalcidas of 387/6 with the King of Persia.

[7] Isocrates frequently mentions the problem of homeless mercenaries (4.168, 5.120, and 8.24). This is a result of the increased use of mercenaries in the fourth

women and children, dishonoring the most beautiful women and stripping from other women the clothing they are wearing; as a result, those who formerly should not properly have been seen by anyone, even fully clothed, are now seen naked by many, while others in rags are wasting away without the bare necessities.

[11] No city that claims to be a leader among the Greeks has been upset by these circumstances, which have existed now for some time, nor have any of its leading men been angered by this, except for your father. Agesilaus alone of all those we know desired for his whole life to free Greece and wage war against the barbarians. In spite of all that, he did err in one respect. [12] And do not be surprised if I mention his mistakes in my discussion with you, for I am accustomed always to compose my discourses with frankness, and I would prefer to be hated for finding fault justly than to be admired for praising inappropriately. [13] This, then, is my view on the subject: that man in all other respects was superior and became the most self-disciplined, most just, and most statesmanlike man; yet he had two desires, each of which separately seemed to be noble but were incompatible with each other and impossible to accomplish at the same time. He wanted to make war against the King, and he also wanted to bring his friends back from exile into their cities and have them regain control of public affairs.[8] [14] It turned out, however, that his efforts to support his allies caused great troubles and dangers for the Greeks, and because of the great turmoil that resulted from this, he had no time or power to make war on the barbarians. Thus, from his ignorant mistakes at that time, it is now easy to understand that those who plan well should not wage war against the King before someone reconciles the Greeks and puts an end to our madness and love of strife. I have spoken on these matters before and will again devote some words to them now.

[15] And yet some people who have no education, but who claim to be able to educate others, dare to fault my words while at the same time striving to imitate me. They might perhaps claim that my concern for the troubles of the Greeks is sheer madness, as if Greece would

---

century and the problems rising from that increasing population. For more on mercenaries, see Parke 1933.

[8] He says the same sort of thing in *To Philip* (5.87–88).

fare better or worse because of my words. But everyone would justly fault them for their great cowardice and mean spiritedness, since they pretend to be philosophers (*philosophein*) but pride themselves on trivialities and are continually grousing at those who are able to give advice about the most important matters. [16] Therefore, they say these things perhaps to support their own weakness and sloth, but I have such great confidence in my own ability—although I am 80 years old and quite worn out—that I think it is particularly fitting for me to speak about these matters and to give you good advice by composing my discourse to you, and I think that something that is needed will perhaps result from these remarks. [17] And I think that the rest of the Greeks too, if they should need to choose from all people the one most able to inspire the Greeks by his eloquence to a campaign against the barbarians and the one who would most quickly complete the tasks that are considered helpful, they would choose no one else but us. And, indeed, would we not be acting shamefully if we neglect those things that are so honorable and that others think we are capable of doing? [18] My contribution is the lesser, of course, for setting out what one thinks is not by nature so very difficult. But for you it is appropriate to attend to what I have said and then consider whether you should set aside the affairs of Greece, since you come from the family I have mentioned a little earlier,[9] you are the leader of the Spartans, are called king, and have the greatest reputation of all Greeks, or whether you should disdain the affairs that now occupy you and set your hand to greater matters.

[19] I say, then, that you must cast aside all else and give your attention to these two things: how to set the Greeks free from the wars and other evils that now beset them and how to stop the barbarians from behaving so arrogantly and taking more than they deserve. That these goals can be accomplished and are advantageous for you and for your city and for all other Greeks, it is now my task to show.[10]

---

[9] In section 3.

[10] The letter seems to be incomplete. This last sentence implies a continued discussion. On the question of the fragmentary nature of this letter and other discourses of Isocrates, see Too 1995.

BIBLIOGRAPHY

Adams, D. C., 1912: "Recent Views on the Political Influence of Isocrates," *Classical Philology* 7:343–350.

Baynes, N. H., 1955: "Isocrates," in *Byzantine Studies and Other Essays*, ed. Baynes. London: 144–167.

Benseler, G. E., and F. Blass, eds., 1978: *Isocratis Orationes*, vol. I, Leipzig.

Bitzer, L., 1968: "The Rhetorical Situation," *Philosophy and Rhetoric* 1:1–14.

Blass, F., 1892: *Die Attische Beredsamkeit.* Hildesheim: [1962 reprint].

Bonner, R. J., 1920: "Notes on Isocrates' *Panegyricus* 188," *Classical Philology* 15: 385–387.

Bons, J., 1993: "AMFIBOLIA: Isocrates and Written Composition," *Mnemosyne* 46: 160–171.

Borza, E., 1990: *In the Shadow of Olympus: The Emergence of Macedon.* Princeton.

Bringmann, K., 1965: *Studien zu den politischen Ideen des Isokrates.* Hypomnemata, Heft 14. Gottingen.

Buchner, E., 1958: *Der Panegyrikos des Isokrates: Eine historisch-philologische Untersuchung.* Historia Einzelschriften 2. Wiesbaden.

Burgess, T., 1902: *Epideictic Literature.* Chicago.

Campbell, D. A., ed. 1967: *Greek Lyric Poetry.* New York.

Carter, L. B., 1986: *The Quiet Athenian.* Oxford.

Cartledge, P., 1979: *Sparta and Lakonia: A Regional History 1300–362 BC.* London.

Cloché, P., 1963: *Isocrate et son temps.* Paris.

Connelly, J. B., 1996: "Parthenon and Parthenoi: A Mythological Interpretation of the Parthenon Frieze," *American Journal of Archaeology* 100: 53–80.

Davidson, J., 1990: "Isocrates against Imperialism: An Analysis of *De Pace*," *Historia* 39: 20–36.

Demand, N., 1996: *A History of Ancient Greece*. Boston.

Eden, K., 1987: "Hermeneutics and the Ancient Rhetorical Tradition," *Rhetorica* 5.1: 59–86.

Edwards, M., 1994: *The Attic Orators*. London.

Ellis, J. R., 1976: *Philip II and Macedonian Imperialism*. Princeton.

Ellis, W. M., 1989: *Alcibiades*. London.

Flory, S., 1990: "The Meaning of τὸ μὴ μυθῶδες (1.22.4) and the Usefulness of Thucydides' *History*," *Classical Journal* 85: 193–208.

Foley, H. P., ed., 1994: *The Homeric Hymn to Demeter: Translation, Commentary, and Interpretive Essays*. Princeton.

Gagarin, M., 2002: *Antiphon the Athenian*. Austin.

Gaines, R., 1990: "Isocrates' *Ep.* 6.8," *Hermes* 118: 165–170.

Gantz, T., 1993: *Early Greek Myth*, 2 vols. Baltimore.

Garland, R., 2001: *The Piraeus*, 2nd edition. London.

Ghirga, Chiara, and Roberta Romussi, eds., 1999: *Isocrate Orazioni*. Milano: 5th edition.

Gillis, D., 1970: "The Structure of Arguments in Isocrates' *De Pace*," *Philologus* 114: 195–210.

———, 1971: "Isocrates' *Panegyricus:* The Rhetorical Texture," *Weiner Studien* 5: 52–73.

Gray, V., 1994: "Images of Sparta: Writer and Audience in Isocrates' *Panathenaicus*," in *The Shadow of Sparta*, eds. A. Powell and S. Hodkinson. London: 223–271.

Grote, G., 1846: *A History of Greece*. London.

Hall, J. M., 2001: "Contested Ethnicities: Perceptions of Macedonia within Evolving Definitions of Greek Identity," in *Ancient Perceptions of Greek Ethnicity*, ed. I. Malkin. Cambridge, MA: 159–186.

Hamilton, C. D., 1979: "Greek Rhetoric and History: The Case of Isocrates," in *Arktouros: Hellenic Studies Presented to Bernard M. W. Knox*, ed. G. Bowersock, W. Burkert, and M. Putnam. Berlin: 290–298.

Hammond, N. G. L., 1986: *A History of Greece to 322 BC*, 3rd edition. Oxford.

Harding, P., 1973: "The Purpose of Isokrates' *Archidamus* and *On the Peace*," *California Studies in Classical Antiquity* 6: 137–149.

Heinimann, F., 1945: *Nomos und Physis*. Basel.

Herman, G., 1987: *Ritualised Friendship and the Greek City.* Cambridge.

How, W. W., and J. Wells, eds., 1928: *A Commentary on Herodotus,* 2 vols. Oxford: corrected version.

Hudson-Williams, H. L., 1948: "Thucydides, Isocrates, and the Rhetorical Method of Composition," *Classical Quarterly* 42: 76–81.

Hutchinson, D. S., 1988: "Doctrines of the Mean and the Debate concerning Skills in Fourth-century Medicine, Rhetoric, and Ethics," *Apeiron* 21.2: 17–52.

Jebb, R., 1962: *The Attic Orators from Antiphon to Isaeus,* 2 vols. New York.

Jehne, M., 1993: *Koine Eirene.* Stuttgart.

Kennedy, G. A., 1958: "Isocrates' Encomium of Helen: A Panhellenic Document," *Transactions of the American Philological Association* 89: 77–83.

―――, 1963: *The Art of Persuasion in Greece.* Princeton.

―――, 1984: *New Testament Interpretation through Rhetorical Criticism.* Chapel Hill.

―――, 1989: "Ancient Antecedents of Modern Literary Theory," *American Journal of Philology* 110: 492–498.

―――, tr., 1991: *Aristotle, On Rhetoric: A Theory of Civic Discourse.* Oxford.

―――, 1994: *A New History of Classical Rhetoric.* Princeton.

―――, 1999: *Classical Rhetoric in Its Christian and Secular Tradition from Ancient to Modern Times,* 2nd edition. Chapel Hill.

Koch, H., 1914: *Quomodo Isocrates Saeculi quinti Res enarraverit.* Giessen.

Laistner, M. L. W., 1921: "Isocratea," *Classical Quarterly* 15: 78–84.

―――, ed., 1927: *De Pace and Philippus.* Ithaca, reprinted 1967.

―――, 1930: "The Influence of Isocrates' Political Doctrines on Some Fourth-century Men of Affairs," *Classical World* 23: 129–131.

Lewis, D. M., J. Boardman, M. Ostwald, and S. Hornblower, eds., 1994: *Cambridge Ancient History VI,* 2nd edition. Cambridge.

Lidov, J. B., 1983: "The Meaning of *Idea* in Isocrates," *La Parola del Passato* 38: 273–287.

Loraux, N., 1986: *The Invention of Athens: The Funeral Oration in the Classical City.* Cambridge, MA.

MacDowell, D. M., 1963: *Athenian Homicide Law in the Age of the Orators.* Manchester.

———, 1978: *The Law in Classical Athens.* Ithaca.

Markle, M. M. III, 1976: "Support of Athenian Intellectuals for Philip," *Journal of Hellenic Studies* 96: 80–99.

Mathieu, G., 1925: *Les Idées politiques d'Isocrate.* Paris.

Mathieu, G., and E. Brémond, eds., 1929–1962: *Isocrate: Discours,* 4 vols. Paris.

May, J. M., 1988: *Trials of Character.* Chapel Hill.

Meiggs, R., and D. Lewis, eds., 1969: *A Selection of Greek Historical Inscriptions to the End of the Fifth Century B.C.* Oxford.

Merlan, P. 1954: "Isocrates, Aristotle and Alexander the Great," *Historia* 3: 60–81.

Mesk, J., 1903: *Isokrates' Panegyrikos.* Leipzig.

Michelini, A. N., 1998: "Isocrates' Civic Invective: *Acharnians* and *On the Peace,*" *TAPhA* 128: 115–133.

Mirhady, D., and Y. L. Too, trs., 2000: *Isocrates I.* Austin.

Morrison, J. S., and J. F. Coates, 1986: *The Athenian Trireme.* Cambridge.

Moysey, R. A., 1982: "Isokrates' On the Peace: Rhetorical Exercise or Political Advice," *American Journal of Ancient History* 7: 118–127.

Müller, C. W., 1991: "Plato und die Panegyrikos des Isokrates," *Philologus* 135: 140–156.

Neils, J., ed., 1992: *Goddess and Polis: The Panathenaic Festival in Ancient Athens.* Princeton.

———, 2001: *The Parthenon Frieze.* Cambridge.

Nickel, D., 1991: "Isokrates und die Geschichtsschreibung des 4. Jahrhunderts v. Chr," *Philologus* 135: 233–239.

Nisetich, F., tr., 1980: *Pindar's Victory Songs.* Baltimore.

Norlin, G., ed., 1928: *Isocrates I.* Loeb Classical Library. Cambridge, MA.

———, ed., 1929: *Isocrates II.* Loeb Classical Library. Cambridge, MA.

Nouhaud, M., 1982: *L'Utilisation de l'histoire par les orateurs attiques.* Paris.

O'Sullivan, N., 1992: *Alcidamas, Aristophanes and the Beginnings of Greek Stylistic Theory.* Hermes Einzelschriften 60. Stuttgart.

Papillon, T. L., 1995: "Isocrates' *Techne* and Rhetorical Pedagogy," *Rhetoric Society Quarterly* 25: 149–163.

———, 1996a: "Isocrates on Gorgias and Helen: The Unity of the *Helen*," *Classical Journal* 91: 377–391.

———, 1996b: "Isocrates and the Use of Myth," *Hermathena* 161: 9–21.

———, 1997a: "Mixed Unities in Isocrates' *Antidosis*," *Rhetoric Society Quarterly* 27: 47–62.

———, 1997b: "The Identity of Gorgias in Isocrates' *Helen*," *Electronic Antiquity* 3.6: http://scholar.lib.vt.edu/ejournals/ElAnt/V3N6/papillon.html

———, 1998a: "Isocrates and the Greek Poetic Tradition," *Scholia* 7: 41–61.

———, 1998b: *Rhetorical Studies in the Aristocratea of Demosthenes.* New York.

Parke, H. W., 1933: *Greek Mercenary Soldiers from the Earliest Times to the Battle of Ipsus.* New York, reprinted by Ares, 1981.

Perelman, S., 1957: "Isocrates' *Philippus:* A Reinterpretation," *Historia* 6: 306–317.

———, 1969: "Isocrates' *Philippus* and Panhellenism," *Historia* 18: 370–374.

Perkins, T. M., 1984: "Isocrates and Plato: Relativism vs. Idealism," *Southern Speech Communication Journal* 50: 49–66.

Poulakos, J., 1995: *Sophistical Rhetoric in Classical Greece.* Columbia, SC.

Poulakos, T., 1997: *Speaking for the Polis: Isocrates' Rhetorical Education.* Columbia, SC.

———, 2001: "Isocrates' Use of *doxa*," *Philosophy and Rhetoric* 34: 61–78.

Race, W., 1978: "*Panathenaicus* 74–90: The Rhetoric of Isocrates' Digression on Agamemnon," *Transactions of the American Philological Association* 108: 175–185.

———, 1982: *The Classical Priamel from Homer to Boethius.* Leiden.

———, ed., 1997: *Pindar: Nemean Odes, Isthmian Odes, Fragments.* Cambridge, MA.

Raubitschek, A. E., 1941: "Two Notes on Isocrates," *Transactions of the American Philological Association* 72: 356–364.

Richter, G. M. A., 1965: *The Portraits of the Greeks,* abridged revision by R. R. Smith (1984). Ithaca.

de Romilly, J., 1958: "Eunoia in Isocrates or the Political Importance of Creating Good Will," *Journal of Hellenic Studies* 78: 92–101.

———, 1992: "Isocrates and Europe," *Greece and Rome* 39: 2–13.

Rummel, E., 1979: "Isocrates' Ideal of Rhetoric: Criteria of Evaluation," *Classical Journal* 75: 25–35.

Russell, D. A., 1983: *Greek Declamation.* Cambridge.

Russell, D. A., and N. G. Wilson, eds., 1981: *Menander Rhetor.* Oxford.

Ryder, T. T. B., 1965: *Koine Eirene.* London.

Said, S., 2001: "The Discourse of Identity in Greek Rhetoric from Isocrates to Aristides," in *Ancient Perceptions of Greek Ethnicity,* ed. I. Malkin, Cambridge, MA: 275–299.

Sandys, J. E., ed., 1872: *Isocrates: Ad Demonicum et Panegyricus.* London, reprinted 1979 by Arno.

Sanneg, J., 1867: "De Schola Isocratea." Diss. Halae.

Schiappa, E., 1991: *Protagoras and Logos: A Study in Greek Philosophy and Rhetoric.* Columbia, SC.

———, 1996: "Toward a Prediscriplinary Analysis of Gorgias' *Helen,*" in *Theory, Text, and Context: Issues in Greek Rhetoric and Oratory,* ed. C. L. Johnstone. Albany: 65–86.

———, 1999: *The Beginnings of Rhetorical Theory in Classical Greece.* New Haven.

Schwarze, S., 1999: "Performing Phronesis: The Case of Isocrates' *Helen,*" *Philosophy and Rhetoric* 32: 78–95.

Seager, R., 1994: "The King's Peace and the Second Athenian Confederacy," in *Cambridge Ancient History, Volume VI,* eds. D. M. Lewis, J. Boardman, S. Hornblower, and M. Ostwald. Cambridge: 156–186.

Sealey, R., 1976: *A History of Greek City States 700–338 B.C.* Berkeley.

Smith, L. F., 1940: *The Genuineness of the Ninth and Third Letters of Isocrates.* Lancaster, PA.

Sullivan, R. G., 2001: "Eidos/idea in Isocrates," *Philosophy and Rhetoric* 24: 79–92.

Sullivan, R., 2004: "Classical Epistolary Theory and the Letters of Isocrates," in *Letter Writing Manuals from Antiquity to the Present,* ed. C. Poster and L. Mitchell. Columbia, SC.

Talbert, R. J. A., ed., 1985: *Atlas of Classical History.* London.

Thompson, W. E., 1983: "Isocrates on the Peace Treaties," *Classical Quarterly* 64: 75–80.

Timmerman, D. M., 1998: "Isocrates' Competing Conceptualization of Philosophy, "*Philosophy & Rhetoric* 31: 145–159.

Too, Y. L., 1995: *The Rhetoric of Identity in Isocrates.* Cambridge.

Usher, S., 1973: "The Style of Isocrates," *Bulletin of the Institute of Classical Studies* 20: 39–67.

———, 1990: *Greek Orators III: Isocrates.* Warminster.

———, 1999: *Greek Oratory: Tradition and Originality.* Oxford.

Van Hook, L., ed., 1945: *Isocrates III.* London.

Welles, C. B., 1966: "Isocrates' View of History," in *The Classical Tradition: Literary and Historical Studies in Honor of Harry Caplan,* ed. L. Wallach. Ithaca: 3–25.

Whitehead, D., 1986: *The Demes of Attica, 508/7–ca. 250 B.C.: A Political and Social Study.* Princeton.

Wilcox, S., 1943: "Isocrates' Genera of Prose," *American Journal of Philology* 64: 427–431.

Wooten, C., tr., 1987: *Hermogenes of Tarsus: On Types of Style.* Chapel Hill.

Worthington, I., 1993: "Two Letters of Isocrates and Ring Composition," *Electronic Antiquity* 1.1: http://scholar.lib.vt.edu/ejournals/ElAnt/V1N1/worthington.html

Wycherley, R. E., 1978: *The Stones of Athens.* Princeton.

INDEX

Tisias, xi, 4
Tissaphernes, 64
Tithraustes, 62, 65
Torone, 183–184
translation, xxvi, 9–11, 18–19
treaties (*synthēkai, homologiae*), 17,
    23, 24, 38, 46, 50, 56, 57, 62, 66,
    69, 70–71, 74, 77, 97, 110, 113,
    116, 122, 123, 128–129, 130, 139,
    150, 157, 183, 193–194, 204–205,
    230, 231–232, 234, 237, 238, 242,
    247, 279
triad, educational (nature, training,
    practice), 8, 268
Triballoi, 147, 217
triremes, 49, 50–51, 54, 62, 87, 111,
    141, 143, 146, 153–154, 157, 181
Trojan War, 41, 47, 66, 71, 72–73,
    106, 179, 180, 185, 186, 211–212,
    214

Troy, 99–100
Tyndareus, 114
Tyre, 67, 97

unity. *See* panhellenism

virtue. *See aretē*

Xenophanes, 29, 35
Xenophon, 94, 135; *Anabasis*, 63,
    94, 157, 193, 253; *Cyropaedaea*,
    90; *Hellenica*, 55, 56, 58, 65, 124,
    142, 152, 155, 157, 229, 232, 238,
    278
Xerxes, 44, 48–51, 84, 180–181,
    204–205, 211, 253

Zeus, 42, 71, 104, 106, 114, 186, 214,
    241, 278